LAND LAW

The University of Law

LAND LAW
SECOND EDITION

Kate Lambert

Published by
The University of Law
2 Bunhill Row
London EC1Y 8HQ

British Library Cataloguing in Publication Data

A catalogue record for this book is available from the British Library

ISBN 978 1 80502 106 3

Preface

This book is part of the 'Foundations of Law' series of textbooks, designed to support postgraduates in their study of the core subjects of English law.

It is anticipated that the reader can then move on to studies for their professional examinations (eg the SQE and BSB assessments) comfortable that they have an understanding of foundational legal principles.

Each textbook aims to provide the reader with a solid knowledge and understanding of fundamental legal principles and rules. The series aims to give the reader the opportunity to identify and explore areas of critical interest whilst also identifying practice-based context.

For those readers who are students at The University of Law, the textbooks are used alongside other learning resources to best prepare students to meet outcomes of the Postgraduate Diploma in Law and related programmes.

We wish you every success as you learn about English Law and in your future career.

The legal principles and rules contained within this textbook are stated as at 1 September 2024.

Contents

Table of Cases

Table of Legislation

Part I Fundamental and Pervasive Concepts of Land Law

1 Introduction to Estates and Third Party Interests in Land

LEARNING OUTCOMES

When you have completed this chapter, you should be able to:

- explain what is meant by 'land' and how it differs from other types of property;
- distinguish between a fixture and a chattel and explain why this distinction is important;
- distinguish between various types of estate in land;
- identify different types of third party rights and interests in land;
- explain how estates and third party rights and interests are validly created;
- explain the two main stages of the system of conveyancing.

1.1 Introduction to estates and third party interests in land

When you are learning about ownership of a piece of land, you will discover that there may be a number of people who claim to have an interest in that land. The most obvious is the 'owner' of the land. However, others (generally referred to as 'third parties') may claim to have rights in the same piece of land. For example, the owner's partner or spouse may claim that they have a right to live there; neighbours may claim rights of way or other rights that would stop the owner from building on their land or using it in a particular way; and there may be mortgages over the property that need to be paid off.

It is important for you to be able to classify interests and rights in land and to be able to ascertain whether or not they have been created correctly. To do this you will need to understand some basic concepts relating to land law, as this underpins your ability to understand land law as a whole. This chapter, together with **Chapters 2** and **3** that make up **Part I**, will provide this understanding. You will then build on your knowledge in the remainder of the textbook using the fundamental and pervasive concepts of land law contained in this part.

1.2 What is land?

1.2.1 Relationship of 'land' and 'property'

The starting point for a course on land law is to examine the meaning of the terms 'land' and 'property'.

We often use the word 'property' to mean land. A person may say that they have bought some property or that they own a lot of property. Many people would assume that they are referring to land, but this is not strictly correct.

When speaking of property, we are strictly referring to rights that confer upon a person a degree of control over a resource. Some examples of rights that may be enjoyed in relation to land are leases, easements and covenants. The resource need not, of course, be land. It may, for example, be a car. Ownership of shares in a company will also confer property rights. In this case, unlike land or a car, there is no physical object. All the shareholder has are rights such as the right to receive income in the form of a dividend, the right to attend and vote at meetings and the right to share in the distribution of available assets if the company is wound up. In this textbook we are going to focus on rights in respect of one resource, namely, land.

1.2.2 What is land?

The meaning of land in an ordinary dictionary would say something like 'the solid part of the earth's surface; ground; soil'. That is usually what we would imagine when we think of the ordinary meaning of the word 'land'. However, for a lawyer, such a definition is inadequate. The legal definition of land is far broader and has multiple dimensions.

Land is defined in s 205(1)(ix) of the Law of Property Act (LPA) 1925 as follows:

> Land includes land of any tenure, and mines and minerals, whether or not held apart from the surface, buildings or parts of buildings (whether the division is horizontal or vertical or made in any other way) and other corporeal hereditaments; also a manor, advowson, and a rent and other incorporeal hereditaments and an easement, right, privilege, or benefit in, over or derived from land ...

This definition can be broken down as follows:

(a) The concept of tenure will be explained in **1.3** below.

(b) Mines and minerals would include, for example, any coal beneath the property. In practice, all interests in coal are now vested in the Coal Authority under the Coal Industry Act 1994.

(c) Corporeal hereditaments refer to the physical and tangible characteristics of land which are capable of being inherited. For example, trees, rocks and clods of earth.

(d) Incorporeal hereditaments are intangible property rights which are capable of being inherited. For example, profits and easements.

(e) The concepts of a manor and advowson reflect the feudal nature of the development of land law and have limited modern application.

(f) Buildings and parts of buildings are included within the definition of land. Buildings can be divided horizontally or vertically, meaning that it is possible for a building to be included within the definition of land although it does not touch the soil. This is called a 'flying freehold'.

Although the definition seems fairly comprehensive, it is not exhaustive. It has been said that possession of land 'extends upwards to infinity and downwards to the centre of the earth'. (In Latin, '*Cujus est solum, ejus est usque ad coelum et ad inferos*'.) However, case law has curtailed the first part of this rule (*Bernstein of Leigh (Baron) v Skyviews & General Ltd* [1977] 3 WLR 136).

It is clearly necessary for a landowner to be entitled to use some of the airspace above their land for otherwise no one would be able to build on land. However, for a person to claim they are entitled to an unlimited amount of airspace above their land would mean that a trespass would be committed every time a satellite passed over a suburban garden.

The courts have to seek to balance the rights of the landowner and those of the general public who, as well as the landowner, also have an interest in the use of airspace. In the *Bernstein* case it was held that the landowner's claim to airspace should be restricted to such height as is necessary for them to enjoy in an ordinary way the land that they own and the structures that are placed upon it. Beyond that they have no more of a claim to airspace than any other member of the public.

1.2.3 Fixtures are part of the land

Now that you have some idea of the meaning of land, we need to look at one final issue. This concerns chattels that become attached to land. A chattel is an item of movable property (such as furniture, pictures, books, a motor car) as opposed to land, which is immovable. If you attach a chattel to land it may cease to be a chattel and become what is known as a fixture. If you buy a house the likelihood is that you will attach all sorts of things to it, for example, shelves, cupboards, mirrors, light fittings. Until you attach them, they are undoubtedly chattels. However, by attaching them you may have converted them into what are known as fixtures. A fixture is treated as though it is part of the land to which it is attached. In other words, it has ceased to be a chattel. This may have important consequences for someone who is buying or selling a house. If you are selling a house, you might want the item to be classed as a chattel so that you are free to take it with you when you move. On the other hand, if you are buying a house, you may want the item to be a fixture so that it is included in the purchase price that you are paying and must be left there by the seller. In practice, the parties' legal advisers will seek to avoid any difficulties by ensuring that the contract for sale which the parties enter into makes it clear which items are included in the sale and which are not. However, if the contract does not contain an appropriate provision dealing with this, the law has developed a two-stage test to determine whether an object is a fixture or a chattel (*Berkley v Poulett* [1977] 1 EGLR 86, CA).

The two tests you have to apply are:

(1) the method and degree of annexation;

(2) the object and purpose of the annexation.

The first test of the method and degree of annexation requires there to be some degree of physical annexation to land in order for the item to be considered a fixture. The legal maxim is whatever is attached to the soil becomes part of it (*quicquid plantatur solo, solo cedit*). So, if an object has been affixed to land, then under the first test, a presumption is raised that the item is a fixture. If an item cannot be removed without causing serious damage to the property, there will be a stronger presumption raised that the item is a fixture rather than if the item is only lightly attached. If the item is not affixed to the land, then under the first test, it will be considered a chattel.

The more important test today is the second test: the object and purpose of the annexation. This means that any presumption raised under the first test can be rebutted when applying the second test.

If the purpose of the annexation was to enhance the realty, for example, an item attached to a wall in a room to make the whole room more beautiful, then the conclusion, after applying the second test, is that the item will remain a fixture. However, if the purpose of affixing the item was so that it could be enjoyed better as an item in itself, it will ultimately be considered to be a chattel after the second test is applied, despite the fact that the item is affixed to the land.

Therefore, applying the second test, it is possible to argue that an object resting on the ground by its own weight alone, and which would therefore be a chattel under the first test, could ultimately be a fixture if the purpose of placing it there was to enhance the realty.

There are two main exceptions to the rule that you cannot remove fixtures. The first is that a person who is selling land may include a provision in the contract for sale that gives a right to remove fixtures.

The second exception arises where the person who has affixed the object is a tenant. A tenant does have the right, in certain circumstances, to remove fixtures known as 'tenant's fixtures', that is, trade, agricultural or ornamental fixtures.

You now know what a fixture is and what two tests to apply to decide if an object has ceased to be a chattel and has become a fixture.

Set out below is a summary of a number of cases in which the courts determined whether items could be treated as fixtures or chattels. Read through the case summaries.

***Berkley v Poulett* [1977] 1 EGLR 86, CA**

The Court of Appeal considered a number of items and reached the following decisions:

Pictures

The pictures had been fixed into recesses in the panelling of the rooms. The panelling had been installed at the beginning of the 20th century and recesses had been left for pictures. Although this pointed to the pictures being fixtures, the Court of Appeal did not accept that they were fixtures because the pictures could not be considered part of a 'composite mural'. They had been put there to be enjoyed as pictures and no more.

Sundial

The sundial was small and had been detached from its pedestal many years before the sale. It no longer formed part of the realty and was not, therefore, a fixture.

Statue

Although the statue was heavy, it was easy to remove it from the plinth on which it stood. Whilst it could be argued that architectural design was the reason for the siting of the statue, it was more likely to be the reason for the siting of the plinth, leaving the owner free to choose what to place upon the plinth. The statue was not, therefore, a fixture.

Plinth

The plinth was firmly fixed to the ground and its siting was architecturally important. It was, therefore, a fixture.

***D'Eyncourt v Gregory* [1866] LR 3 Eq 382**

A number of freestanding items were considered by Lord Romilly MR to be fixtures as they were part of the architectural design of the property. Tapestries were fixed into panelling in the walls. A particular portrait was hung in a certain location. Although these items could be removed easily and without damage, it was held that they were essentially a part of the building itself. Carved kneeling figures in the great hall and sculptured marbled vases in the hall were considered to be part of the architectural design of the hall and staircase. The lions at the head of the steps in the garden and the 16 stone garden seats in the garden were also considered to be fixtures. Although they were freestanding items, they were placed in the garden as part of the overall architectural design of the property.

Leigh v Taylor **[1902] AC 157**

Certain tapestries were displayed by being stretched over canvas and then tacked to a framework of wood which was then nailed to the walls. Each tapestry was surrounded by a moulding which was also fastened firmly to the wall. The House of Lords considered that the tapestries never lost their character as chattels. The only way that they could be properly displayed was for them to be fixed to the walls in this manner.

Elitestone Ltd v Morris and another **[1997] 2 All ER 513**

A bungalow consisting of two bedrooms, a living room, kitchen and bathroom rested on concrete foundation blocks set into the ground. The tenants of the bungalow claimed that it was a fixture and that they had security of tenure.

The freehold owner claimed that the bungalow was a chattel and that the tenancy consisted only of the site, so the tenants could not claim the protection of the Rent Act 1977. The House of Lords adopted a common sense approach and concluded that a house that is constructed so as to be removable, whether as a unit or in sections, may well remain a chattel. A house which is constructed in such a way that it cannot be removed at all, save by destruction, cannot have been intended to remain as a chattel. It must have been intended to form part of the realty.

Botham v TSB Bank plc **(1997) 73 P & CR D1**

This decision involved a number of commonplace items that a mortgagee claimed were fixtures and therefore part of the land that was repossessed by the mortgagee. The Court of Appeal held that fitted carpets and curtains were not fixtures. Light fittings were also chattels, as were gas fires connected to the building only by a gas pipe. White goods manufactured to standard sizes and fitted into standard sized holes were held to be chattels, although fitted kitchen units were fixtures.

ACTIVITY 1 Fixtures and chattels

Imagine that you have entered into a contract to buy a piece of land. The reason you are buying it is because there is a house built on it that you have always dreamt you would live in one day. When you were shown around it by the estate agent you were struck by the magnificent carpets and curtains, the panelled walls containing pictures, the gas fire, the dishwasher, the washing machine, the cooker and the light fittings. Out in the garden there is a greenhouse and garden shed. There is also a large statue. At the top of the long drive there is a spacious garage, which houses the seller's car, and on the drive itself there is parked a caravan.

In the table below, we have listed the items mentioned above. Can you identify which of them you expect to be included in the sale and which you do not expect to be included in the sale? Place a tick in the appropriate column. If you are not certain, insert a question mark. Make a note of the reasons for your answer.

Item	Fixture (included in sale)	Chattel (not included in sale)
1. land		
2. house		
3. carpets		
4. curtains		
5. pictures		
6. gas fire		
7. dishwasher		
8. washing machine		
9. cooker		
10. light fittings		
11. greenhouse		
12. garden shed		
13. statue		
14. garage		
15. car		
16. caravan		

COMMENT

Item 1

The land is obviously included in the sale.

Items 2 and 14

The house and garage are part and parcel of the realty (*Elitestone*).

Items 3 and 4

Carpets and curtains will be chattels and not included in the sale (*Botham*).

Item 5

If the pictures are hung merely to display them, they will be chattels (*Leigh v Taylor*). However, if they are hung within the panelled walls as part of the overall architectural design of the room, they may be fixtures (*D'Eyncourt v Gregory*).

Item 6

It will depend on how the gas fire is connected. If it is merely standing by its own weight and is only connected to the building by a gas pipe, it will not be a fixture, as the connection is only necessary to enable it to be used (*Botham*).

Items 7 and 8

White goods will usually be classed as chattels (*Botham*).

Item 9

Whether the cooker is a fixture or a chattel will again depend on how it is fixed. If it is free standing and connected only by a flex it will be a chattel. If it is a split level cooker with the hob set into a work surface and the oven being part of a kitchen cabinet, it will be a fixture (*Botham*).

Item 10

The light fittings are probably easy to remove and are, therefore, likely to be chattels (*Botham*).

Items 11 and 12

It will depend on how the greenhouse and garden shed have been constructed. If they are capable of being easily dismantled and moved to other areas of the garden, they will be classed as chattels; otherwise they are fixtures (*Elitestone*).

Item 13

If the statue is capable of being removed without causing damage and does not form part of the architectural design, it is a chattel (*Berkley v Poulett; D'Eyncourt v Gregory*).

Items 15 and 16

The car and caravan present no difficulty: they are chattels.

1.3 Concepts of ownership

Now that you have an idea of what land is and its relationship to property, we need to look at some aspects of ownership. In relation to land, what is it that a person actually owns?

Example

Imagine a situation where you are renting a small house with a garden attached. You have agreed to occupy the land for a period of three years. You discover that your neighbour regularly crosses your garden to get to the local pub in the next road. You are also aware that your landlord lets their nephew store their motorbike in the shed at the bottom of the garden. Who owns what, if anything, of the property?

To answer this question, you will need to understand what is meant by concepts of ownership in land law. We need to consider two concepts or doctrines: tenures and estates.

1.3.1 The doctrine of tenure

The doctrine of tenure concerns the way in which land is held - from whom and on what terms. Its origins lie in the feudal system of landholding and all modern land law has developed from this.

Theoretically, since the time of the Norman Conquest in 1066, all land belongs to the Crown. William the Conqueror claimed ownership of all England by right of conquest and rewarded his most important subjects by granting them land he had captured. These subjects were allowed to keep the land provided that they performed some service for the Crown, for example service of a military nature. In turn, they would reward lesser subjects with land, again in return for services. In this way a pyramid or hierarchy developed with the king at the top. All persons in possession of land were 'tenants' (from the French 'tenir' meaning 'to hold'), that is to say they held their land either immediately or mediately of the Crown.

Over time this method of land holding became obsolete. As a result the doctrine of tenure has lost much of its importance, although it is still technically correct to say that only the Crown owns land whilst everyone else is a 'tenant' holding either immediately or mediately of the Crown.

This concept of tenure is, however, still to be found in the area of leases. You will undoubtedly have come across situations where a person occupies land as what we still refer to today as a tenant. In this situation, the tenant will be paying money - a rent - to someone we call a landlord, for the right to occupy. Leases, however, developed at a later stage and outside the feudal system, although borrowing from it the notion of tenure.

1.3.2 The concept of the estate

A lawyer does not think of a person as owning land itself but rather as owning a period of time. An estate is a period of time. Land therefore acquires a fourth dimension, that of time. This can be illustrated as follows:

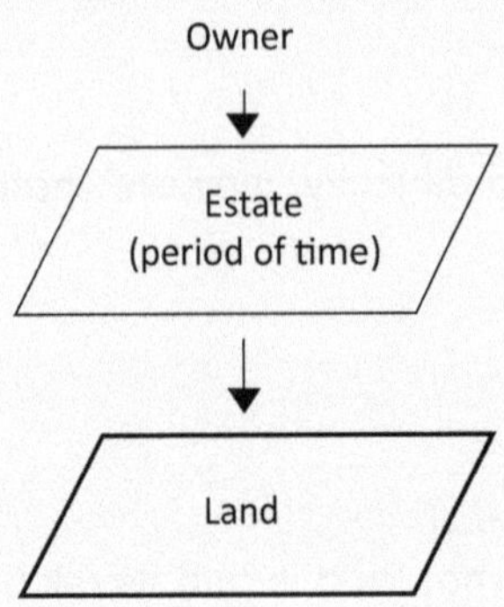

As an estate is a period of time, like time it is capable of division. Thus a person owning an estate can create out of it a lesser estate, or shorter period of time, and confer the benefit of such lesser estate on others.

Whilst you own an estate in land you have the right to enjoy or possess that land, or to receive any rents or profits produced from that land. Historically it was possible to have many different types of estate in land. However, since the LPA 1925 there are only two estates in land which are recognised by the law today.

The only two estates in land which are capable of subsisting or of being conveyed or created at law are set out in s 1(1) of the LPA 1925:

(a) An estate in fee simple absolute in possession (known as freehold).

(b) A term of years absolute (known as leasehold).

1.3.2.1 Freehold estate

Section 1(1)(a) of the LPA 1925 recognises that an estate in fee simple absolute in possession is capable of existing at law. This is also known as 'freehold' or the 'freehold estate'.

The word 'fee' denotes that the estate is one that is capable of being inherited and the word 'simple' signifies that it may pass to any class of heir. Thus on the death of such an estate owner who had no direct lineal descendants the estate might pass, for example, to brothers and sisters or uncles and aunts. As it is unlikely that a person will die without any heir at all, such an estate was unlikely to come to an end and is, therefore, capable of lasting for as long as the land itself lasts, ie, effectively, forever. To have the fee simple estate is therefore equivalent to having permanent ownership of the land.

A person owning a fee simple is free to do with it as they wish. They may sell it or give it away and, on their death, it may be inherited. Where such an estate is disposed of, the person acquiring it will acquire an estate that lasts for as long as they, the person acquiring it, has heirs: in other words, they will acquire an estate that is capable of lasting forever.

The word 'absolute' indicates that this estate is not determinable or conditional on any event. It is not limited in any way. It is a legal estate in land absolutely.

Lastly, the meaning of 'in possession' is entitlement to possession of the land now. It is not an entitlement to possession at some time in the future, dependent upon some event, but current entitlement.

In conclusion, if you hold a fee simple absolute in possession - the freehold estate - you have the equivalent to outright ownership of the land at the current time. The only situation in which a freehold will come to an end is when the owner dies leaving no will and no heirs to whom the property could pass. This situation is rare but in the event that it does occur, the property reverts to the Crown. In reality the property passes to the Treasury Department which will resell the freehold.

Note that there is a relatively new type of land ownership known as 'commonhold'. This is a form of freehold estate and is not a different type of tenure. It relates to the separate ownership of units within a commonhold scheme. However, this is beyond the scope of this textbook.

1.3.2.2 Leasehold estate

Section 1(1)(b) of the LPA 1925 identifies a term of years absolute as the other type of estate that is capable of existing at law. This is also known as 'leasehold' or the 'leasehold estate'.

We will consider leaseholds in detail in **Chapter 5**. The leasehold estate is inferior to the freehold estate as it is of limited duration.

If a fee simple owner wishes to derive an income from land, one way of doing it is to grant another person (a tenant) the right to use the land for a fixed or determinable period of time. The fee simple owner (now the landlord) retains their freehold estate. All they lose is the right to occupy and use the land. In return the tenant has to pay them a rent. This is illustrated in the following diagram:

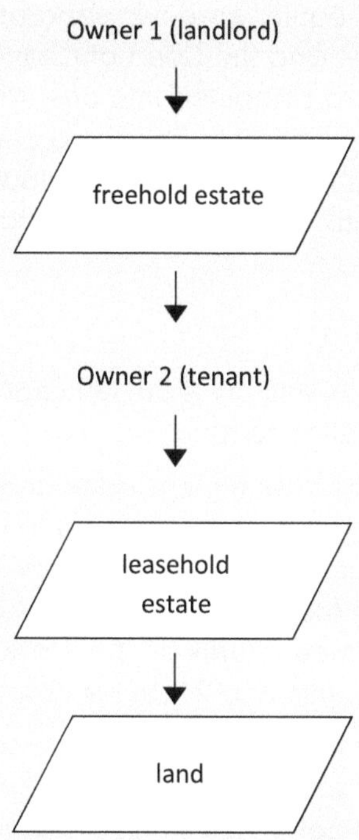

The tenant's interest will last for the duration of the lease and may be sold, given away or inherited.

To qualify as a leasehold estate, the tenant (ie the owner of the leasehold estate) must have exclusive possession of the property for a fixed and certain duration. These characteristics of exclusive possession and certainty of duration are essential for a leasehold estate. You will examine these characteristics in more detail in **Chapter 5**. Briefly, exclusive possession means that the tenant must be able to exclude everyone from the property, including the landlord. For certainty of duration, the commencement date and the duration of the lease must be clearly ascertained at the start of the lease. So the landlord and tenant must both know when the legal estate will commence and for how long it will last; that is, the lease must be 'for a term certain'.

The length of the lease will vary. Some will be granted for a fixed term, such as 7, 25 or 99 years. Others will be periodic, that is to say, they will be weekly, monthly, quarterly or yearly and, unless ended by one of the parties, will renew themselves at the end of each period. All of these are periods of certain or fixed duration and therefore satisfy the requirement for 'a term of years'. Section 205(1)(xxvii) of the LPA 1925 defines the expression 'term of years' as including a term for less than a year, or for a year or years, and a fraction of a year or from year to year. When referring to the leasehold estate, the term 'absolute' does not add anything to the meaning of a term of years. A lease will be determinable and is not therefore absolute in the sense that the freehold estate is absolute.

When referring to ownership, therefore, we are not referring to ownership of the land but rather to the concept of an estate or period of time in land.

Consider again the example at the beginning of **1.3** above. You should now be able to understand that you would have the leasehold estate in the house and garden, and your landlord would have the freehold estate. It is therefore possible for there to be two legal estates in the same piece of land at the same time.

1.3.3 Relationship between common law and equity

The freehold estate and the leasehold estate are recognised at common law. They are capable of existing at law and therefore equate to legal ownership of land.

Originally the common law and equity were two separate systems administered by separate courts: the courts of common law and the Court of Chancery. As a result of the Judicature Acts 1873–1875 these courts were combined into one system, so that the rules of common law and the rules of equity are now applied by the same court. However, the distinction between what is legal (and therefore enforceable at common law) and what is equitable still remains important. Where there is a conflict between common law and equitable rules, the equitable rules will prevail.

1.3.3.1 Equity and the concept of the trust

One of equity's most important inventions is the concept of the trust. It is necessary to explain briefly the role of the trust in relation to land.

Let us go back in time to the period of the crusades and imagine a knight, Sir Henry, about to depart for some far-off land. He is leaving behind land that he owns and also an infant son, Nigel. Whilst he is away fighting, he needs to know that someone will take care of his land. He therefore transfers it to his brother, Sir Rodney, on the understanding that it will be transferred back to him when he returns or, if he fails to return, to Nigel on attaining his majority, ie, full age. Historically, this was 21, but is now 18 years of age.

To the outside world Sir Rodney appears to own the land, but in reality he is holding it for the benefit of Sir Henry and his son. What happens if Sir Henry fails to return and Sir Rodney refuses to transfer the land to Nigel on his coming of age? The answer given by the common law was a simple one: Sir Rodney is the owner; no one else is entitled to the land. Nigel is without a remedy.

Nigel decides to appeal to the King as the fountain of justice. The King passes the matter to the Chancellor, who is trained in civil and canon law and is the keeper of the royal conscience. The Chancellor interrogates Sir Rodney and threatens to imprison him if he does not fulfil his obligations. So we have the beginnings of the Court of Chancery, which develops a system of rules which become known as equity.

1.3.3.2 Legal ownership and equitable ownership

You now see the emergence of two types of ownership: a legal one (recognised by the common law) and an equitable one (recognised by equity). We can illustrate this in the following way:

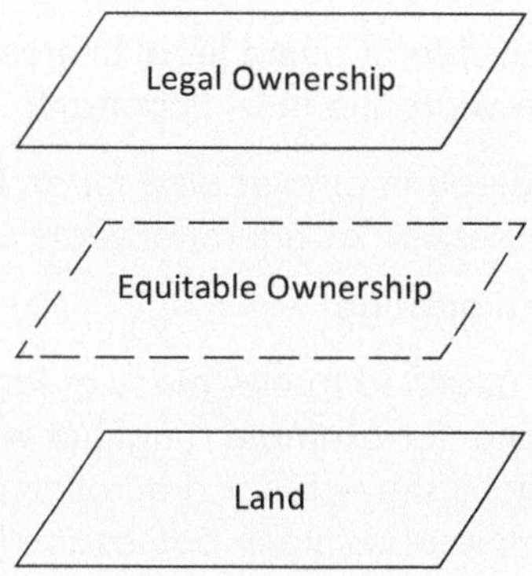

The common law courts still insisted that Sir Rodney was the legal owner. The Court of Chancery, however, forced him to carry out his duties. Today we would refer to Sir Rodney as a 'trustee' and Nigel as a 'beneficiary'. Because Sir Rodney was recognised as the owner by the courts of common law, we say he is the legal owner – he has the legal estate vested in him. Because Nigel's interest in the property was protected by the Court of Chancery, we say that he has an equitable interest in the property.

As mentioned, we do not today have separate courts of law and equity. The one court administers both rules, but the distinction between legal ownership and equitable ownership remains.

So you now have the foundations for a division of property ownership. There is dual ownership of the same piece of land at the same time. The legal owner has rights recognised at common law, whereas the equitable owner has rights recognised in equity. This is not shared ownership but different types of ownership. If I buy a piece of land in my sole name and for my own benefit, I become the owner of the legal estate and also of the equitable interest. I am the sole beneficial owner. However, if I buy the land and declare that I hold it for the benefit of my children, I am still the owner of the legal estate but I no longer own the equitable interest. My children are the beneficiaries; it is they who own the equitable interest. We thus have a horizontal split in ownership.

What happens if I decide to sell the land? As we have seen, the legal estate can be sold, given away or inherited (see **1.3.2** above). It is the legal owner who has the right to do this. Where a trust exists, the legal estate is vested in the trustee. What happens to the equitable interest of the beneficiaries if the trustee decides to sell the land?

You will see in **2.3.5.2**, **3.3.1.3** and **4.4.1** that if the buyer pays the purchase money to a minimum of two trustees and obtains their receipt, the buyer will take the property free from equitable interests that arise under a trust. The equitable interests are transferred to the proceeds of sale. This is known as overreaching.

1.4 Third party rights and interests over land

When considering estates we are, in effect, looking at the question of ownership. Owners are able to create, in favour of others, rights over their land that fall short of ownership of an estate. The interests thus acquired by non-owners are generally known as 'third party interests'. These third party interests may be legal or they may be equitable or they may arise under statute.

1.4.1 Legal interests

The five interests which are capable of being legal interests are listed in s 1(2) of the LPA 1925. Of these, the following two are the most important:

(a) an easement, right or privilege in or over land for an interest equivalent to an estate in fee simple absolute in possession or a term of years absolute;

(b) a charge by way of legal mortgage.

An easement is a right that is attached to one piece of land and imposes a corresponding burden on another piece of land, for example a right of way (see **Chapter 8**). Easements are only capable of being legal if they are for a duration equivalent to one of the two legal estates, ie an estate in fee simple absolute in possession (freehold) or for a term of years absolute (leasehold). Only easements lasting forever or for a fixed duration are capable of being legal. This this means that an easement for an uncertain duration is not capable of being legal.

A mortgage is an interest in land given as security for a loan (see **Chapter 9**).

Whenever you have to decide whether an estate or an interest in land is legal or equitable, you have to begin by looking at s 1(1) and (2) of the LPA 1925. If the estate or interest is mentioned there, it is *capable* of being a legal estate or interest in land. It does not necessarily follow that it is a legal estate or interest because, as you will discover later, in order to create a legal estate or interest you usually have to comply with specific formalities. Of the legal interests listed in s 1(2) we are going to concern ourselves only with easements and charges by way of legal mortgage.

Consider again the example at the beginning of **1.3** above. You should now be able to understand that your neighbour has an easement over the garden of the property that you rent. This will be capable of being legal if it was granted for an interest equivalent to an estate in fee simple absolute in possession or a term of years absolute. You will also see, when you look at easements in more detail in **Chapter 8**, that your landlord's nephew may have an easement in relation to the shed in the garden. Therefore, in addition to the legal freehold and the legal leasehold, there may be two easements that affect the property.

1.4.2 Equitable interests

If an estate or interest in land does not fall within the lists in s 1(1) or (2) of the LPA 1925, it can only take effect in equity (LPA 1925, s 1(3)). These third party interests are therefore equitable interests in land. There are two types of equitable interest: the rights of beneficiaries under a trust; and equitable interests in land where no trust is involved.

1.4.2.1 Equitable interests under trusts

In **1.3.3.1** you were introduced to the concept of the trust. Where there is a trust of land, the legal estate is held by the trustee and the equitable interest is held by the beneficiary. There may be more than one trustee and there may be more than one beneficiary. The trust structure enables the legal estate to be held by the trustee(s) for the benefit of the person(s) who has (have) the equitable interest. This may be seen in the diagram below:

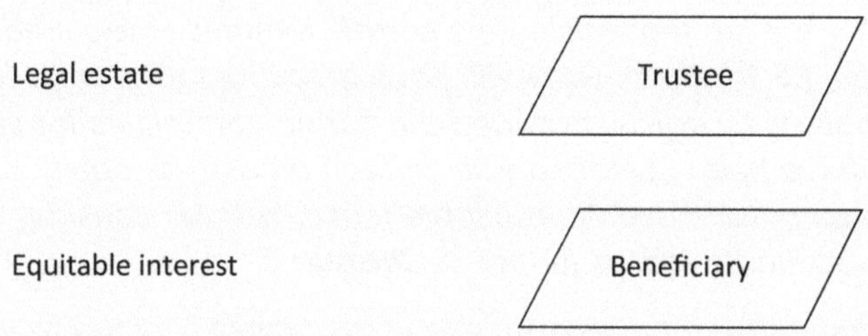

It is important to remember to keep the two types of ownership separate. The trustee has the legal ownership of the land and therefore has rights recognised at common law, whereas the beneficiary has the equitable ownership of the land and therefore has rights recognised in equity. The beneficial interest in the land equates to the equitable interest under a trust and is recognised by s 1(3) of the LPA 1925.

1.4.2.2 Equitable interests where no trust is involved

There are other interests in land that can exist where there is no trust structure.

Restrictive covenants

These are promises made by one party (the 'covenantor') in favour of the other party (the 'covenantee') that the covenantor will not use their land in a particular way. Restrictive covenants are often created on a sale of part (see **Chapter 7**) and are equitable interests.

Estate contract

This is a contract to create or convey a legal estate in the land. The buyer under the contract has an equitable interest in the land. Applying the equitable maxim, 'equity sees that as done which ought to be done', equity treats the contract as having already been specifically enforced. So the person with the benefit of the contract (the buyer) is seen as having an immediate (equitable) interest in the land.

Examples of estate contracts

(a) Jim, the owner of a freehold property, decides to sell the property to a buyer, Bill. They exchange contracts. After exchange and until completion of the purchase, Bill holds an equitable interest in the property. This type of equitable interest is an estate contract – a contract to buy a freehold estate in land.

(b) Jim also owns a large undeveloped plot of land in which the Waitway Supermarket is interested as the site for a new store. However, Waitway is not sure that it will be

able to get planning permission for the development of the site for retail purposes. To ensure that Jim does not sell the property to another company whilst its planning application is being considered, Waitway enters into an agreement with Jim under which Jim grants Waitway the option to buy the land for £500,000 at any time in the next 12 months. Waitway has an option to purchase the property and this is an equitable interest - also an estate contract.

(c) *Another estate contract is a contract to grant a lease. Jim has another freehold property and he grants Larry a 10-year lease of that property. However, he does not grant the lease using the correct formalities required to create a legal lease (see* ***1.5.1*** *below). Larry will have a contract to grant a lease, which will be recognised by equity, provided the correct formalities for creating an estate contract have been complied with. In such a case, as equity will recognise the contract, Larry will have an equitable lease. You will consider this method of creating equitable leases further in* ***Chapter 5****.*

(d) *If Jim granted a right of way for five years across his land to his neighbour, Andy, this is a right that is capable of being legal under s 1(2)(a) of the LPA 1925. However, if Jim used a document to create the easement that did not satisfy the correct formalities required to grant a legal easement (see* ***1.5.1*** *below), then equity will still recognise the easement provided that the formalities required for an estate contract have been complied with. So if the document meets these requirements then Andy will have an equitable easement, another form of estate contract.*

Certain formalities must be met to create an estate contract (see **1.5.3.2** below).

Equitable easements

You have seen at **1.4.1** above that an easement for an interest equivalent to an estate in fee simple absolute in possession or a term of years absolute is capable of being a legal interest. An easement for an uncertain period does not fall within s 1(2) of the LPA 1925 and so is not capable of being legal. It will, however, be recognised as an equitable easement if the formalities for creating equitable interests that are not estate contracts are fulfilled (see **1.5.3.2** below).

It is important to be aware of the distinction between the formalities required to create an equitable interest such as easement of uncertain duration, or a restrictive covenant, and the formalities required for the creation of an estate contract, a right recognised in equity (see **1.5.3.2** below).

1.4.3 Statute

Certain third party rights have arisen by virtue of statutory provisions, eg s 30 of the Family Law Act (FLA) 1996.

Although spouses may live together in the matrimonial home, it may be that only one of them owns the legal estate, ie the conveyance was in the name of only one of them. Parliament has given the non-owning spouse certain rights (now known as 'home rights'), principally a right of occupation as against the other spouse. This right arises provided that:

(a) the parties are legally married (not divorced);

(b) the home is, has been or is intended to be the matrimonial home.

Home rights usually last only so long as the marriage subsists. They would normally end, therefore, on death or divorce.

The right of a non-owner to occupy the matrimonial home under s 30 of the FLA 1996 extends to couples who have registered their partnership under the Civil Partnership Act 2004.

The right is independent of and in addition to any equitable interest arising under a trust which the non-legal owning spouse or civil partner may have (see **Chapter 4**).

This is the only type of statutory third party right that you will encounter in this textbook. It has evolved from Parliament, whereas all other property rights that you will encounter in this textbook have evolved either through the common law or the Chancery Courts.

1.4.4 Licences

1.4.4.1 Introduction

So far we have been looking at interests that are proprietary in nature, that is, they are capable of binding successive owners of land. However, there will be many situations in which landowners, whilst allowing persons to use their land in some way, do not intend to create any kind of proprietary interest in it. The person using the land will, instead, usually have a licence of some kind. Licences are important as they often constitute the default position if the right created by the landowner does not fall into one of the categories of proprietary interest.

1.4.4.2 What is a licence?

A licence is a familiar concept. Most people have a licence of some kind. It may be a licence to drive a car, to sell alcohol to the public, to run a betting shop, or simply a licence for the television that they watch at home in the evening. The licence gives them permission to do something that they are not otherwise authorised to do. In each of these situations it is the law that imposes the requirement for a licence and makes it an offence to carry out the activity without one.

However, we have to think of the licence in broader terms. It is a permission to do something you would not normally be allowed to do, but it is not confined to authorisation given by the State. You, as a private individual, may grant a licence to someone.

1.4.4.3 Terminology

The person granting the licence is known as a 'licensor' and the person to whom the licence is granted as a 'licensee'. Our concern in this textbook is, of course, with licences affecting land, and the person granting the licence, or who is deemed to have granted it, will be a landowner of some kind.

1.4.4.4 General characteristics of a licence

Every day, probably without realising it, you are either granting or being granted a licence over land.

Examples of licences

Allowing a child into your garden to retrieve a ball is an example of a licence. You have given someone permission to enter your land but have no intention of conferring on them a permanent right to do so. Other examples of situations where a person will have only a licence to be on someone's land include staying at a hotel overnight, taking up lodgings in someone's house, going to a pub for a drink, going to the cinema or the theatre and entering a shop.

You can see that a licence is capable of authorising anything, from a simple right of access (going into a shop) to temporary occupation (becoming a lodger), and that its length can vary. In *Thomas v Sorrell* (1673) Vaugh 330, Vaughan CJ stated the effect of a licence to be that it 'properly passeth no interest, nor alters or transfers property in anything, but only makes an action lawful, which without it had been unlawful'.

So put very simply, a licence does not create any proprietary interest in land. It is no more than a permission that rescues you from being regarded as a trespasser on someone's land. It is purely a personal matter affecting only the licensor and the licensee. It is not assignable and can be revoked at any time. That, however, is putting it very simply. There are several different types of licence. The only ones you are going to consider are the bare licence and the contractual licence.

1.4.4.5 Bare licence

Nature

The first licence we will consider is known as a bare licence, that is to say, it is a licence granted for no consideration. If, for example, I own a field and give you permission to take a short cut across my land, that would be a bare licence. It only, of course, entitles you to cross my land. It does not authorise you to do anything else on my land, such as riding your horse around the field. Scrutton LJ expressed it in the following way: 'when you invite a person into your house to use the staircase, you do not invite him to slide down the banisters' (*The Calgarth* [1927] P 93).

Revocation?

If a friend invites you to come and stay for the weekend, the friend may phone you up and say you cannot come. You cannot turn round and say to your friend: 'Try and stop me!' Such a licence does not give you any proprietary interest in the land and can be revoked.

1.4.4.6 Contractual licence

Nature

A contractual licence is one that is supported by consideration.

Revocation?

If you visit the cinema, you have a licence to enter the cinema and remain there whilst the film is being shown. The purchase of your ticket has given you a contractual right to see the film and the licence to enter the cinema is essential to the fulfilment of the contract. If you are thrown out of the cinema before the film ends, without any apparent justification, what rights do you have? At common law, revocation of a contractual licence may give rise to damages for breach of contract. In equity, it may be possible, in some situations, to restrain wrongful revocation by means of an injunction.

1.5 Formalities for the creation of estates and interests

So far in this chapter, we have looked at the various legal and equitable estates and interests that can exist in land. We now need to consider the formalities required for the creation of such estates and interests.

1.5.1 Creation of legal estates and interests

Section 52(1) of the LPA 1925 sets out the general rule that a deed is required to create legal estates and interests in land. If this formality is not followed, the purported transaction will be void at law. This means that the estates and interests appearing respectively in s 1(1) and (2) of the LPA 1925 must be created by deed in order to be legal.

The requirements for a deed are set out in s 1 of the Law of Property (Miscellaneous Provisions) Act (LP(MP)A) 1989 which are that it must:

- make it clear on the face of the document that it is intended to be a deed (whether describing itself as a deed or being executed by the parties as a deed); and
- be signed, witnessed and delivered.

These provisions apply to deeds made on or after 31 July 1990. Delivery does not have to be physical delivery. It may be a matter of intention only, evidenced by a signatory executing the deed with the intention that they will be bound by it.

However, there are some exceptions to this general rule contained in s 52(2) of the LPA 1925. An important one is the exception in s 52(2)(d) – leases that are not required by law to be made in writing. This is known as the parol lease exception. Section 54(2) of the LPA 1925 describes such leases.

Where the transaction involves the grant of a lease for a term of three years or less, the lease can be granted without a deed and can even be granted orally. There are two other conditions set out in s 54(2) of the LPA 1925 that must be satisfied before the lease can be created without a deed. The first condition is that the lease must take effect immediately in possession (ie the tenant must be entitled to take possession as soon as the lease is granted). The second is that the lease must have been granted at the best rent which can be reasonably obtained (ie market rent) without taking a fine (also known as a premium). Payment of a fine (or premium) means the tenant paying the landlord a lump sum at the beginning of the lease. This fine (or premium) could be paid instead of rent or in addition to it.

There are other exceptions to s 52(1). Usually, the creation of a legal easement requires the formality of a deed; however, certain easements (as a consequence of their method of creation) do not require this formality. This will be considered in more detail in **Chapter 8**.

1.5.2 Disposition of legal estates and interests

So far, we have considered the formalities required for the creation of legal estates and interests in land. We should also consider the formalities required to dispose of or transfer an existing legal estate or interest.

In considering any disposition of an estate or interest in land we are looking at any sale or gift, or other disposal of an existing estate or interest, that is, one that has already been created. There are formalities that need to be satisfied for such dispositions to be valid at law. Section 52 of the LPA 1925 also provides that a deed is required to transfer a legal estate or interest.

Examples

(a) The sale of an existing legal lease where the lease was originally granted for a term of 20 years falls within s 52 of the LPA 1925. This means that the sale of the lease must be effected by deed.

(b) The sale of an existing legal lease where the lease was originally granted for two years needs to be effected by deed as s 54(2) of the LPA 1925 applies only to the creation of a lease.

(c) The sale of a freehold falls within s 52 of the LPA 1925 and so the transaction must be completed with a deed.

If the title is unregistered, the deed transferring ownership is called a 'conveyance', and if the title is registered, the deed is called 'a transfer'.

With a registered property, regardless of the date on which the deed was executed, the legal title does not pass to the purchaser until their name is entered in the register as the new proprietor of the land (see **Chapter 3**).

1.5.3 Creation of equitable interests

Equitable interests can come into existence because they have arisen under a trust of land, or in a number of other ways (see **1.3** and **1.4**). The formalities for the creation of equitable interests which arise under trusts are different from the formalities for the creation of other equitable interests.

1.5.3.1 Equitable interests under trusts

Remember that trusts can be established expressly, for example in a property owner's will or during the property owner's lifetime. So if two people want to make a declaration of trust on buying a house together in order to evidence that they are both beneficial owners, they can do so expressly. Express trusts over land must satisfy s 53(1)(b) of the LPA 1925. The declaration of trust must be evidenced in writing and must be signed.

Trusts can also come into existence without the need for formalities (LPA 1925, s 53(2)). These trusts are known as 'implied' trusts. An implied trust arises automatically as a result of the property owner's actions, for example where one party makes a financial contribution to the purchase of property, which is not a gift or a loan, but that party is not named as a legal owner. In this situation, the legal owner would hold the property on trust for themselves and the party who made the contribution. We shall look at these trusts further in **Chapter 4**.

1.5.3.2 Equitable interests where no trust is involved

All other equitable interests can be categorised as non-trust interests. You have already seen that these include restrictive covenants and easements for an uncertain period, as well as estate contracts (see **1.4.2.2**). The formalities required to create a purely equitable interest, and those required to create an estate contract (recognised as an equitable interest), are different.

Estate contracts

The formalities for contracts relating to land that are entered into on or after 27 September 1989 are governed by s 2 of the LP(MP)A 1989. The contract must:

- be in writing;
- incorporate all the expressly agreed terms in one document (or where contracts are exchanged in each document); and
- be signed by or on behalf of all the parties.

Section 2 does not apply in relation to a contract:

(a) to grant such a lease created under s 54(2) of the LPA 1925 (short leases);

(b) made in the course of a public auction.

Examples

Vikki Vincent owns the freehold of her house, Rosemead. Jason claims that she has entered into a binding contract for the sale of Rosemead to him. She denies this. The following examples demonstrate whether a binding estate contract has been created:

(a) Vikki put the freehold of Rosemead up for auction. Jason went to the auction and made the highest bid, and the house was knocked down to him. There is nothing in writing to record what has happened.

Under s 2(5)(b) of the LP(MP)A 1989, a contract for the sale of land made at a public auction does not have to be in writing and so there is a binding contract with Jason for the sale of Rosemead.

(b) Vikki and Jason have signed a written contract prepared by a solicitor for the sale of the freehold of Rosemead. The solicitor forgot to include a term (agreed by Vikki and Jason) in the contract that Vikki will take her mahogany toilet seat when she moves out.

The contract does not fulfil all of the requirements of s 2 of the LP(MP)A 1989 as it does not contain all of the agreed terms. It is, therefore, not a valid contract for the sale of land.

(c) Jason and Vikki instructed a solicitor to draft a contract for the sale of the freehold of Rosemead to Jason. The contract contained all the agreed terms and Vikki and Jason have signed it.

This contract does fulfil the requirements of s 2 of the LP(MP)A 1989 and is a valid contract for the sale of Vikki's house.

(d) Vikki and Jason have a conversation in which Vikki agrees to grant Jason a legal lease of Rosemead for one year. There is nothing in writing.

Under s 2(5)(a) of the LP(MP)A 1989, an agreement to grant a short lease falling within s 54(2) of the LPA 1925 (see ***1.5.1*** *above) does not need to be in writing. So the agreement to grant the one-year lease could be created without complying with the conditions set out in s 2 of the LP(MP)A 1989 and it could be created orally. So Vikki has entered into a contract to grant the lease.*

(e) Vikki and Jason have a conversation in which Vikki agrees to grant Jason a legal lease of Rosemead for seven years. There is nothing in writing.

The agreement to grant the lease for a term of seven years does not fall within the exception under s 54(2) of the LPA 1925. The requirements of s 2 of the LP(MP)A 1989 therefore apply to this contract. The contract to grant the lease for seven years is therefore not valid as it was created orally.

Other equitable interests

The minimum formality requirement for the creation of equitable interests where no trust is involved (other than estate contracts) is that the interest be created by signed writing (LPA 1925, s 53(1)(a)).

So, if an easement is granted for an uncertain period, eg a right of way granted until the land over which the right is granted is developed, that easement is not capable of being legal under s 1(2)(a) of the LPA 1925. As a result, it is only capable of being an equitable easement (LPA 1925, s 1(3)). Therefore, the formalities required to create an equitable easement are that it should be created in writing, signed by the person creating it (LPA 1925, s 53(1)(a)).

A restrictive covenant is an interest which is only capable of being equitable (LPA 1925, s 1(3)). Restrictive covenants are usually created when land is sold. As you have seen in **1.5.1** above, the sale of land requires there to be a deed, and as such restrictive covenants will usually be contained in a deed as part of that sale transaction. The formalities required for the creation of a restrictive covenant are signed writing (LPA 1925, s 53(1)(a)). A deed is *not* required to create a valid equitable interest, but a valid deed will automatically comply with the requirement of signed writing; therefore, a restrictive covenant contained in a deed is a valid equitable interest.

1.5.4 Disposition of equitable interests

Any sale, gift or other disposition of an equitable interest must be in writing and signed by the parties to the document (LPA 1925, s 53(1)(c)). For example, if a beneficiary under a trust wished to dispose of their equitable interest, they would need to do this in a written document which they then signed. They would not need a deed as they are dealing with an equitable interest.

1.6 Introduction to the conveyancing of land

In order for you to have a full understanding of how land law operates today, it is necessary to look at how the system of conveyancing operates in England and Wales. The term 'conveyancing' is used to describe the procedure followed to transfer title to (ie ownership of) land. In this section we will give you a basic outline of the conveyancing procedure.

1.6.1 The stages in a conveyancing transaction

In any conveyancing transaction in England and Wales there are two distinct stages. The first is the stage leading up to exchange of contracts. The second important stage is completion, which typically takes place a few weeks after exchange of contracts.

1.6.1.1 The contract

Prior to entering into the contract, the buyer will investigate the property fully. This will include: looking at a copy of the documentary evidence of title; asking the seller questions about the property; searching for public local information; and inspecting the property. This pre-contract stage is very important, as it is at this stage that the buyer will hope to find out about all the rights and interests that exist over the property.

As you now know, to be valid, a contract for the sale of land must satisfy s 2 of the LP(MP)A 1989. Thus the contract must be in writing and must contain all the express terms agreed between the parties; other terms may be implied by common law or statute. The contract must be signed by or on behalf of each party. Where duplicate contracts are produced and exchanged, both parties to the contract must sign it, but not necessarily the same part. Usually the seller and purchaser sign identical but separate contracts which they exchange. On exchange the contract becomes fully effective.

Until contracts are exchanged either party may withdraw from the transaction without penalty. However once contracts have been exchanged, the parties are contractually bound to each other, and if they fail to complete as provided for in their contract, they will face penalties. This is why people who are in the process of buying or selling their homes will be extremely relieved once their solicitor tells them that they have exchanged contracts. They know that the deal will go ahead and can think about practical arrangements such as removal of furniture, changing telephone numbers and finalising bills for services such as gas and electricity.

You will find an example of a standard contract for the sale of land in **Reading 1** in the **Appendix**.

Effect of the contract

After exchange of contracts, the seller still has the legal title to the land. They must look after the property and not sell it to anyone else. The seller may remain in the property until completion when the buyer must pay the balance of the purchase price. Between contract and completion, the buyer has an equitable interest in the property. This corresponds to the estate or interest to be sold. The equitable interest is known as an estate contract, as you saw in **1.4.2** above. Even though the price has not been paid, and the buyer is not entitled to physical possession of the land, the binding contract gives them an equitable interest.

The legal title to the property does not pass to the buyer until the second stage of the conveyancing transaction has been carried out and the legal formalities completed.

1.6.1.2 The conveyance or transfer

The second stage in the conveyancing transaction is completion. As you will know, to transfer the title to a legal estate or interest in land, the parties must execute a deed (LPA 1925, s 52). On completion, the legal title to the property is transferred to the purchaser using a conveyance or transfer. You will find an example of each of these documents at **Readings 2** and **3** respectively in the **Appendix**. The day on which the conveyance or deed is completed is the day when the balance of the purchase money is paid over and the parties actually move. However, as you will see in **Chapter 3**, after that the new owner must be registered at Land Registry.

1.6.2 Electronic conveyancing

As you may be aware, it is intended that land will be conveyed by means of electronic conveyancing in the future. Contracts for the sale of land and deeds will be made in electronic form and signed electronically by the parties or their agents. However, the current system of conveying land is as explained at **1.6.1** above.

1.7 Summary of interests and formalities

Now that you have been introduced to estates and third party interests in land, you will be able to identify different types of estates and interests in land and the formalities required to ensure that they are validly created. The following summary will provide you with a suggested approach to enable you to do this.

1.7.1 Identify the estate or interest

At this stage you have been introduced to various different types of estates and third party interests that can exist in relation to land. It is important that you correctly ascertain the type of estate or interest you are dealing with, for example, an easement, a lease, a restrictive covenant. These will each be studied in more detail in the later chapters of this textbook.

1.7.2 Is it capable of being legal?

You will now know that s 1(1) of the LPA 1925 lists the estates that are capable of being legal - the freehold (fee simple absolute in possession) and the leasehold (term of years absolute), whilst s 1(2) of the LPA 1925 lists the third party interests that are capable of being legal. The two most important are the easement and the mortgage. If the estate or interest does not fall within these lists, it is not capable of being legal; it can only take effect in equity (LPA 1925, s 1(3)). The only type of statutory third party right that you will be concerned with is the 'home right' under the FLA 1996.

1.7.3 Formalities

In order to determine whether an estate or interest in land is valid, it is necessary to consider whether the correct formalities have been used to create it. You are now aware that there are several levels of formality.

1.7.3.1 Creation by deed

Generally, to be valid, all legal estates and interests must be created by deed (LPA 1925, s 52). The requirements for a deed are contained in s 1 of the LP(MP)A 1989. This covers all the estates and interests listed in s 1(1) and (2) of the LPA 1925.

There are some exceptions to this rule. You have been introduced to the parol lease exception - a valid legal lease can be created without a deed if it satisfies the conditions in s 54(2) of the LPA 1925. In **Chapter 8** you will also discover that a valid legal easement may arise without the need for a deed or any other formality.

1.7.3.2 Creation in a contract

Where there is a contract to create or convey a legal estate in land, equity will recognise that contract as creating an equitable interest in land, so long as it satisfies the requirements for a contract under s 2 of the LP(MP)A 1989. This is because where there is a contract that is specifically enforceable at common law, then equity will see as done that which ought to be done. Rights recognised by equity include a contract to buy a freehold estate in land and an option. In addition, equity will recognise as an estate contract a lease, or an easement which satisfies s 1 of the LPA 1925 but which has not been granted by deed. Where the instrument creating a lease or an easement satisfies the requirements of s 2 of the LP(MP)A 1989 then these will also be treated as estate contracts.

1.7.3.3 Creation by signed writing

There are certain minimum formalities for the creation of other equitable interests such as restrictive covenants and easements of uncertain duration. These equitable interests are only valid if they are created in signed writing (LPA 1925, s 53(1)(a)). Express trust interests relating to land must be evidenced in writing (LPA 1925, s 53(1)(b)).

1.7.3.4 No formalities

As stated in **1.7.3.1** above, there are certain legal estates and interests that are valid at law without a deed being used - the parol lease exception and certain easements. You will now also be aware that implied trusts may be created without any formality according to s 53(2) of the LPA 1925. In addition, the statutory right under the Family Law Act 1996 does not require any formality and will arise if the conditions in s 30 have been satisfied. This is the only statutory right with which you will be concerned in this textbook.

1.7.4 Legal, equitable or statutory?

By applying your knowledge relating to whether an estate or interest is capable of being legal or not and your knowledge of the necessary formalities, you can conclude whether it is legal, equitable or statutory.

If it is capable of being legal and has been created by deed or satisfies one of the exceptions, it will be a valid legal estate or interest. However, if the formalities are not met, equity may save the estate or interest (for example a lease or easement) if it satisfies the formalities for an estate contract.

If it is only capable of being equitable, eg a trust interest or a restrictive covenant, it will only be a valid equitable interest if it satisfies the appropriate rules.

If the formality rules are not complied with then there can be no valid interest in the land. The claimant would have a licence only.

ACTIVITY 2 Test your knowledge

The aim of this activity is to test your understanding of the material covered in **Chapter 1**.

Your client, Heathersage Ltd, has instructed your firm to act in relation to a proposed purchase of Seagrove Farm owned by Geoffrey Wainwright. Your investigations have revealed the following:

(1) Geoffrey Wainwright's son, Roland, has provided you with a copy of a document containing an express declaration of trust relating to Seagrove Farm for the benefit of Roland, signed by his father in January last year.

(2) Two years ago, Geoffrey agreed that his neighbour could lay, and then use, drains across part of Seagrove Farm. A document allowing the neighbour to do this was drawn up between them.

(3) One of the outbuildings is occupied by Geoffrey's brother, who runs a motorcycle repair business from that outbuilding. To put the arrangement on a formal basis, Geoffrey wrote a letter to his brother saying, 'I give you the exclusive right to occupy my outbuilding for five years to use as a motorcycle repair business, provided you pay me £500 each year.'

(4) In June last year, Geoffrey executed a deed in which he promised Soames Feeders Ltd, a business run from an adjacent property, that he would not grow winter wheat on any part of Seagrove Farm for 10 years.

Identify the types of third party interests that have been revealed, whether each interest has been created by the correct formalities, and whether the interest is legal or equitable. Make reference to statutory authority where relevant.

COMMENT

(1) Roland Wainwright

Roland appears to have an equitable interest under a trust. It has been created expressly, and therefore must be evidenced in writing and must be signed to be valid (LPA 1925, s 53(1)(b)).

On the facts this appears to be the case, and therefore Roland has a valid equitable interest under a trust.

(2) Geoffrey's neighbour

The right to lay and use the drains is capable of being a legal easement under s 1(2)(a) of the LPA 1925. As there is no time limit imposed on the right, it is of unlimited duration. It is therefore an easement for an interest equivalent to the fee simple absolute in possession.

It has been created in a document. If that document satisfies the requirements for a deed under s 1 of the LP(MP)A 1989 - namely, it is clear on the face of the document that it is intended to be a deed and it is signed, witnessed and delivered - then the neighbour will have a valid legal easement (LPA 1925, s 52(1)). However, if the document only complies with s 2 of the LP(MP)A 1989, namely, it is in writing, signed by both parties and contains all the agreed terms, then the neighbour will have a valid equitable easement. Even though it is capable of being legal, it has not been created with the correct formalities to make it legal. However, if the correct formalities have been used for a valid estate contract, then it will be recognised in equity.

(3) Geoffrey's brother

Geoffrey's brother's right is capable of being a legal lease. He has been granted exclusive possession of the outbuilding for a fixed term of five years; therefore the right comes within s 1(1)(b) of the LPA 1925.

To create a valid legal lease, a deed is required under s 52(1) of the LPA 1925. Geoffrey has set out the arrangement in a letter which is unlikely to satisfy the requirements for a deed in s 1 of the LP(MP)A 1989. Nor can Geoffrey's brother rely upon the parol lease exception under s 54(2) of the LPA 1925, as this lease is for a term of five years.

In the absence of the correct formalities to create a legal lease, Geoffrey's brother may have an equitable lease. As an equitable lease is a type of estate contract, to be valid in equity it would need to be created in accordance with s 2 of the LP(MP)A 1989. There must be an agreement in writing, containing all the agreed terms and signed by both parties. It is unlikely that a letter would satisfy these requirements and, therefore, Geoffrey's brother would not have an equitable lease.

In the absence of a valid deed or a valid estate contract, Geoffrey's brother may have a legal periodic tenancy as rent is paid and received on a regular basis. To be a valid legal periodic tenancy, the arrangement must satisfy s 54(2) of the LPA 1925. As you will see in **Chapter 5**, a periodic tenancy may be implied where rent is paid by reference to a period. Here, rent is paid annually and this may give rise to an annual periodic tenancy. However, this arrangement is unlikely to satisfy the conditions in s 54(2) of the LPA 1925 for a legal periodic tenancy as £500 per annum is unlikely to be the 'best rent'.

It seems that Geoffrey's brother will have only a licence to occupy the outbuilding. However, as he is paying rent, it will be a contractual licence. The rent will equate to consideration.

(4) Soames Feeders Ltd

Geoffrey has given a promise not to grow winter wheat on Seagrove Farm. This is a restrictive covenant. It has been created in a deed, which is standard for the creation of a restrictive covenant. Despite the fact that a deed has been used, the restrictive covenant is equitable as it does not come within s 1(1) or (2) of the LPA 1925, and therefore can only be equitable in accordance with s 1(3) of the LPA 1925. (As an equitable interest, the minimum requirement for creation of a restrictive covenant is signed writing in compliance with s 53(1)(a) of the LPA 1925; however, as you will see in **Chapter 7**, restrictive covenants are commonly created by deed.)

SUMMARY

- Land ownership is not always clear and straightforward. As you have now seen, there may be issues about what actually comprises land and what interests or rights exist in relation to land.
- You now have sufficient background knowledge to be able to identify what is meant by land and to identify estates and third party interests in land. You could advise on whether those estates and third party interests are valid at law or in equity, as you will now understand the particular rules required for the creation and transfer of estates and interests in land.
- You will be able to use this knowledge in your study of the unregistered system in **Chapter 2** and the registered system in **Chapter 3**.

2 Overview of the Unregistered System

LEARNING OUTCOMES

When you have completed this chapter, you should be able to:

- understand the basics of the unregistered system of land law;
- explain and apply the rules governing enforceability of third party rights and interests in the unregistered system.

2.1 Introduction

In **Chapter 1** you considered the nature of the estates and interests that can exist in land today. We are now going to look at how those estates and interests are treated in the unregistered system of land law. This was the only system in existence prior to 1925. In that year it became codified by the Law of Property Act (LPA) 1925, and at the same time the registered system was introduced by the Land Registration Act (LRA) 1925.

Since 1925, the unregistered system has been replaced largely by the modern registered system that will be covered in **Chapter 3**. However, more than 40% of England and Wales by area still remains unregistered. This comprises about 10% of all titles to land. It is therefore necessary to have an understanding of the unregistered system in order to be able to apply the relevant law to such land.

2.2 Unregistered conveyancing

2.2.1 Proof of ownership of title

As we saw in **Chapter 1**, there are two stages to the conveyancing transaction. Stage one leads up to the exchange of contracts. At that stage, the buyer obtains an equitable interest in the land. Stage two is completion, when the parties execute a deed to transfer legal ownership of the land. Where title to the land is unregistered, the buyer becomes the legal owner of the land at the date of the conveyance. You will see in **Chapter 3** (at **3.2**) that the conveyance of an unregistered title triggers an obligation to register the title.

Where the title to the property is not registered at Land Registry, sellers prove that they have the right to possession of the land by producing documents that show that they and their predecessors in title have been entitled to possession of the land for a given number of years. The deed used to transfer ownership of land from sellers to buyers is called a conveyance. Owners of unregistered titles prove their ownership by showing prospective buyers a bundle of deeds, most of them conveyances. The bundle of deeds and documents is called an 'epitome of title'. By studying the epitome, you can tell who has the right to possession of the land (and therefore has title to the land) and for what period, and some of the things they have done with it, eg granted leases, created mortgages, etc. The epitome provides a picture of who has been in possession of the land for the period of years covered by the deeds. The buyer of an unregistered title becomes the owner of that title at the date of the conveyance.

2.2.2 Proof of ownership of title

Imagine that Kamal wants to sell his unregistered freehold title to Ben. Kamal must show Ben an unbroken chain of title to prove his ownership of the land. So, Kamal will show Ben a copy of the conveyance proving that Xavier conveyed title to the land to Kamal. Ben might then enquire whether Xavier owned the land and was entitled to pass ownership of that land to Kamal. Kamal gives him a copy of a conveyance showing that Yvonne conveyed title to that land to Xavier. Ben might then ask for proof that Yvonne was entitled to convey the land to Xavier and be given a copy of a conveyance from Zoe to Yvonne. Ben again asks for proof that Zoe was entitled to sell the land to Yvonne, and Kamal provides him with a copy of a conveyance from Alan to Zoe. The result is a bundle of conveyances proving that Kamal has an unbroken chain of title.

The arrow diagram below shows how the land has changed hands.

X → K	2005
Y → X	1989
Z → Y	1979
A → Z	1976

So, Kamal has an unbroken chain of conveyances, starting with the 1976 conveyance and ending with the last conveyance in his favour. Note that Alan was not the first person to have title to the land. Someone else had title to it before Alan, and someone else before that person. As long as the documents have not been lost or destroyed, it may be possible to trace title back for centuries.

However, proving the title back a number of centuries would be expensive and time-consuming. Instead, the LPA 1925 provides that, unless the contract between the seller and the buyer provides to the contrary, the seller need only produce title deeds proving ownership of the land for the last 15 years, culminating in the conveyance to the seller (LPA 1925, s 44).

So, Kamal need only show Ben that he and his predecessors in title have enjoyed lawful possession of the land back to a good root of title that is at least 15 years old. The 2005 conveyance is old enough to be the root of title. (Note: you will see in **Chapter 3** (at **3.2**) that the conveyance to Kamal in 2005 required registration and this would have brought the land within the registered system. However, the theory that the 2005 conveyance is a good root of title is correct.)

Kamal need not show the 1976, 1979 or 1989 conveyances to Ben. Ben has the right to see all the conveyances since (and including) the 2005 conveyance.

So, in unregistered conveyancing, landowners' title deeds are used to prove their ownership of their land. The conveyances can also be used to find out about some third party rights (for example, covenants and easements) which bind the land.

2.2.3 Disadvantages of the unregistered system

The unregistered system of proving ownership of land has many disadvantages. The first problem that buyers face is that of forged title deeds. The conveyances proving ownership may look genuine but buyers have no guarantee that these documents are not forgeries.

There is also a risk that the title deeds shown to buyers to prove the sellers' ownership of the land may be genuine but may not include documents that record those transactions about which buyers may need to know before buying the land. Remember that buyers do not usually need to see any conveyance prior to the root of title document. Sellers do not have to show buyers conveyances dated prior to that root. These documents may be missing by design or accident. Buyers of an unregistered title can never be absolutely certain that the title they investigate is a good title, even if the title deeds they see indicate that title is good.

Another problem stems from the fact that no two unregistered titles look the same. Each transaction is individual, with the parties entering into a unique contract. Each time the land is sold, buyers have to read the old conveyances to establish ownership, and this system of proving title is time-consuming and repetitive. It is also expensive, as most buyers will instruct and pay a solicitor to do this work for them.

Landowners prove their ownership by using a bundle of original documents. Problems can occur if this bundle of original documents is lost, destroyed or stolen. Effectively this method of proving ownership is lost. In addition, original deeds are sometimes hard to read.

2.3 Enforceability of third party rights in the unregistered system

2.3.1 Introduction

As we saw in **Chapter 1**, ownership of land can amount to ownership of a legal estate, freehold or leasehold, but it can also include ownership of a third party interest or right which can be legal or equitable.

You will remember that some interests in land are 'proprietary interests', ie they can bind someone who buys the land but was not a party to creating the proprietary interest. For example, if you claim that you have a right of way over a particular piece of land, you are not claiming the right to own that piece of land but simply that you have the right to do one thing with that land - cross it. The same third party rights or incumbrances can exist in relation to land that is still unregistered and land that is now within the registered system that you will study in **Chapter 3**. The way in which you decide whether or not those third party rights bind the land (and therefore anyone who buys that land) differs, however, depending on whether you are dealing with an unregistered or a registered title.

In this section you will examine the rules governing enforceability of third party rights over unregistered land. These rules are relevant whenever unregistered land is being sold to a purchaser, to determine whether the purchaser is bound by any third party interests that exist in the land. Note that these rules apply even where first registration of the title is required after completion.

Generally, all that is necessary is to consider the statutory rules found in the Land Charges Act (LCA) 1972. This Act replaces the earlier Land Charges Act (LCA) 1925. However, the LCA 1972 does not apply to every third party interest. If the interest falls outside of the LCA rules, you must apply the rules which operated before the LCA 1925 came into force. That Act came into force on 1 January 1926 so we will refer to the old rules as the 'pre-1926 rules' (see **2.3.3** and **2.3.4** below for an explanation of the pre-1926 rules). As the pre-1926 rules now apply only to a very few interests, we will consider the position under the LCA 1972 first.

2.3.2 The land charges system

From 1 January 1926, a system of registration of incumbrances came into existence. Certain third party rights became registrable on the Land Charges Register. This is a public register kept at the Central Land Charges Department in Plymouth. Note that the Land Charges Register is a different register from that contained at Land Registry. The Land Charges Register is essentially a register of third party rights that affect unregistered land. Land Registry is a register dealing with both the ownership of the title and third party rights in registered land. You will learn about this system in **Chapter 3**.

The Land Charges Register is a register of names. Details of the third party interests should be registered by the person with the interest against the name of the estate owner who has created the interest and whose land is to be burdened by it (LCA 1972, s 3). This should be done at the time the interest is created.

Not all third party rights can be registered on the Land Charges Register. The third party rights that are registrable at the Land Charges Department are listed in s 2 of the LCA 1972. The key classes are as follows:

C(iv)	an estate contract
D(ii)	a restrictive covenant
D(iii)	an equitable easement
F	a home right
C(i)	puisne mortgage

Example

Adam owns the unregistered freehold of his house, Church Cottage. He enters into a contract for the creation of a lease in favour of Mayuko. This is an estate contract. In order to protect her estate contract, Mayuko would need to register a C(iv) land charge against Adam's full name as it appears in the title deeds.

2.3.2.1 Effect of registration of land charges

Registration of those interests capable of being registered as a land charge is deemed to constitute actual notice of the incumbrance and of the fact of registration to all persons connected with the land affected, as from the date of registration (LPA 1925, s 198). In effect this means that where a land charge has been registered on the Land Charges Register, anyone who buys the land is deemed to buy with actual knowledge of the land charge and so will be bound by it. In order to bind a purchaser, the land charge must be registered by the date of completion of the sale. In unregistered land, this means the date of the conveyance when the purchaser becomes the legal owner of the land.

As a consequence, purchasers need to find out about any registered land charge before committing themselves to buying the land.

Remember that sellers of unregistered titles prove their ownership by sending their purchasers copies of their title deeds showing an unbroken chain of ownership going back at least 15 years. Purchasers can then search the Land Charges Register against the names of previous estate owners revealed by the sellers' title deeds. Any land charges that have been registered will then be revealed. You will find an example of the result of a search at the Land Charges Registry at **Reading 5** in the **Appendix**. This document shows that a restrictive covenant has been registered against the name of George Handel at the Land Charges Registry.

2.3.2.2 Effect of failure to register a land charge

Section 4 of the LCA 1972 deals with the effect of non-registration and provides that purchasers of the land can take free of the unregistered land charge. It is therefore essential for the owner of a third party right to register it as a land charge, to ensure that it binds any purchaser.

The term 'purchaser', for the purposes of the LCA 1972, includes a mortgagee and a lessee but not someone who has taken a gift of the property. A person who receives property as a gift takes subject to all the third party rights, whether registered or not.

Example

*Continuing with the Example in **2.3.2** above, Adam enters into a contract for the creation of a lease in favour of Mayuko. This is an estate contract. Mayuko fails to register a C(iv) land charge against Adam's name. Adam subsequently sells the land to Sol for full market price. Is Sol bound by the estate contract?*

Sol is not bound. He has purchased a legal estate for money or money's worth and the land charge was not registered before completion of the purchase. Sol takes free of the estate contract.

2.3.2.3 What if the buyer has actual knowledge of the interest?

A farmer granted his son an option to purchase the farm. An option is an estate contract. The son failed to register a C(iv) land charge. The farmer and son then fell out. The farmer subsequently conveyed the farm to his wife for the sum of £500 (much less than the true value of the farm). The son argued that his mother should be bound by his option as she knew about it when she purchased the land from her husband.

The court held that if a land charge was not protected by registration, the knowledge of the buyer is irrelevant. This was the outcome in *Midland Bank Trust Co Ltd v Green* [1981] 1 AC 513. The farmer's wife was not bound by her son's option.

2.3.3 The pre-1926 rules: legal estates and interests

To have the complete picture of how the system for enforcing third party rights works where title to land is unregistered, you need to know the pre-1926 rules.

One way of categorising third party rights is to divide them into legal and equitable interests. The pre-1926 rules use this as a starting point for deciding whether or not third party rights bind the land. Under the pre-1926 rules, legal estates and interests bind the whole world. This means that a legal third party interest will bind the purchaser of the legal estate, even if the purchaser has no knowledge of the existence of the interest when they buy the property.

Example

If A gives a legal lease to B and then sells the fee simple to C, B's legal lease is binding on and enforceable against C. It is irrelevant whether or not C knew about B's legal lease when they bought from A.

2.3.4 The pre-1926 rules: equitable interests

A person who holds an equitable interest is not as secure as a person with a legal interest.

Example

Two trustees, T1 and T2, hold the legal estate of a house on trust for A and, in breach of trust, they sell the house to P. A could sue the trustees for breach of trust and recover the monetary value of the house. But suppose that the trustees were bankrupt or had disappeared, or A really wanted the house back and not compensation in money. Could they sue P?

The basic rule is that equitable interests are enforceable against anyone *except* the *bona fide purchaser of the legal estate for value without notice* ('equity's darling'). The question you will have to consider is whether or not the buyer comes within the definition of 'equity's darling'.

2.3.4.1 Meaning of equity's darling

First, the buyer must be *bona fide* - this means they must be acting in good faith (without fraud).

Next, the buyer must come within the definition of a *purchaser* - this includes a mortgagee or a lessee. A purchaser is a person who receives property other than by operation of law. Therefore, if A sells land to B, or gives it to B, or leaves it to B in their will, then B is a purchaser. If, however, A died intestate and X inherited A's property through the intestacy rules, then X would not be a purchaser. Similarly, if A went bankrupt and their property passed to their trustee in bankruptcy, T, then T would not be a purchaser. Both of these situations result in the property passing by operation of law.

Third, the buyer must have bought the property *for value* - this means they must have given consideration for the purchase of the estate. Value includes any form of consideration which would be classed as valuable consideration in the law of contract, namely: money, money's worth (eg land, stocks and shares), marriage or the promise of marriage, and payment of an existing debt. It does not have to amount to full consideration. It may be worth noting that a person who gives no valuable consideration is called a 'volunteer'.

Fourth, the buyer must have taken the *legal estate* in the property - they must have purchased a fee simple absolute in possession or a term of years absolute (LPA 1925, s 1(1)).

Lastly, the buyer must have bought the property *without notice* that the equitable interest exists. There are three recognised forms of notice, which we will now examine further.

2.3.4.2 Types of notice

A buyer can take free of an equitable interest only if they had no notice of it. Notice may be actual, constructive or imputed:

(a) *Actual notice.* A person has actual notice of all facts of which they have (or have had) actual knowledge, however that knowledge was acquired; but they are not regarded as having actual notice of facts which have come to their ears only in the form of vague rumours.

(b) *Constructive notice.* A buyer is deemed to have constructive notice of any matter or fact which 'would have come to his knowledge if such inquiries and inspections had been made as ought reasonably to have been made by him' (LPA 1925, s 199(1)).

(c) *Imputed notice.* A purchaser is deemed to have imputed notice of any matter of which their solicitor (or other agent) had actual or constructive notice.

The meaning of 'actual notice' is probably obvious, but what are the meanings and effects of constructive and imputed notice? How should a purchaser avoid being fixed with constructive or imputed notice of an equitable interest?

The answer is that the purchaser (or their agent) should investigate the seller's title and they should follow up anything that appears inconsistent with that title. Section 44(1) of the LPA 1925 gives the purchaser the right to inspect the seller's title deeds back to a good root of title, which is, unless otherwise provided in the contract, at least 15 years old (see **2.2.2** above). They should also inspect the land to see who is in occupation. If they find someone other than the seller (eg the seller's spouse or adult children) in occupation then the purchaser should enquire what interest, if any, the occupier has. If they (or their agent) do not take these steps, they will have constructive or imputed notice of any right that the occupier may have.

In *Kingsnorth Finance Co Ltd v Tizard* [1986] 1 WLR 783, the House of Lords explored this important area of law. Consider a purchaser of a house who is buying it from the owner, Mr T, who lives in the house with Mrs T. We will see in **Chapter 4** that Mrs T may have an equitable interest in the house (eg because she has contributed to the purchase price). Suppose the purchaser does not know of Mrs T's rights and buys the house; does the purchaser have constructive notice of her equitable interest? The *Kingsnorth* case made it clear that the purchaser or their agent must make all inquiries and inspections that, in the circumstances, ought reasonably to have been made. Otherwise, the purchaser will not be equity's darling, as they will be deemed to have constructive notice of Mrs T's equitable interest in the house.

ACTIVITY 1 Notice

Set out below is a series of events involving dealings by Hakim in various plots of land. In each case there exists a prior equitable interest under a trust. In all cases Hakim was a bona fide purchaser. Consider for each event whether or not Hakim would be bound by the prior equitable interest.

(1) Hakim bought the legal freehold of a two-acre plot of land outside Malham for £180,000. He made all the inquiries and searches required of a purchaser and had no notice of the interest.

(2) Hakim's brother, Mandla, gave Hakim the legal freehold of a lodge house at the entrance to Mandla's main residence. Again, Hakim made all the inquiries and searches required of a purchaser and had no notice of the equitable interest.

(3) Mandla has also exchanged his freehold ownership of Foley Farm for Hakim's freehold ownership of Roma Cottage together with three acres of land. Hakim exchanged the land without notice of the equitable interest in Foley Farm.

(4) Hakim bought the legal freehold of a small house in Beaconsfield. The house was owned by Mr Smith. Mr and Mrs Smith lived in the house, and Mrs Smith had contributed £5,000 towards the original purchase price. Hakim was aware that Mrs Smith lived in the house.

(5) Mandla also sold the equitable interest he held in Longrange Shooting Park to Hakim. Hakim had no notice of the prior equitable interest that existed in the Park.

COMMENT

(1) Hakim will not be bound by the equitable interest under a trust that exists in the plot of land as he is a bona fide purchaser of the legal estate for value without notice – equity's darling.

(2) Hakim will be bound by the equitable interest under a trust that exists in the lodge house as, although he has no notice of the equitable interest, he did not purchase the legal freehold for value but was given the house. He is treated as a purchaser, in that he acquires the property other than by operation of law. However, he has given no valuable consideration. He is a 'volunteer'.

(3) An exchange of one piece of land for another is treated as valuable consideration. As Hakim has acquired the freehold of Foley Farm without notice of the equitable interest, he is not bound by it. He is equity's darling.

(4) Since Hakim will have constructive notice of Mrs Smith's equitable interest under a trust through her occupation of the house, he will be bound by her interest as he does not purchase the house without notice of the interest – *Kingsnorth*. He would need to overreach her interest to take the land free of it (see **2.3.5.2**).

(5) Hakim will be bound by the prior equitable interest as he has not purchased the legal estate in the Park and therefore, he is not equity's darling.

The question of whether or not purchasers have constructive or imputed notice of a particular third party right causes difficulties for purchasers. They must ensure that they take all of the steps that a prudent purchaser would take to ensure that they do not have notice of an equitable interest and that, if they employ an agent, such as a solicitor, that agent passes on to them all relevant information about third party rights. As the issue of notice is crucial to the pre-1926 rules, the concept of considering whether or not a buyer is equity's darling is also known as the doctrine of notice.

The doctrine of notice, as you now know, has largely been superseded by the reforms introduced by the 1925 legislation.

2.3.5 'Unregistrable' interests and estates

The system of land charges was intended to replace the old pre-1926 rules, in particular the doctrine of notice which applies to the pre-1926 equitable rules. There are now only a very few interests to which the pre-1926 rules apply. The LCA 1972 does not cover all third party incumbrances, and the following list identifies the interests not covered in the classes of land charge:

(a) equitable interests arising under a trust;

(b) most legal interests (eg legal leases, legal easements, legal mortgages protected by title deeds); and

(c) pre-1926 equitable interests (including restrictive covenants and equitable easements created before 1 January 1926).

So far as these are concerned, the old rules as to enforceability must be applied. So, the equitable interests arising under a trust and the pre-1926 restrictive covenants and equitable easements will bind everyone except equity's darling. The legal interests will bind the whole world.

2.3.5.1 Removal of third party interests

A purchaser who discovers a third party interest before they buy the property may be able to take action to ensure that it is removed from the property before they complete the purchase.

If a lease, easement, mortgage or covenant is discovered, the buyer may be able to negotiate with the person who holds the benefit of the interest and get them to release their interest. This may involve a payment of money either by the seller, eg the repayment of a mortgage loan, or by the buyer, eg for the release of a covenant. If the person with the benefit of the interest refuses to remove it, the buyer will have to reconsider their purchase of the property.

2.3.5.2 Equitable interests under a trust and overreaching

If the buyer discovers an equitable interest under an express or implied trust, there is a special device that the buyer can use to remove the interest from the property – overreaching.

A legal owner can freely sell, give away or bequeath a legal estate in land. However, where a trust exists in relation to that land, the equitable interests of the beneficiaries need to be considered.

A buyer who satisfies the conditions for overreaching takes the land free of the interests of the beneficiaries under any express or implied trust. If overreaching occurs, the interests of the beneficiaries cease to be attached to the land but attach instead to the sale proceeds in the hands of the selling trustees.

To overreach a beneficial interest:

(a) the buyer must be acquiring the legal estate in the property;

(b) the buyer must pay the purchase money to all the trustees; and

(c) there must be at least two trustees (or a trust corporation).

(Note that overreaching also applies to registered titles, see **Chapter 3**.)

2.3.6 Enforceability in the unregistered system

Set out below is a flowchart showing how to apply the rules relating to the enforceability of third party rights in the unregistered system:

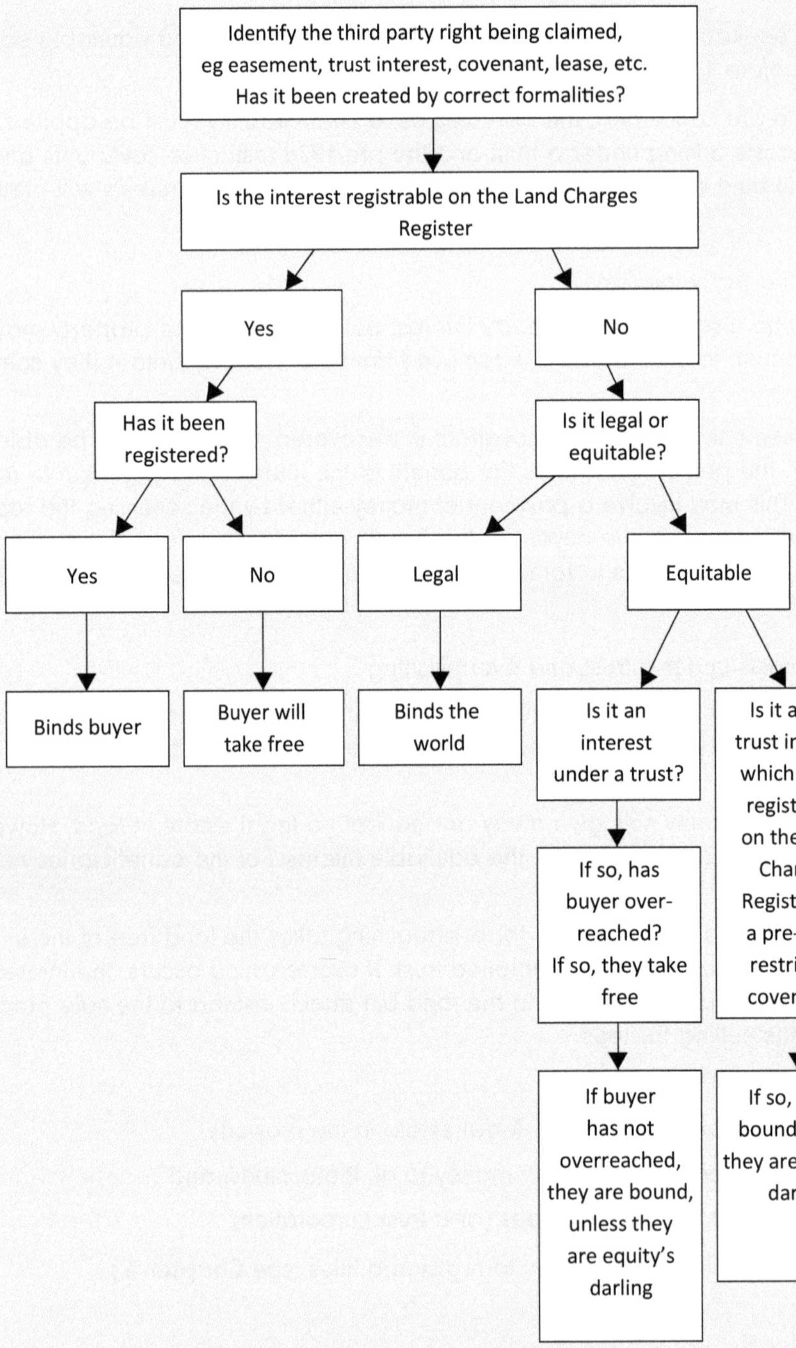

ACTIVITY 2 Test your knowledge: enforceability in the unregistered system

Complete the following table by indicating how each third party interest will be protected in the unregistered system. Assume all rights were created after 1925 unless stated otherwise.

Third party right	Registrable and class of land charge?	Binds the world?	Binds everyone except equity's darling?
Legal mortgage where lender has the title deeds			
Equitable lease			
Restrictive covenant			
Legal easement			
Equitable easement			
Legal lease for five years			
Legal lease for 10 years			
Option to buy freehold			
Non-legal owning spouse's/civil partner's right to occupy – Family Law Act 1996			
Restrictive covenant created in 1922			
Equitable interest under a trust of land			
Contract for the sale of land			

COMMENT

Third party right	Registrable and class of land charge?	Binds the world?	Binds everyone except equity's darling?
Legal mortgage where lender has the title deeds		√	
Equitable lease	C(iv) land charge		
Restrictive covenant	D(ii) land charge		
Legal easement		√ (however created)	
Equitable easement	D(iii) land charge		
Legal lease for five years		√	
Legal lease for 10 years		√	
Option to buy freehold	C(iv) land charge		

Third party right	Registrable and class of land charge?	Binds the world?	Binds everyone except equity's darling?
Non-legal owning spouse's/ civil partner's right to occupy – Family Law Act 1996	F land charge		
Restrictive covenant created in 1922			√
Equitable interest under a trust of land			√ (but can be overreached by purchaser)
Contract for the sale of land	C(iv) land charge		

ACTIVITY 3 Test your knowledge: types of interests and enforceability

You are acting for Satterthwaite Construction Ltd, which is buying a plot of unregistered land in Wigan from Blake Enterprises. Your investigations have revealed that, last year, the seller created the following interests in the land. Advise as to the types of interest that exist and explain whether, or in what circumstances, those interests will be binding on your client if it goes ahead with the proposed purchase.

(1) Blake Enterprises executed a deed in which they gave Ralph Gregson, the owner of an adjoining property, and any future owners of his land, the right to use a driveway over a field on the plot for 30 years. The use of the driveway was shared with Blake Enterprises.

(2) Blake Enterprises executed a deed with the owner of another adjoining property, in which Blake Enterprises promised that they and their successors would never build a supermarket on the land.

(3) How, if at all, would your answer to (2) differ if the deed had been signed in 1922?

COMMENT

(1) As Blake Enterprises did not grant exclusive use of the driveway (so did not grant a lease), it looks as if Ralph Gregson has an easement over the plot.

As the right is granted to Ralph Gregson and any future owners of his land for 30 years, it is an interest equivalent to a term of years absolute. It is therefore capable of being legal, as it comes within s 1(2)(a) of the LPA 1925.

It is created expressly, so to be legal it must be in a deed according to s 52 of the LPA 1925. It is granted in a deed and therefore it is legal.

The land is unregistered and the legal easement cannot be registered as a land charge on the Land Charges Register. However, legal rights bind the world, so Satterthwaite Construction Ltd will be bound by the right until 2036.

(2) This appears to be a restrictive covenant. It is created by deed, which is standard for a restrictive covenant (although it need only satisfy s 53(1)(a) of the LPA 1925 to be valid). Notwithstanding the fact that a deed has been used, the restrictive covenant is equitable only as it is not listed in s 1(1) or (2) of the LPA 1925, and therefore s 1(3) of the LPA 1925 applies.

The restrictive covenant can be registered on the Land Charges Register, and will bind Satterthwaite Construction Ltd if the adjoining owner registered a Class D(ii) land charge against the name of Blake Enterprises on the Land Charges Register before completion of the sale to Satterthwaite Construction Ltd. If it is not so registered, Satterthwaite Construction Ltd takes the land free of the restrictive covenant.

(3) A restrictive covenant created before 1925 cannot be protected as a land charge, so Satterthwaite Construction Ltd will be bound by the restrictive covenant unless it is equity's darling, ie a bona fide purchaser for value of the legal estate without notice of the covenant.

A purchaser is entitled to inspect the title deeds under s 44 of the LPA 1925, unless otherwise provided in the contract. It is likely that the restrictive covenant is mentioned in later conveyances, so it is likely that Satterthwaite Construction Ltd will have notice of the restrictive covenant and hence be bound by it.

SUMMARY

- You will now be able to appreciate that when dealing with a transaction involving unregistered land, you need to be able to build up a picture of estates, interests and rights that may affect the land and bind a purchaser.
- The starting point is the title deeds which a seller needs to produce to a purchaser to prove ownership of the legal estate. The deeds themselves may reveal third party interests as well. However, these will not bind a purchaser of the land unless they are either legal interests that bind the world or interests registered under the LCA 1972, or interests protected by the doctrine of notice. The system of protection under the LCA 1972 also applies to other third party interests that are not revealed by the title deeds. Where these are registrable as land charges, they must be registered to bind a purchaser.
- The residual interests and rights that do not come within the LCA 1972 are usually binding, as only in rare situations will the purchaser be equity's darling.
- It will now be apparent to you that you need to have an understanding of these three aspects – the title deeds themselves; the LCA 1972; and the doctrine of notice – to be able to appreciate the mechanics of transactions involving unregistered land and to advise a client in this context.

3 The Registered System

LEARNING OUTCOMES

When you have completed this chapter, you should be able to:

- understand the basics of the registered system of conveyancing and how to interpret official copies taken from the register at Land Registry;
- explain and apply the rules governing the enforceability of third party interests in the registered system of conveyancing, in both residential and commercial scenarios;
- understand the importance of the Land Registration Act 2002, Sch 3, para 2, and how it overlaps with the other categories of interest in the registered system.

3.1 Registered conveyancing

When we looked at the formalities involved in the sale of land, we saw that the transaction happens in two stages. At the first stage, exchange of contracts, the parties enter into a contract for sale of the land. At the second stage, completion, the parties execute a deed to transfer ownership of the land from one to the other. Where title to the land is registered, the deed takes the form of a transfer.

The law relating to the transfer of registered titles is contained in the Land Registration Act (LRA) 2002 and the Land Registration Rules 2003 (SI 2003/1417) which both came into force on the 13 October 2003. These repealed the Land Registration Act (LRA) 1925 and the Land Registration Rules 1925 and introduced a number of important changes to the registered system.

3.1.1 Proof of ownership

In registered conveyancing, the seller proves ownership by showing the buyer an 'official copy' of the entries on the register at Land Registry. The register of titles to land is maintained by Land Registry and it is open to the public. Each title has its own unique title number. The register will reveal who the current owner is and what other interests exist over the property (although not all of them). The register is divided into three parts:

- property register;
- proprietorship register; and
- charges register.

You will find a specimen register at **Reading 4** in the **Appendix**.

3.1.1.1 Property register

This contains a description of the land by reference to a title plan and to the address of the property. The title plan shows edged red the extent of the land which Land Registry (ie the State) guarantees. It also reveals the legal estate which has been registered under this title number - freehold or leasehold (eg see entry 1 in the specimen register at **Reading 4**). Rights for the benefit of the registered title are also set out in the property register (eg see entry 2 in the specimen register at **Reading 4** - the property has the benefit of an easement).

3.1.1.2 Proprietorship register

This register states the class of title. Absolute title is the best and most common grade. The Land Registry can award lesser grades of title, being possessory and qualified. It also reveals the name and address of the legal owners of the land, ie the 'registered proprietors'. This register also indicates any restrictions affecting the ability of the registered proprietors to deal with the legal estate in land and records the price paid for the land by the current owners if the land has been sold since 1 April 2000. The specimen register at **Reading 4** shows that there are two registered proprietors (entry 1), the price paid was £180,00 (entry 2) and there are limitations known as 'restrictions' placed on the register - there is a co-ownership restriction (entry 3) and a restriction placed by the mortgage lender (entry 4).

3.1.1.3 Charges register

This contains notices of any third party rights registered against the title which burden the land. There will also be a note of any registrable leases created out of the registered title. It also records any mortgage by registered charge created out of the registered title. The specimen register at **Reading 4** contains entries which show that the land is subject to covenants, an easement and a mortgage. You will learn more about these interests in **Part IV**.

3.1.2 The transfer

The deed used to transfer the ownership of a registered title is called a transfer. You will find a copy of a transfer in Land Registry Form TR1 at **Reading 3** in the **Appendix**. A transfer does not have quite the same effect as a conveyance in unregistered land. Section 27 of the LRA 2002 provides that on the sale of a registered title, completion of the transfer does not transfer the legal estate from seller to buyer. The legal estate remains with the seller and will pass to the buyer only when the buyer's name is put on the register as the new owner of the land. Contrast this with the sale of an unregistered title, where completion of the conveyance does pass the legal estate to the buyer.

3.2 The registered system

The system of registered titles was introduced to try to remedy the problems with the unregistered title system. A body called Land Registry was set up to administer registration of title. England and Wales is divided up into administrative areas, each with its own centrally funded district land registry.

This reform did not involve an overnight conversion of all unregistered titles into registered ones. Instead, a policy of creeping first registration was adopted. When owners of an unregistered title sell or otherwise deal with their land, the transaction may trigger compulsory first registration. The recipients of the land may have to apply to convert the unregistered title into a registered one.

3.2.1 Estates capable of registration

First, we will consider the titles capable of being registered at Land Registry.

The introduction of the registration of title (by the LRA 1925) progressed quite slowly, being introduced county by county over a long period of years. The whole of England and Wales became an area of compulsory registration as from 1 December 1990. This meant that if an unregistered property was leased or sold after this date, the transaction had to be followed by first registration of the title.

The law relating to land registration was updated by the LRA 2002, which came into effect on 13 October 2003.

All freehold estates are capable of registration with separate title. This is known as 'substantive registration'. In addition, some leasehold estates may be registered with separate title, but some are excluded. For example, under the LRA 2002, a lease which has seven years or less to run is incapable of registration with its own title. But a lease with more than seven years to run can be registered at Land Registry (under the LRA 1925, only leases for more than 21 years were capable of substantive registration).

It is important to remember that it is the title to the estate in the land that is registered and not the land itself. The result is there can be more than one register of title existing in relation to one piece of land.

Example

Richmond House Property Limited is a company which owns the freehold of a Victorian house, Richmond House. The house is converted into five flats, each held on a 99-year legal lease. One of the flats has been sublet by its buy-to-let owner on a one-year legal lease. The freehold is registered at Land Registry with its own title number in the name of Richmond House Property Limited. Each of the five 99-year leases are also registered with their own title number, as the leases are for more than seven years. The one-year sublease is not registrable. As a result, six different registered titles now exist over the same property.

3.2.2 Compulsory first registration

So, unregistered titles are gradually being converted into registered ones. Once this happens, ownership of the land and most third party rights burdening the land should appear on the register.

There are two ways in which first registration can happen - voluntary or compulsory first registration. First, landowners can convert their titles voluntarily (voluntary first registration). This does not often happen as there is a fee to pay.

Secondly, when landowners deal with their land in particular ways (for example, by selling it), the transaction can trigger an obligation to register the title (compulsory first registration). Section 4(1) of the LRA 2002 sets out the trigger events for first registration. The list of events triggering first registration is wider than the original LRA 1925 with the purpose of ensuring that more land in England and Wales is registered.

The events that are subject to compulsory first registration are as set out below.

3.2.2.1 Qualifying estates

A qualifying estate is defined as:

- an unregistered freehold estate; and
- an unregistered leasehold estate with more than seven years to run.

The transfer of a qualifying estate by sale, gift, court order or assent triggers first registration.

An assent is where personal representatives transfer land to a beneficiary under a will. An example of a court order would be on divorce, where one party to the marriage transfers the matrimonial home to the other in compliance with a court order.

3.2.2.2 Legal leases

A legal lease created (granted) for more than seven years must be registered. On registration, the lease will be given its own title number. This means (as explained in **3.2.1** above) that one parcel of land may have more than one registered title. The registration of a legal lease for more than seven years does not trigger the registration of the freehold reversion, and it is possible to have an unregistered freehold title with a registered lease.

Why can only legal leases of more than seven years be registered with a separate title? One of the policies of the 1925 and 2002 legislation was to simplify conveyancing. Equitable leases are excluded from registration with a separate title, as they are not legal estates in land. Shorter legal leases are usually excluded, as otherwise any tenants with a shorter legal lease, such as a lease for one year, could register their title and this would create many new registers of title for short-lived estates in land. Instead, short legal leases and equitable leases are protected as proprietary third party interests in the land (see **3.3.1.2**).

3.2.2.3 Mortgages

The creation of a first legal mortgage of a qualifying estate triggers first registration of the estate mortgaged. Thus, a mortgage of freehold unregistered land or the mortgage of an unregistered lease with more than seven years left to run would trigger the registration of the freehold or lease respectively.

ACTIVITY 1 First registration

Christine owns the freehold of an unregistered property. She is considering the transactions set out below. Which events would trigger an application for first registration?

(1) The sale of the freehold estate

(2) Mortgaging the land to a bank by way of legal mortgage

(3) Giving the freehold estate to a friend

(4) Leaving the freehold estate to her brother in her will

(5) Granting a legal lease for a term of 25 years to a tenant

(6) Granting a legal lease for a term of seven years to a tenant

COMMENT

(1) Under s 4(1)(a) of the LRA 2002, any transfer of a qualifying estate for valuable consideration will trigger compulsory first registration. A freehold is a 'qualifying estate' under s 4(2)(a). The purchaser of the land from Christine would have to apply for first registration.

(2) The mortgage will also trigger first registration as it is a legal mortgage of the freehold estate (LRA 2002, s 4(1)(g)). Christine would have to apply for first registration of the title after she had entered into the mortgage.

(3) Under s 4(1)(a) of the LRA 2002, any transfer of the freehold by way of a gift will also trigger compulsory first registration. Even if the estate transferred has a negative value,

it will still be regarded as a transfer for valuable consideration. The friend would therefore have to apply for first registration.

(4) The gift in the will to her brother does not trigger first registration. (However, when Christine dies, her personal representatives will transfer the freehold estate in the house to her brother by an assent, which will trigger compulsory first registration of the freehold title under s 4(1)(a)(ii).)

(5) The grant of a lease for a term of more than seven years triggers compulsory first registration (LRA 2002, s 4(1)(c)). The obligation to register affects the leasehold estate, but not Christine's freehold estate. The tenant must register the lease, but Christine's freehold estate can remain unregistered.

(6) This would not trigger registration as, since 13 October 2003 when the LRA 2002 came into force, only leases with more than seven years need to be substantively registered.

3.2.2.4 The application

Where there is an obligation to apply for first registration, the application must be made within two months of completion of the transaction that triggered first registration. Landowners make their application for first registration to the relevant district Land Registry. The Land Registry creates a new register for the title and allocates a title number to that register.

If the estate owner fails to apply for first registration within the two-month period, the transaction will be void with regard to the passing of the legal estate to the buyer. In this situation, the seller would need to transfer the land to the buyer again, at the buyer's cost.

3.3 Enforceability of third party interests in the registered system

The same third party rights that exist in relation to unregistered titles can also exist over registered titles. The way in which they can be made to bind purchasers of registered titles differs from the unregistered title rules – when dealing with enforcement of third party rights over registered titles, there are an entirely different set of rules.

With registered titles, the register is meant to provide a mirror reflecting who owns the land and the third party rights that burden the land. As you have seen, the proprietorship register names the owner of the land, and the charges register contains details of the third party rights burdening the land. The register is not, however, a perfect mirror. The charges register will not contain every third party interest burdening the land.

In order to advise a purchaser of a registered estate about whether they would be bound by a third party right, we need to know about the three categories of rights that exist over registered titles and how each is protected against a purchaser. These categories are:

(a) registrable dispositions;

(b) interests which affect a registered estate; and

(c) unregistered interests which override.

Some third party rights may fall within more than one category, as we shall see later. Trust interests are also treated differently.

The LRA 2002, which is the current Act governing registered titles, came into force on 13 October 2003. Before that date, the appropriate Act was the LRA 1925. As you will come across third party interests that were created before the LRA 2002 came into force, you will need to know something about the protection of third party interests under the LRA 1925. Where relevant, the most important changes are mentioned.

3.3.1 Interests that bind a purchaser of a registered title on or after 13 October 2003

Under s 29 of the LRA 2002, a purchaser for valuable consideration of a registered freehold title takes the legal estate subject to:

(a) entries appearing on the register (ie entries completing 'registrable dispositions' and notices protecting 'interests affecting that registered estate'); and

(b) unregistered interests which override that registered disposition (which do not appear on the register).

Valuable consideration is defined in s 132 of the LRA 2002 and does not include marriage consideration or nominal consideration in money.

The first step to take when assessing whether or not a third party right binds a registered title is to decide into which of the categories the third party right falls.

3.3.1.1 Registrable dispositions

The LRA 2002 sets out certain categories of disposition of registered land which must be completed by registration in order to take full effect. These are listed in s 27 and include the creation of a legal mortgage and the express creation of a legal easement. Once they have been completed by registration, these interests will both become legal and bind any purchaser of the land. For more detail on these interests, see **Chapters 8** and **9**.

Also included as a registrable disposition under s 27 is the creation of a leasehold estate for a term of more than seven years. We saw at **3.2.2** that such estates must be registered in their own right, with their own title numbers. However, they can also be considered as third party interests as against a freehold or superior leasehold estate and must also be noted against such titles if the freehold or superior leasehold is already registered, in order to become valid legal estates in the land. (The second element of this dual registration requirement will not apply where the superior title remains unregistered.)

Under the LRA 1925, only leases for a term in excess of 21 years were registrable. Thus many more leasehold estates now appear on the register than was the case in the past. Many of them are commercial leases of shops, offices and warehouses, for example.

3.3.1.2 Interests affecting a registered estate

This category of third party interest affecting registered title covers all other non-trust interests which do not fall into the categories of registrable dispositions or overriding interests.

The interests in this category will not bind a purchaser unless they are the subject of a notice on the register (LRA 2002, s 32) by the date of registration of the transfer to the purchaser (LRA 2002, s 29).

Examples of these are restrictive covenants over freehold land, estate contracts (such as options and equitable leases) and Family Law Act (FLA) 1996 rights. These rights should be protected by a notice in the charges register of the owner's title. The notice may be 'agreed' (ie entered by or with the consent of the registered proprietor) or 'unilateral' (entered without the consent of the registered proprietor). Remember that these interests cannot be overreached.

The provisions set out above replace those under the LRA 1925, whereby these interests could be protected by an entry on the register, which could take a number of different forms. However, any such entries placed on the register before 13 October 2003 will remain and will continue to bind a purchaser of the land.

Whenever you are considering the enforceability of a third party interest over registered land, always consider whether Sch 3, para 2 will protect the interest if the holder of the right is in actual occupation of the relevant land. Provided the conditions are fulfilled, the interest may be protected by Sch 3, para 2 even if it has *not* been protected on the register. Note: this alternative does not apply to FLA 1996 rights - see **3.3.1.4**.

3.3.1.3 Interests of beneficiaries under trusts of land (trust interests)

These interests are treated differently from interests affecting a registered estate (and cannot be protected by a notice - LRA 2002, s 33). They should be recorded by a restriction (LRA 2002, s 40) in the proprietorship register of the owner's title.

Remember, however, that interests of beneficiaries under trusts can be overreached if the buyer pays the purchase money to all the trustees being at least two in number (LPA 1925, ss 2 and 27). Thus a restriction will alert a buyer to the need to overreach, rather than 'protecting' the beneficiary's interest. However, if overreaching occurs, then the beneficiary's interest will transfer from the property to the proceeds of sale. If the buyer fails to overreach, the restriction will prevent the buyer being registered as the new owner. The buyer in this situation would have to get their money back from the seller or try to negotiate with the beneficiary to remove the restriction.

3.3.1.4 Unregistered interests which override

These are interests which will bind a purchaser if in existence at the date of the disposition to the purchaser. They are not required to be entered on the register and so pose a potential problem for purchasers, who must check carefully to see if any exist.

One of the aims of the LRA 2002 is to ensure that the register is not only accurate but as complete as possible. The concept of interests which do not require registration but which are binding on the purchaser of the property is one which appears to be at odds with the concept of land registration. The LRA 2002 is designed to reduce the impact of such unregistered interests.

The list of interests which override is in Sch 3 to the LRA 2002. This list is considerably narrower than the list of overriding interests that was in the LRA 1925. This is because people are generally uncomfortable with the idea that a purchaser handing over money when buying a registered title should find themselves bound by an interest which is neither entered on the register nor easy to discover.

The interests listed in Sch 3 are:

(a) Legal leases granted for a term not exceeding seven years - Sch 3, para 1 to the LRA 2002. Leases will be considered further in **Chapter 5**.

(b) Legal easements which are not created expressly by deed (ie those created by implication or prescription) - Sch 3, para 3 to the LRA 2002. (The LRA 1925 gave similar protection. Easements already protected before the LRA 2002 came into force will continue to be overriding (Sch 12, para 9).) Easements will be considered further in **Chapter 8**.

There are, however, important limitations on the easements which will be granted overriding status under Sch 3, para 3 to the LRA 2002. As mentioned above, the provision only applies to easements created by prescription or implication. In addition, the easement will be an overriding interest and binding on the purchaser only if, since 13 October 2006:

(i) the purchaser actually knew of the easement before the purchase of the property; or

(ii) the easement would have been obvious on a reasonably careful inspection of the land; or

(iii) the easement has been used by the person entitled to it in the year preceding the disposition of the land.

(c) An interest belonging to a person in actual occupation of the land over which the interest arises – Sch 3, para 2 to the LRA 2002. (This provision replaces s 70(1)(g) of the LRA 1925 but is narrower in its application.)

To qualify under para 2, the interest must be proprietary in nature, ie not a personal right. In *Strand Securities v Caswell* [1965] Ch 958 (a case on s 70(1)(g)), the right to occupy property under the terms of a licence to occupy was not an interest in land and could not be an overriding interest. An equitable lease would, however, enjoy such protection as an interest in the land.

The non-owning spouse's or civil partner's right to occupy the matrimonial or civil partnership home under s 30 of the FLA 1996 is incapable of being an overriding interest as it has been specifically excluded from this provision by s 31(10)(b) of the FLA 1996.

In the case of *Williams & Glyn's Bank v Boland* [1981] AC 487, a husband and wife bought their matrimonial home together. It had a registered title. The legal estate in the house was transferred into the husband's sole name. The husband held the legal estate on trust for himself and his wife in equity as she had made contributions towards the purchase price. So, the husband held the legal estate in the land subject to his wife's equitable interest. The husband then mortgaged the land to the Williams & Glyn's Bank by way of a legal mortgage. The question before the court was whether the bank's mortgage took effect subject to the wife's equitable interest (remember that lenders must be treated in the same way as purchasers of the legal title). The class of overriding interest at issue in the *Boland* case was one arising under s 70(1)(g) of the LRA 1925 (now Sch 3, para 2 to the LRA 2002): this protects the 'rights of every person in actual occupation of the land'.

The two questions that the House of Lords had to answer resulted from the wording of s 70(1)(g) (now replaced by Sch 3, para 2 to the LRA 2002). The claimant had to show two elements. The first element was that the claimant had a right or interest in land. The second element was that the right was protected if the owner of that right or interest in land was in actual occupation of the land.

Comment

The first question was whether a wife who owns an equitable interest in land under a trust had a 'right' capable of protection. For a right to be protected under this provision, it must be an interest in land. If the wife's interest was capable of being an overriding interest, it could bind the land without the need for any entry on the register of title (if the wife was also in actual occupation).

The second question was whether the wife was in actual occupation of the land. The wife was in 'actual occupation'. This phrase had to be interpreted as ordinary words of plain English.

Judgment

Lord Wilberforce stated that:

> There was physical presence, with all of the rights that occupiers have ... The house was a matrimonial home, intended to be occupied, and in fact occupied by both spouses, both of whom have an interest in it: it would involve some special doctrine of law to avoid the result that each is in occupation.

In *Boland*, the wife had an equitable interest under a trust. She could have registered that interest but failed to do so. Her occupation brought her right within s 70(1)(g), now Sch 3, para 2 to the 2002 Act. She had an overriding interest which bound the lender irrespective of notice.

The *Boland* case gives us a good example of the most common type of overriding interest - the one arising under Sch 3, para 2 (previously s 70(1)(g)).

It also helps us with a guide as to what 'actual occupation' means, as it is not defined in the statute. Lord Wilberforce clearly required there to be physical presence on the land by the claimant, not just the right to occupy. But how far does this go?

In the case of *Abbey National Building Society v Cann* [1991] 1 AC 56, a mother who had an equitable interest in the property was held not to be in actual occupation by merely sending her son to move in her furniture and put up curtains. The court held that the action amounted to 'no more than taking the preparatory steps leading to the assumption of actual residential occupation'.

However, in the case of *Lloyds Bank plc v Rosset* [1989] Ch 350, it was suggested that the claimant, Mrs Rosset, was in actual occupation by visiting the property regularly while it was being renovated in order to supervise the building contractors. In this case she was occupying, so far as it was possible to occupy, a semi-derelict property.

In *Link Lending Ltd v Bustard* [2010] EWCA Civ 424, Ms Bustard was deemed to have been in actual occupation at the time a mortgage over her property was created even though she had been absent for over a year in residential psychiatric care. The Court of Appeal agreed that the original judge could have properly concluded that Ms Bustard was in actual occupation given that her possessions were still in the property, she made regular visits there, bills for the property were paid on her behalf and that she regarded it as home and intended to return to live there, an aspiration that her doctors had not yet ruled out on medical grounds. By contrast, in *Thompson v Foy* [2010] 1 P&CR 16, the judge held that although the fact that Mrs Thompson's possessions were still in the property during her temporary absence could be sufficient to establish actual occupation, it was not so in this case because Mrs Thompson had decided that she was never going to return to live there.

So it seems that actual occupation does not necessarily mean residing on the property if, for example, the property is not fit for occupation or if the person claiming to be in occupation has left temporarily. What amounts to actual occupation also seems to depend upon the nature of the property itself. In *Kling v Keston Properties Ltd* (1983) 49 P&CR 212, a car was parked regularly in a garage. It was held that this was the normal use of the property and hence could amount to actual occupation.

So far you have looked at situations where the owner of the registered title sells or mortgages the land some time after an overriding interest under Sch 3, para 2 has come into existence. In these cases, it is clear that the overriding interest exists and the owner of it is in occupation long before the sale or mortgage of the registered title. Now you will look at a less clear-cut situation. Imagine that an unmarried couple buy a property together, both contributing towards the purchase price but the legal estate being vested in the name of the man alone. In that situation (as you will see in **Chapter 4** on co-ownership), the non-legal owner acquires an equitable interest under an implied trust of land. That right comes into existence as soon as the property is purchased. If the woman occupies the land, she will have an overriding interest under Sch 3, para 2 of the LRA 2002. Imagine that some of the purchase price came from a mortgage taken out by the man to fund the purchase. Immediately after the purchase of the legal estate is completed, the mortgage will be completed. The question is whether the woman's overriding interest binds the lender or whether the lender takes free of her interest.

This will be important if the man later defaults on the mortgage and the lender wants to sell the property with vacant possession.

Schedule 3, para 2 to the LRA 2002 gives overriding status to a person in actual occupation at 'the time of the disposition'. This means the date of completion.

So in the scenario above involving the lender and the woman with the overriding interest, since the woman went into occupation after completion of the purchase and the mortgage, any overriding interest she may have acquired under Sch 3, para 2 to the LRA 2002 does not bind the lender.

Further conditions to satisfy under Sch 3, para 2

There are some important limitations to the protection afforded by the provision in Sch 3, para 2 to the LRA 2002.

The interest will override only if:

- the *occupation* (not the interest) would have been obvious on a reasonably careful inspection of the land at the time of the sale; or
- the purchaser had actual knowledge of the *interest* at the time of the sale.

In addition, if enquiries were made of the person holding the interest before the sale, that person must have disclosed it if they could reasonably have been expected to do so.

These conditions were considered in *Thomas v Clydesdale Bank Plc* [2010] EWHC 2775 (QB). On the first condition, what is required is 'visible signs of occupation which have to be obvious on inspection': there is no requirement on the person inspecting to have any particular knowledge or make reasonable enquiries. On the second condition, 'actual knowledge' means actual knowledge of the facts which give rise to the interest, not receipt of formal evidence of it as in a legal document.

Overreaching

It is important to remember that if a buyer discovers that someone other than the seller has a beneficial interest under a trust in the property protected by Sch 3, para 2, that beneficial interest can always be overreached if the buyer pays the purchase money to all the trustees being at least two in number (see **2.3.5.2** and **3.3.1.3**). This operates in connection with registered titles as well as unregistered ones. For an example of its operation, see *City of London Building Society v Flegg* [1988] AC 54, where the mortgage loan was paid to two trustees.

Summary of the effect of Sch 3, para 2

There are four requirements that must all be satisfied to claim the protection of Sch 3, para 2:

Interest in the land	Actual occupation	**EITHER** occupation obvious on reasonably careful inspection **OR** purchaser actually knew of interest	If inquiry made of person claiming the right, they must disclose it (unless unreasonable to do so)

3.3.2 Summary of enforceability in the registered system

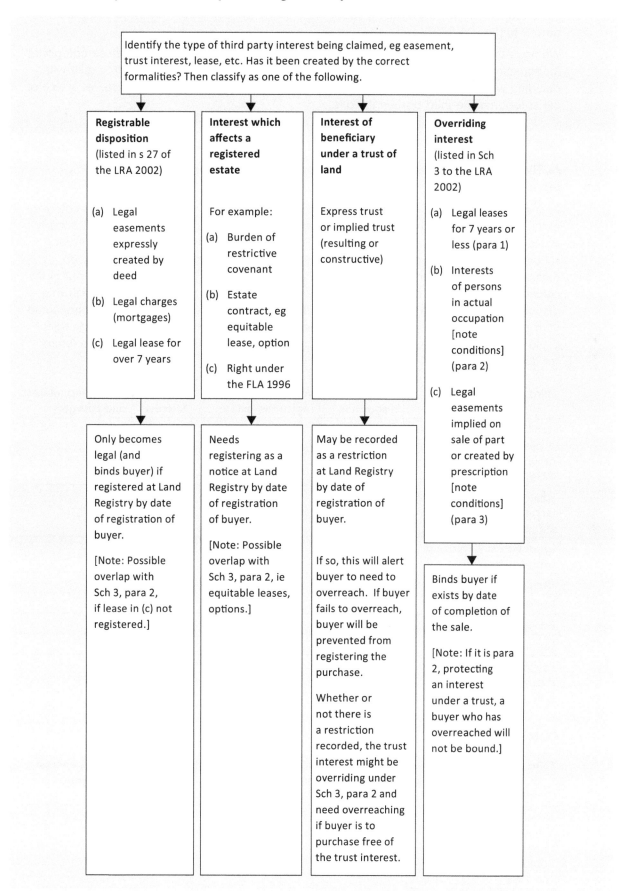

Identify the type of third party interest being claimed, eg easement, trust interest, lease, etc. Has it been created by the correct formalities? Then classify as one of the following.

Registrable disposition (listed in s 27 of the LRA 2002)	**Interest which affects a registered estate**	**Interest of beneficiary under a trust of land**	**Overriding interest** (listed in Sch 3 to the LRA 2002)
(a) Legal easements expressly created by deed (b) Legal charges (mortgages) (c) Legal lease for over 7 years	For example: (a) Burden of restrictive covenant (b) Estate contract, eg equitable lease, option (c) Right under the FLA 1996	Express trust or implied trust (resulting or constructive)	(a) Legal leases for 7 years or less (para 1) (b) Interests of persons in actual occupation [note conditions] (para 2) (c) Legal easements implied on sale of part or created by prescription [note conditions] (para 3)
Only becomes legal (and binds buyer) if registered at Land Registry by date of registration of buyer. [Note: Possible overlap with Sch 3, para 2, if lease in (c) not registered.]	Needs registering as a notice at Land Registry by date of registration of buyer. [Note: Possible overlap with Sch 3, para 2, ie equitable leases, options.]	May be recorded as a restriction at Land Registry by date of registration of buyer. If so, this will alert buyer to need to overreach. If buyer fails to overreach, buyer will be prevented from registering the purchase. Whether or not there is a restriction recorded, the trust interest might be overriding under Sch 3, para 2 and need overreaching if buyer is to purchase free of the trust interest.	Binds buyer if exists by date of completion of the sale. [Note: If it is para 2, protecting an interest under a trust, a buyer who has overreached will not be bound.]

Note: Transitional provisions

Easements which were overriding under the old law will continue to override under Sch 12, para 9 to the LRA 2002.

We have seen that third party rights over registered titles fall within one of these categories (or sometimes within more than one category). As stated in **3.3**, the first step to take when deciding whether or not a third party right binds a registered title is to decide into which of the categories the third party right falls.

ACTIVITY 2 Test your knowledge: the categories of third party rights in the registered system

In this question, you will look at specific third party rights and decide within which category of third party rights each one falls. In the left-hand column you will find a list of third party rights that can exist over a registered title. For each third party right, decide whether it should be protected as a registrable disposition, as an interest affecting a registered estate, or as a trust interest or overriding interest by putting a tick under one or more of the columns in the chart. If, for example, you decide that the third party right is a 'registrable disposition', put a tick in the column headed 'Registrable disposition'. Remember that some third party rights can fall into more than one category. If you think that a third party right could be protected under more than one category, put a tick in the two relevant columns. Jot down the reasons for your decision.

Third party right	Registrable disposition	Interest affecting a registered estate	Trust Interest	Overriding interest and category
Non-legal owning spouse's or civil partner's right of occupation under the FLA 1996				
Equitable lease where the tenant is in occupation of the land				
Legal easement granted expressly by deed				
Restrictive covenant				
Equitable easement				
Estate contract				
Legal mortgage				
Equitable interest under a trust where the beneficiary is in occupation of the land				

COMMENT

Third party right	Registrable disposition	Interest affecting a registered estate	Trust interest	Overriding interest and category
Non-legal owning spouse's or civil partner's right of occupation under the FLA 1996		√		

Third party right	Registrable disposition	Interest affecting a registered estate	Trust interest	Overriding interest and category
Equitable lease where the tenant is in occupation of the land		√		√ (Sch 3, para 2)
Legal easement granted expressly by deed	√			
Restrictive covenant		√		
Equitable easement		√		
Estate contract		√		√ (Sch 3, para 2)
Legal mortgage	√			
Equitable interest under a trust where the beneficiary is in occupation of the land			√ (restriction entered but can be overreached)	√ (Sch 3, para 2 - but can be overreached)

The restrictive covenant, equitable lease, estate contract, equitable easement and non-legal owning spouse's or civil partner's right to occupy under the FLA 1996 are all interests affecting a registered estate and as such must be protected by a notice on the register. The tenant under the equitable lease (which is also an estate contract) is in actual occupation. Their 'right', ie their lease, is therefore protected as an overriding interest (LRA 2002, Sch 3, para 2). The party with the estate contract may, similarly, be protected if they are in actual occupation.

The legal mortgage over a registered title is always a registrable disposition. It cannot take effect as a legal mortgage until it is registered on the title of the property it affects.

An equitable interest arising under a trust may be registered as a restriction, which will alert a buyer to the need to overreach and does not protect the interest; but where the owner of the equitable interest under the trust occupies the land, that equitable interest can fall within the category of overriding interest (LRA 2002, Sch 3, para 2). Remember, though, that these interests can be overreached.

Legal easements created by express grant in a deed are registrable dispositions and must be completed by registration against the title over which they are exercised (see **Chapter 8** for more details).

ACTIVITY 3 Test your knowledge: using the categories in the registered system to advise a purchaser

Ibrahim buys a house with registered title from Asha. Using your knowledge from **Chapter 1**, work out the nature of each of the third party rights below, as the first stage in advising Ibrahim whether he is likely to be bound by them:

(1) A right claimed by Asha's civil partner Teresa (who did not contribute to the purchase of the land).

(2) A right of way over the driveway granted by deed last year by Asha to her neighbour Vernon.

(3) Asha's mortgage with Barclays Bank.

(4) A lease of part of the back garden for a term of five years to Wendy, another neighbour. This was created in a written document (not a deed) earlier this year.

COMMENT

(1) Teresa made no contribution to the original purchase of the land, so she does not have an interest under an implied trust. She appears to have a statutory right to occupy the land under s 30 of the FLA 1996 if certain conditions are satisfied, ie the parties are in a legal civil partnership, the legal owner (Asha) is still alive and it is the civil partnership home.

(2) Vernon appears to have the benefit of an easement. The right is capable of being legal as it appears to satisfy s 1(2)(a) of the LPA 1925. Being of unlimited duration (this is assumed if the deed is silent as to duration) it is equivalent to a fee simple absolute in possession. It must comply with the formalities in s 52(1) of the LPA 1925, ie it must be created by deed. A valid deed must comply with s 1(2) of the Law of Property (Miscellaneous Provisions) Act (LP(MP)A) 1989, making it clear on its face that is intended to be a deed, and being signed, witnessed and delivered as a deed. On the facts, this is the case.

(3) Barclays' mortgage will be a charge, which is capable of being a legal interest under s 1(2)(c) of the LPA 1925 if it complies with the formalities in s 52(1) of the LPA 1925. It appears to, as it is likely that Barclays will have ensured that the loan was completed correctly in a deed. A valid deed must comply with s 1(2) of the LP(MP)A, as in (2) above. This is likely to be the case here.

(4) Wendy's lease is capable of being legal under s 1(1)(b) of the LPA 1925 as it is for a fixed and certain duration, but it has not satisfied the formalities for a legal lease as it has not been created by deed under s 52 of the LPA 1925. Equity will recognise the lease as an estate contract provided that it has been created in writing, contains all the agreed terms and is signed by or on behalf of both parties, in accordance with s 2 of the LP(MP)A 1989. Accordingly, it seems that Wendy has an equitable lease of the land.

Now complete your advice to Ibrahim by explaining into which category each interest falls in the registered system and whether it is likely to bind him.

COMMENT

(1) Teresa's FLA 1996 right

In registered title, Teresa's right is an interest affecting a registered estate. To bind Ibrahim, Teresa must have protected her right by a notice on the register before Ibrahim was registered as the new owner. If not, Teresa's right will not bind Ibrahim – s 29 of the LRA 2002.

Remember that FLA 1996 rights cannot be protected by Sch 3, para 2 to the LRA 2002 even though Teresa is in occupation here – FLA 1996, s 31(10)(b).

(2) Vernon's easement

Vernon's easement (as it is capable of being legal) is a registrable disposition under s 27 of the LRA 2002. It needs to be completed by registration on the charges register before Ibrahim is registered as the new owner, in order to become legal and to bind Ibrahim. If Vernon has registered it, Ibrahim will be bound – s 29 of the LRA 2002.

(3) Barclays' mortgage

The mortgage is also a registrable disposition under s 27 of the LRA 2002. It needs to be completed by registration on the charges register before Ibrahim is registered as the new owner, in order to be legal and to bind Ibrahim. It is likely that Barclays has ensured this was done so Ibrahim will be bound – s 29 of the LRA 2002.

(4) Wendy's equitable lease

Wendy has an equitable lease which she should have protected as an interest affecting a registered estate by a notice on the register (LRA 2002, s 32) before Ibrahim is registered – s 29 of the LRA 2002.

However, even if she has not done so, as she appears to be in actual occupation of the garden, her lease will override under Sch 3, para 2 to the LRA 2002, provided her occupation would have been obvious on a reasonably careful inspection of the land or Ibrahim knew about her lease when he bought the property. It would have been reasonable for Wendy to disclose the existence of her lease had Ibrahim asked her. If overriding, her lease will bind Ibrahim until the five-year term has expired.

SUMMARY

- The system of land registration forms the backbone of buying and selling land in England and Wales. Understanding how it works gives you a valuable insight into how conveyancing lawyers have played their part in property transactions.
- You now have sufficient background knowledge to identify and advise on the main third party issues that may arise in a standard conveyancing transaction. For example, you could advise a property investor thinking of buying a portfolio of properties whether there are any adverse entries on any of its registered titles which would affect the overall value of the portfolio.
- Conversely, you could also advise those holding third party rights how to protect themselves against an unexpected sale, for example tenants whose landlord decides to part with the freehold estate.

Part II Trusts of Land

4 Trusts of Land and Co-ownership

LEARNING OUTCOMES

When you have completed this chapter you should be able to:

- explain and apply the provisions of the Trusts of Land and Appointment of Trustees Act 1996 to a domestic or commercial problem scenario;
- explain how co-ownership can arise and the different forms it may take, having regard to statutory provisions and case law you have reviewed;
- analyse fact patterns and recognise potential examples of severance and explain the effect on the pattern of co-ownership;
- understand when implied trusts may arise and suggest when a claimant may or may not be successful in a claim over land;
- demonstrate a sound knowledge and understanding of the enforceability of co-owners' interests against a prospective buyer.

4.1 Introduction

You have already encountered the concept of the trust and the people involved in it in **Chapter 1**. Land has been held under trusts since the Middle Ages but this particular kind of trust, the 'trust of land', is a relatively new creature in land law as it has existed only since 1 January 1997. This means that we have few cases interpreting the effect of the provisions of the statute that created the trust of land – the Trusts of Land and Appointment of Trustees Act (TLATA) 1996. In this chapter, we shall therefore apply the provisions of TLATA 1996 to a number of factual situations.

We will also be looking at the law relating to joint ownership of land. When two or more people buy a house together, a trust is automatically created. The fact that there is a trust becomes important should a dispute arise between the joint owners, as TLATA 1996 also allows either party to apply to court to resolve the dispute.

We will be looking at what happens when somebody who owns land jointly dies. Who inherits their share in the land? You will discover that it does not necessarily pass under their will but in certain circumstances passes automatically to the other joint owner(s).

Another area we will be looking at is implied trusts over land (ie implied co-ownership). Your study of this area of law will help you understand how a person may acquire an equitable interest in land which is legally owned by another. As a result, they will also be entitled to a share in the proceeds of sale of the land. Implied trusts are very important in resolving land disputes between partners who are neither legally married nor civil partners.

There is no such thing as the concept of a 'common law' husband or wife in English law, so an unmarried partner who is not a legal owner may need to claim an interest under an implied trust if they are to claim any interest over the property they both lived in before the relationship broke down.

If couples who were married or were civil partners divorce or obtain a dissolution, the divorce courts can make 'property adjustment orders' which redistribute legal ownership of the property between them, so implied trust law is not so important in resolving disputes between married couples or civil partners.

4.1.1 Trusts of Land and Appointment of Trustees Act 1996

The broad effect of TLATA 1996 was to replace the two types of trust which could exist previously - the strict settlement and the trust for sale - with one single trust to be used whenever land is held under a trust. The new trust is called a trust of land.

Where a new trust is created over land after 1 January 1997, instead of taking the form of a strict settlement or trust for sale, it can only take the form of a trust of land.

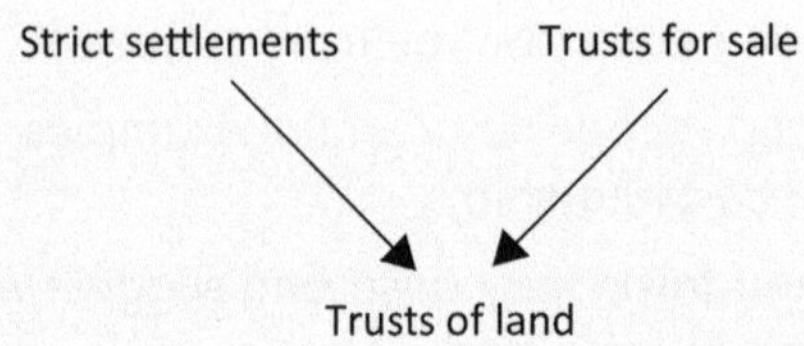

Examples of trusts

(1) Adam gave his land to trustees to hold on trust for Sam for life with remainder to Jack in fee simple after 1 January 1997 and so the trust must take the form of a trust of land. The trustees hold the legal estate in the land on trust for Sam and Jack. Sam and Jack have an equitable (beneficial) interest in the land. The trustees of land manage the trust and make the decisions about whether and when to sell the land.

(2) Land is sold to Alison and Brian jointly and therefore a trust of land automatically arises, with Alison and Brian being both trustees and beneficiaries of that trust.

*(3) Another trust of land would be created where Katrina buys a house in her sole name but her boyfriend Leon contributes towards the deposit. This is an example of an implied trust (see **4.3.1**). Katrina is the sole trustee, holding the legal estate in the land on trust for herself and Leon as beneficiaries (equitable owners).*

4.1.2 Trustees of land and their powers

Once a trust of land comes into existence, either expressly or by implication, TLATA 1996 contains provisions setting out the powers of the trustees and the rights of the beneficiaries whilst that trust subsists.

Trustees of land are in an extremely strong position. They are the legal owners of the land and manage the trust land. But what precisely are the trustees' powers and duties under a trust of land?

4.1.2.1 Trustees' powers generally

The starting point for looking at the powers enjoyed by trustees of land is s 6 of TLATA 1996. This section sets out in general terms the powers enjoyed by the trustees. Later sections then go on to set out boundaries within which the trustees can exercise the wide powers given to them under s 6.

Section 6(1) of TLATA 1996 sets out the general powers of the trustees of land and provides that: 'For the purposes of exercising their functions as trustees, the trustees of land have in relation to the land subject to the trust all of the powers of an absolute owner.'

Section 6(2) and (3) of TLATA 1996, and s 8 of the Trustee Act (TA) 2000 (which repealed s 6(4) of TLATA 1996), give trustees new powers not previously enjoyed. The structure of a trust of land means that the trustees of land are the legal owners of the land. As such, they have the right to sell the trust land as a result of their ownership of the legal estate. Broadly, s 6 of TLATA 1996 sets out the circumstances in which the trustees are authorised to sell the trust land, and s 8 of the TA 2000 the circumstances in which trustees can acquire land.

Section 6(2) gives trustees the authority to exercise the power to dispose of the legal estate in a specified way, ie by transferring it to a beneficiary who is of full age and capacity and absolutely entitled to the land and thus to end the trust. This gives the trustees of land authority to end the trust even if the beneficiaries have not requested them to do so.

Section 6(3) gives the trustees power, ie permission, to buy land in England and Wales for the wide purposes set out in s 8 of the TA 2000.

Section 6(5) requires the trustees to 'have regard to the rights of the beneficiaries' when exercising their powers. However, the trustees already had to comply with this rule under the general law.

Section 6(6) requires the trustees not to exercise the powers they are given under s 6 'in contravention of, or of any order made in pursuance of, any enactment or any rule of law or equity'. Again, this is something the trustees already had to do under the general law.

Example

Tom and Tim are the trustees of a trust of land created inter vivos last year. Under the terms of the trust, they hold the legal estate on trust for Juji for life with remainder to Arafa in fee simple. Tom and Tim want to sell some of the trust land to invest in a house for Juji to live in.

Under s 6 of TLATA 1996, the trustees have all of the powers of an absolute owner. These powers are wider than the old powers given to trustees under a trust for sale and include the power to sell or mortgage the trust land. However, the trustees must remember that they are not in fact absolute owners, they are trustees, and s 6 also limits the ways in which the trustees can exercise the wide powers they have been given. Under s 6(6), these powers have to be exercised to comply with general rules of equity and law. They are permitted to sell (or mortgage) the property under s 6(3). The trustees have the power to buy a legal estate in England and Wales, and s 8(1) of the TA 2000 sets out when the power to purchase land can be exercised. One of the situations is as here, where land is to be bought for occupation by a beneficiary. Section 6(3) of TLATA 1996 (and s 8(2) of the TA 2000) only allows the trustees to buy a legal estate and does not permit the purchase of an equitable interest in land.

4.1.2.2 Restrictions on the trustees' powers

Trustees of land therefore have all of the powers of an absolute owner under s 6 of TLATA 1996. However, there are restrictions on the trustees in the exercise of their powers – the duty to consult with certain beneficiaries before exercising their powers and, where the trust of land is expressly created, the duty to comply with restrictions imposed on the trustees by the settlor.

Duty to consult beneficiaries

When selling trust land, the trustees under s 11 of TLATA 1996 must consult with the beneficiaries who are of full age (18 or over) and who have an interest in possession (entitled to an immediate interest in the land) and comply (as far as is consistent with the general interests of the trust) with the wishes of the majority in value. If the beneficiaries decide that they do not wish the land to be sold, but the trustees then decide that it is in the best interests of the trust that the land should be sold, the trustees can go ahead and sell. Ultimately, it is for the trustees to make the decision. Settlors can exclude this requirement for the trustees to consult in the trust deed. For example, under the terms of the trust in the example in **4.1.2.1** above, Tom and Tim must consult Juji as she has an interest in possession (assuming that she is of full age) before selling the trust property. The trustees do not have to consult Arafa, as she only has an interest in remainder.

Example

Tom and Tim are also trustees of another express trust of land created 12 years ago. Under the terms of that trust of land, they hold the land for Sam and George in unequal shares. Sam owns two-thirds and George one-third.

Here Tom and Tim are under a duty to consult with both beneficiaries (assuming they are of full age) as they both have interests in possession; and because Sam owns the largest share of the equitable interest, they have to comply so far as is practicable with his wishes under s 11 of TLATA 1996.

You are now familiar with the idea that, under a trust of land, the basic principle is that the trustees make all of the decisions about the trust. Once settlors have transferred ownership of their land to the trustees, they have handed over control of the trust property to the trustees. One of the ways in which settlors can try to control the way in which the trustees exercise their powers is under s 8 of TLATA 1996 which allows settlors, when creating a trust of land, to place restrictions on the trustees' powers.

Section 8 allows settlors of an express private trust to place restrictions on the power of the trustees contained in s 6 (giving trustees all of the powers of an absolute owner). A fairly common restriction would be one preventing the trustees from selling the land without first obtaining the consent of a named person or persons. If the trustees sell without first obtaining the consents, they will be acting in breach of trust.

4.1.3 The rights of beneficiaries

Most of the rights of the beneficiaries under a trust of land are a consequence of the trustees' duties dealt with above. These include the rights to be consulted (under s 11 of TLATA 1996) and to give permission before the trustees exercise their powers (under s 8).

The beneficiaries may also have the right to occupy the trust land. The right to occupy is contained in ss 12 and 13 of TLATA 1996. Not all beneficiaries have the right to occupy the trust land. Under s 12, to have the right to occupy, certain conditions must be satisfied. The beneficiaries must be entitled to an interest in possession under the trust, the purposes of the trust must include making the land available for the beneficiaries to occupy, or the trustees must hold the land so that it is available for them to occupy. So, looking again at the example in **4.1.2.1**, only Juji (and not Arafa) can have the right to occupy the trust land under s 12, as she is the beneficiary who is entitled to an interest in possession under the trust. However, if the trust land was occupied by a tenant, it would be the tenant under the lease that had the right to occupy the land and so the land would not be available for occupation by the beneficiaries, and therefore Juji would not have the right to occupy. Similarly, if the beneficiary is, for example, a wheelchair user and the land is not suitable for occupation by a wheelchair user, then the trustees can refuse to allow the beneficiary to occupy the land.

Under s 13 of TLATA 1996, where the trustees do allow the beneficiary to occupy, they can attach conditions to that occupation (for example, imposing a condition that the beneficiary pays the outgoings on the property).

4.1.4 Resolving disputes

There will be situations where the trustees cannot agree whether or not to exercise a particular power (for example, the power to sell). Disputes can also arise between the trustees and the beneficiaries (for example, over whether or not a beneficiary should be allowed to occupy the trust land). If the dispute cannot be resolved amicably, the parties must apply to court for an order resolving the dispute. Applications are made under s 14 of TLATA 1996. An application could also be made under s 14 where the trustees are required to obtain the consent of a named person before selling if, when the trustees try to sell the land, they discover that the named person either cannot be found or refuses to give permission for the sale. Again, the trustees could apply to court under s 14 for an order under s 14(2)(a), relieving the trustees of their obligation to obtain these consents.

Under s 14, 'Any person who is a trustee of land or has an interest in property subject to a trust of land may make an application to the court.' So, the trustees of land can clearly make a s 14 application. In addition, as beneficiaries under a trust of land have an interest in the property subject to the trust, they too can make an application to court under s 14.

When an application to court is made under s 14 of TLATA 1996, the court has the power to make such order as it thinks fit relating to the 'exercise by the trustees of any of their functions' or to 'declaring the nature or extent of a person's interest'. So, the court could simply declare the parties' interests or rights under the trust or could make orders obliging the trustees to exercise one of their functions such as sale. Applications to court can be made to prevent a proposed sale, or for an order relating to the use and occupation of the land.

When the court makes an order under s 14, it has to take into account factors including those listed in s 15. Section 15 sets out a range of factors the court must consider when making an order under s 14. These include looking at the purpose of the trust, the intention of the settlor when creating the trust, the welfare of any minor who occupies or may occupy the trust land, and the interests of any secured creditor of a beneficiary. The list in s 15 is not exhaustive and the court can take into account any other relevant factors.

So, where there is a dispute between the trustees or between the trustees and beneficiaries about whether or not the trustees should sell the trust land, the parties can resolve this by making an application to the court.

4.1.5 Protection of buyers from trust interests

Buyers who buy trust land from the trustees of that land want to ensure that they buy the land free of the equitable interests of the beneficiaries under the trust.

You saw in **Chapters 2** and **3** how the mechanism of overreaching may protect the buyer, and we will revisit this at **4.4.1** below.

Another protection where there is an express trust is provided to buyers in s 10 of TLATA 1996. Section 10(1) provides that where a trust deed requires the trustees to obtain consents before exercising any function such as sale and the buyer has knowledge of that requirement, a buyer need only check that two consents have been obtained. In addition, where one of the persons whose consent is needed to a particular disposition is not of full age, buyers do not have to ensure that this consent is obtained (s 10(3)).

Example

Tim and Tom are the trustees of another trust of land. The trust was created expressly and the settlor, when creating the trust, included a condition that the trustees could not sell the land without first obtaining the consent of the beneficiaries, Jamie, Shanvi and Amy. Amy, Jamie and Shanvi are aged 19, 10 and 11 respectively. Tim and Tom have decided to sell the trust land to Mohamed.

Mohamed never needs to see consent from all three beneficiaries, only from two of them, and as Shanvi and Jamie are aged 10 and 11, Mohamed only needs to see that Amy's consent to the transaction has been obtained.

This protection offered to buyers does not protect the trustees – they are still bound by their duty to obtain the necessary consents.

This section applies to both registered and unregistered titles.

4.2 Co-ownership

4.2.1 Introduction

Co-ownership arises where two or more people have concurrent interests in the same estate in one piece of land. Co-ownership may arise expressly, for example, where land is transferred to joint legal owners, or where there is an express declaration of trust over land for the benefit of more than one person. It can also arise where land is held on trust for beneficiaries having concurrent equitable interests (eg where more than one person has contributed to the purchase price, but they are not named as legal owners of the property).

Any land subject to co-ownership is held on trust (Law of Property Act (LPA) 1925, ss 34 and 36, as amended by TLATA 1996). The trust is a 'trust of land' governed by TLATA 1996.

4.2.2 Forms of co-ownership – joint tenancy and tenancy in common

When there is co-ownership of land, the co-owners can own the land either as *joint tenants*, or as *tenants in common*.

4.2.2.1 Joint tenants

If the co-owners own the land as joint tenants, they are not treated by the outside world as having separate shares in the land. The world treats them as being a single person and not two individuals (think of the land as a large cake: if the co-owners own that cake as joint tenants together, they are entitled to eat it all, but individually they cannot point to any part of the cake and claim that one of them alone can eat it). The right of survivorship applies to joint tenants. This means that when either co-owner dies, the survivor becomes the sole owner of the land. If a joint tenant makes a gift in their will of their interest to a third party, that gift will not be effective; neither will the intestacy rules apply if the joint tenant did not leave a will. Before the gift in the will takes effect, the right of survivorship will vest ownership of the land in the surviving joint tenant(s).

If, however, land held as joint tenants is sold, the joint tenants share the proceeds of sale equally. This means if there are two joint tenants, they will receive half each; if there are three of them, they will receive one-third each and so on.

4.2.2.2 Tenants in common

If, on the other hand, the co-owners own the land as tenants in common, the law treats them as owning distinct shares in the land that may be equal or unequal in size. They hold the land in 'undivided shares' (imagine a cake again: this time, if the co-owners own the cake as tenants in common, although the cake has not yet been divided up into slices, the slices have been marked out and they could each point to a particular slice as belonging to one of them). If one of the co-owners dies, this time their share of the land does not automatically pass to the surviving co-owner. Instead, it falls into their estate and passes under the terms of their will (or, if they left no will, under the intestacy rules).

It is possible for co-owners to change their minds after they have bought a property about which sort of co-ownership they wish to use. Where the parties originally purchased land as joint tenants, they can convert it into a tenancy in common by a process known as 'severance' (see **4.2.5** below).

If land is held as tenants in common, the tenants in common receive a share of the proceeds of sale equivalent to the size of their distinct shares in the land. These shares may be equal or unequal in size.

Wherever there is co-ownership, the co-owners will either expressly declare that they hold the land on a trust of land or, if not, the law will impose an implied trust of land.

4.2.3 The position at law

We shall now look at how these two forms of co-ownership fit in with the two aspects of the land held under the trust - the legal estate and the equitable interest.

Section 1(6) of the LPA 1925 provides that 'A legal estate is not capable of subsisting or being created in an undivided share in land' ('undivided shares' indicate a tenancy in common - see **4.2.2.2** above). This means that it is only possible for co-owners of the legal estate (the trustees) to hold the legal title as joint tenants (LPA 1925, s 36(1)). In addition, s 36(2) of the LPA 1925 states that it is not possible to sever a joint tenancy of the legal estate in order to turn it into a tenancy in common.

Only a person over the age of 18 can act as a trustee (LPA 1925, s 1(6)). Section 34(2) of the LPA 1925 permits a maximum of four trustees. Where a property is conveyed to more than four people, the first four named adults will be the trustees. There is no minimum number of trustees.

4.2.4 Ascertaining how the equitable interest is held

However, co-owners can hold the equitable (beneficial) interest as either joint tenants or tenants in common. To find out if co-owners hold the equitable interest in the land as joint tenants or tenants in common, we have to apply a number of tests. We shall now look at the first test.

4.2.4.1 The first test: are all four unities present?

The four unities are:

(a) *Unity of interest.* This unity requires that all co-owners have exactly the same interest in the property. That is, the interest must be of the same nature and for the same duration.

(b) *Unity of title.* Under this unity, all of the co-owners must receive their interest in the land under the same document.

(c) *Unity of time.* For this unity to be present, each co-owner's interest must vest at the same time.

(d) *Unity of possession.* For this unity to be satisfied, the co-owners must each be entitled to possession of the whole of the land and cannot exclude the other co-owners.

All four unities must be present if the co-ownership is to be capable of taking the form of an equitable joint tenancy. If the co-ownership is to take the form of an equitable tenancy in common, the only essential unity is that of possession. If all four unities are present, then the co-ownership is capable of being either a joint tenancy or a tenancy in common. To decide which kind of co-ownership applies, we need to move on and apply the second test.

4.2.4.2 The second test: does the deed transferring the land to the co-owners contain an express declaration?

Where the deed in favour of the co-owners contains an express declaration of how the co-owners should hold the equitable interest in the land, that declaration is conclusive (*Goodman v Gallant* [1986] Fam 106). If title to the land is unregistered, we would need to look at the conveyance to the co-owners. Look at the sample conveyance at **Reading 2** in the **Appendix**. Clause 1.5 sets out the express declaration that the buyers of the land have made.

If title is registered, the express declaration would be included in the transfer to the co-owners. If it is in Form TR1, as at **Reading 3** in the **Appendix**, any declaration would be included in section 10. That declaration would be conclusive and the co-owners would hold the equitable interest accordingly. In **Reading 3** the co-owners have chosen to hold the land as tenants in common.

Where there is no express declaration in the transfer or conveyance, you need to apply the third test. This involves looking at the same deed to see if it contains words of severance.

4.2.4.3 The third test: does the deed transferring the land to the co-owners contain words of severance?

Words of severance are words indicating that the co-owners intend to own separate and distinct shares in the property. Where the conveyance or transfer contains words of severance, the co-owners take the equitable interest in the land as tenants in common in equity. Any words indicating the co-owner's intention to hold separate shares should suffice. For example:

'To A and B in equal shares'

'To A and B equally'

'Among A and B'

'Between A and B'

'Half to A, half to B'

Where the conveyance or transfer does not contain an express declaration or words of severance, apply the fourth and last test.

4.2.4.4 The fourth test: does equity presume a tenancy in common?

The last test involves looking at the circumstances of the purchase to see if they are such that equity presumes a tenancy in common.

The three situations where equity will presume a tenancy in common are: where co-owners buy the land as partnership property; lend money on mortgage; or make unequal contributions towards the purchase price. Looking at each of these situations in turn:

(a) *Partnership property*. Where the co-owners are business partners and they buy the land as a partnership asset, equity presumes that they buy the land as tenants in common in equity.

(b) *Lenders*. Where more than one person lends money to a borrower, the relationship between the lenders is that of tenants in common (rare in practice).

(c) *Unequal contributions towards the purchase price*. Where two or more people buy land together and make unequal contributions towards the purchase price, equity presumes that they buy as tenants in common in equity. The size of each tenant in common's share is in proportion to their contribution.

Finally, if all four unities are present, there is no express declaration as to how the equitable interest is held, no words of severance and none of the equitable presumptions apply, the co-owners will hold as joint tenants, ie 'equity follows the law', as the legal estate has to be held on a joint tenancy.

Examples

Harriet and Lottie, two friends, purchase a house. The legal estate is held by them as trustees as joint tenants – s 1(6) and s 36(1) of the LPA 1925. Assume that the four unities are present and that the house was not bought as a partnership property. The following examples demonstrate whether the equitable interest is held as a joint tenancy or a tenancy in common:

(a) Harriet contributed 75% of the purchase price and Lottie contributed 25%. The transfer to them contains no declaration or words of severance.

In this example, because Harriet and Lottie made unequal contributions toward the purchase price, equity presumes that they will hold the land as tenants in common in equity, in proportion to their contributions.

(b) Harriet contributed 75% of the purchase price and Lottie contributed 25%. The transfer to them contains an express declaration that they are to hold as joint tenants.

Here, although Harriet and Lottie made unequal contributions, because the transfer contains an express declaration that they hold as joint tenants, that declaration is conclusive. They therefore took the equitable interest as joint tenants.

(c) Harriet and Lottie each contributed half of the purchase price. The transfer does not contain a declaration or words of severance.

The equal contributions towards the purchase price and the absence of any declaration/words of severance or equitable presumption of a tenancy in common mean that Harriet and Lottie will hold as joint tenants – equity follows the law.

(d) Harriet and Lottie each contributed half of the purchase price. The transfer to them states that they took the property 'in equal shares'.

The words of severance in the transfer mean that Harriet and Lottie will hold the land as tenants in common in equal shares

Once co-owners have bought the land, what will their title look like? Where title to the land is unregistered, the fact that the last conveyance is to more than one buyer indicates that there is co-ownership of that land. If the conveyance to the co-owners declares how the co-owners decided to hold the equitable interest, that tells you how they initially owned the equitable interest in the land.

Where title to the land is registered, the co-owners will be the registered proprietors. If they hold the land as tenants in common in equity then a restriction should be placed on the proprietorship register recording that fact. Look at the extract from official copies in **Reading 4** in the **Appendix**. Entry 3 in the proprietorship register shows the standard restriction which Land Registry will enter. If, on the other hand, they hold the land as joint tenants in equity, there will be no restriction on the register.

4.2.5 Severance of an equitable joint tenancy

Even if co-owners initially acquire land as equitable joint tenants, it is possible that this may change over time. It is possible to convert an equitable joint tenancy into a tenancy in common. This process is called severance.

When severance occurs, the 'new' tenants in common will acquire equal shares in the land, regardless of the proportions of their contributions to the original purchase price.

So if two equitable joint tenants, J and K, sever their joint tenancy, both J and K will obtain a half share in the property:

(J, K) joint tenants —severance→ J – $^1/_2$, K – $^1/_2$, tenants in common

If three equitable joint tenants, J, K and L, sever their joint tenancy, J, K and L will receive a one-third share each, and so on:

(J, K, L) joint tenants —severance→ J – $^1/_3$, K – $^1/_3$, L – $^1/_3$, tenants in common

Sometimes severance is desired only by one and not all of the joint tenants. If there are two joint tenants, J and K, and only J severs, then both J and K become tenants in common because there is no-one else for K to continue a joint tenancy with (see above).

However, if there are more than two joint tenants and only one wishes to sever, then the position may be different. Only the severing party's share will be held under a tenancy in common and the remaining joint tenants will stay as they were, holding the remaining 'share' of the property between them:

(J, K, L) joint tenants —severance by J only→ J – $^1/_3$ tenant in common, (LK) – $^2/_3$ as joint tenants

We shall learn below which of the possible methods of severance allow one of the equitable joint tenants to act alone in this way.

There are four different methods that co-owners can use to sever a joint tenancy in equity. Some of the methods of severance available to joint tenants come from the LPA 1925; others arise from the common law that applied prior to 1 January 1926. It is important to remember that severance must be inter vivos, ie only while a joint tenant is alive; it is not possible to sever via a will.

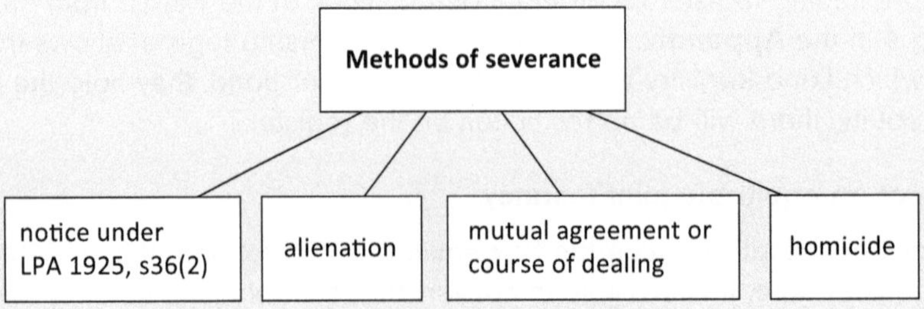

4.2.5.1 Severance by notice

The most common form of severance is severance by notice under s 36(2) of the LPA 1925. Giving written notice is a unilateral act and does not require the consent of the other joint tenants.

There are three requirements for a valid notice under s 36(2):

(a) The notice must be given in writing.

(b) The notice must show the correct intention.

(c) The notice must be correctly served (LPA 1925, s 196).

The notice must be drafted so that it shows an intention 'to bring about the wanted result immediately. A notice in writing which expresses a desire to bring about the desired result at some time in the future is not ... a notice in writing within section 36(2).' In *Harris v Goddard* [1983] 1 WLR 1203, a prayer in a divorce petition was not effective to sever the joint tenancy as it did 'no more than invite the court to consider at some future time whether to exercise its jurisdiction'. So, the notice of severance must show an intention to sever the joint tenancy immediately, and not at some later date. The prayer in the divorce petition at issue in *Harris v Goddard* did not show the required intention and did not operate as a notice of severance. However, in *Re Draper's Conveyance* [1969] 1 Ch 486, on similar facts, the wife's affidavit stated, 'I am entitled to a half share in the matrimonial home.' This was held to show the requisite intention.

Note also that there is no requirement in s 36(2) for a signature, so the notice does not have to be signed.

Once the notice has been drafted so as to show an intention to sever the joint tenancy immediately, the notice must then be correctly served. It must be served on all of the other joint tenants.

The joint tenant who wishes to sever the joint tenancy could of course simply hand the notice to all of the other joint tenants. But if the serving joint tenant does not wish to do this, it is possible to serve the notice in other ways - for example, by post. If posted, reliance can be placed on the deeming provisions of s 196 of the LPA 1925. This provision does not dictate methods of service; it is a method of proving service of notices.

Under s 196(3) of the LPA 1925, any notice is sufficiently served if it is left at the last known place of abode or business in the UK of the person to be served.

Example

Tim left a notice of severance for his co-owner with the reception of his fellow co-owner's hotel while they were at a conference. The co-owner received the notice and wants to know if the joint tenancy has been severed.

This notice was not correctly served as it was not left at the fellow co-owner's last known abode or place of business (LPA 1925, s 196(3)). The co-owner's joint tenancy was not severed.

In *Kinch v Bullard* [1998] 4 All ER 650, the property was owned by a married couple as joint tenants in law and equity. The wife sent notice of severance via ordinary post. The postman put the letter through the letter box. The wife subsequently picked up the letter and destroyed it as she had changed her mind about severance. The husband died shortly afterwards.

If severance had occurred, then the property would be held as tenants in common. This would mean that the deceased husband's interest would go to his estate.

If severance had not occurred, then the property would be held as a joint tenancy. This would mean that when the husband died, the rule of survivorship would apply and the wife would survive him and become sole owner of the property.

The court found that the severance was effective as the letter had been left at the last known place of abode of the husband, even though it was not received by the intended recipient. The court explained that, under s 196(3) of the LPA 1925, it does not matter who left the notice of severance. It could be left by the sender or their agent, or by a postman if the notice has been sent by post. The notice of severance is validly served if the sender can prove that, however it was delivered, the notice was actually left at the last known abode or place of business of the other joint tenants.

Under s 196(4) of the LPA 1925, if the notice is sent by registered or recorded letter, it is deemed to be sufficiently served if the letter is not returned (via the post office) undelivered. So, if a joint tenant chooses to send the notice via recorded letter, they can rely on the presumption set out in s 196(4). In *Re 88 Berkeley Road* [1971] 1 All ER 650, one joint tenant (X) sent notice of severance to the other joint tenant (Y) via recorded delivery. X themselves received and signed for the letter (in order to prove notice) and died soon afterwards. Y, the recipient of the letter, stated they had never seen the letter. The court confirmed that the notice was correctly served even though the serving co-owner had signed on behalf of the recipient to prove receipt of the notice. The equitable joint tenancy was severed. The notice would have been deemed to have been served if it was not returned by the Post Office as undelivered, even if it never actually arrived at its destination.

Other methods of severance

Now we have considered severance by notice, we shall look at the other methods of severance available to co-owners. The other methods of severance are methods that existed at common law before 1926.

4.2.5.2 Severance by alienation

'An act of a joint tenant operating on his own share' is known as severance by alienation. This may occur when the joint tenant sells, gives or mortgages their equitable interest to a third party. To be effective, the gift, sale or mortgage must be in signed writing (LPA 1925, s 53(1)(c)). A contract to dispose of the equitable interest will also sever the joint tenancy in equity provided it complies with the requirements in s 2 of the Law of Property (Miscellaneous Provisions) Act 1989 and is capable of being specifically enforceable (on the basis that equity regards as done that which ought to be done).

The joint tenant cannot transfer their interest in the legal estate (if they have one) at the same time, as this would require severance of the legal joint tenancy, prohibited by s 36(2) of the LPA 1925. They would remain a trustee despite disposing of their equitable interest. Any dealing with the legal estate requires all the trustees to participate.

Bankruptcy of a co-owner also has the effect of automatically severing their equitable joint tenancy, as it results in involuntary alienation of the equitable interest to vest in their trustee in bankruptcy.

Assume J, K and L hold both the legal estate and equitable interest as joint tenants. What happens if J sells their interest to (a) X or (b) K, complying with s 53(1)(c) of the LPA 1925 in each case?

(a)	**Legal estate**	(JKL) joint tenants	J sells to X →	(JKL) joint tenants
	Equitable interest	(JKL) joint tenants		X – $^1/_3$ tenant in common (KL) – $^2/_3$ as joint tenants
(b)	**Legal estate**	(JKL) joint tenants	J sells to K →	(JKL) joint tenants
	Equitable interest	(JKL) joint tenants		K – $^1/_3$ tenant in common (KL) – $^2/_3$ as joint tenants

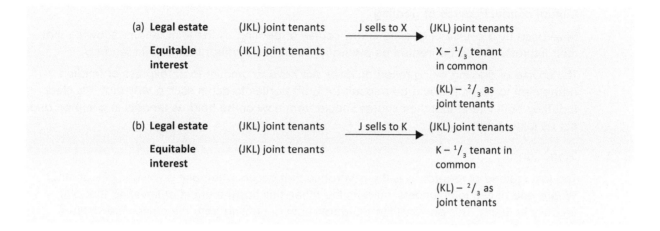

Note that in (b), K cannot 'combine' their two interests as they are held in different ways (although of course if the land was sold, they would be entitled to two-thirds of the sale proceeds).

4.2.5.3 Severance by mutual agreement or a course of dealing

Mutual agreement

This method of severance applies where the co-owners expressly agree to sever the joint tenancy in equity, or where the parties agree to deal with the land in a certain way and that method of dealing would have the effect of severing.

An oral agreement will suffice and the agreement does not need to be carried through to performance. The significance of the agreement is not that it binds the parties, but that it expresses an intention to sever the joint tenancy.

Example

Elderly widowed lovers, Mr Honick and Mrs Rawnsley, purchased a house as beneficial joint tenants. It became apparent that Mrs Rawnsley would not marry Mr Honick and it was subsequently agreed that Mr Honick would purchase Mrs Rawnsley's interest for £750. Mrs Rawnsley then changed her mind and requested a payment of £1,000. No further action was taken by either party and three years later Mr Honick died.

Was there a severance?

Yes, there was an agreement supported by an intention to give valuable consideration (£750) which provided an indication of a common intention to server (notwithstanding Mrs Rawnsley's repudiation of the agreement).

These are the facts and decision from *Burgess v Rawnsley* [1975] 1 Ch 429. In that case, Lord Denning stated:

> I think there was evidence that Mr Honick and Mrs Rawnsley did come to an agreement that he would buy her share for £750. That agreement was not in writing and it was not specifically enforceable. Yet it was sufficient to effect a severance.

If there are more than two equitable joint tenants who all agree to sever, then all of them will become tenants in common with equal shares by this method.

Mutual conduct/course of dealing

Severance by a course of dealing is any course of dealing by the joint tenants showing that their interests should be treated as a tenancy in common rather than a joint tenancy.

The course of dealing being relied on does not have to amount to an express or implied agreement to sever. It would be enough for both parties to act in such a way that it is clear that they both intend that their shares should from now on be held as tenants in common and not as joint tenants.

4.2.5.4 'Homicide'

The last method of severance is the severance that occurs when one co-owner kills another. Where one of two joint tenants murders the other, this has the effect of severing the joint tenancy in equity. This prevents the murderer from benefiting from the crime. The victim's equitable interest in the land passes to the beneficiaries under their will or intestacy. The murderer takes the legal estate in the land as a result of survivorship. The legal estate is held on trust of land for the murderer and the victim's estate as equitable tenants in common (*Re K* [1985] Ch 85).

4.2.5.5 The effect of severance

When equitable joint tenants sever the joint tenancy in equity, the result is that the severing joint tenant takes a share in the property as a tenant in common. (Remember that it is not possible to sever the joint tenancy of the legal estate.) The precise effect depends on the number of joint tenants (*Bedson v Bedson* [1965] 2 QB 666 and *Goodman v Gallant* [1986] Fam 106):

- Where there are two joint tenants in equity, they both become tenants in common in equal shares.
- Where there are three or more joint tenants in equity, only the co-owner who severs their joint tenancy becomes a tenant in common. The other joint co-owners continue to hold a joint tenancy in equity of the remaining interest.
- Their 'share' of the property is proportionate to the number of joint tenants. So, if there are three joint tenants, the co-owner who severs their joint tenancy will hold one-third as a tenant in common and the remaining co-owners will continue to hold two-thirds as joint tenants.
- When severance occurs, the individual co-owner's contribution to the purchase price is irrelevant.

Example (two joint tenants)

Freddie and Mia bought a cottage together and made unequal contributions to the purchase price. Freddie contributed one-quarter of the money and Mia three-quarters of the money. The transfer in their favour contained an express declaration that they were to hold as beneficial joint tenants. Two years later, Mia decided to sever the joint tenancy in equity. She did this by handing Freddie a valid notice of severance. Mia subsequently died.

When Freddie and Mia bought the cottage, they bought as legal and beneficial joint tenants.

When Mia serves notice of severance on Freddie, this has the effect of severing the joint tenancy in equity. The legal estate remains unaffected. Freddie and Mia continue to hold the legal estate as joint tenants under a statutory trust of land. The equitable interest has been converted into a tenancy in common. From the date of service of the notice of severance, Freddie and Mia hold the equitable interest as tenants in common. As there were two co-owners, the effect of severance is that they each get one-half of the equitable interest as tenants in common (irrespective of the fact that they contributed unequal amounts initially, as their declarations of joint tenancy overrode this). Freddie becomes a tenant in common despite taking no action himself, as he cannot remain a joint tenant on his own.

When Mia died, the legal estate automatically vested in Freddie by survivorship. He becomes the sole legal owner as a result of survivorship. Freddie and Mia held the equitable interest as tenants in common. When Mia dies, her share in the property passes into her estate and passes to the beneficiaries under her will or intestacy.

ACTIVITY 1 Severance (more than two joint tenants)

Ten years ago, Reena, Simon, Tariq and Ursula bought a freehold office for their recruitment business. Title to the property was registered. The transfer to the four stated they held the beneficial interest 'as joint tenants'.

Five years ago, Ursula needed money and so signed a document selling her interest in the property to Reena.

Last year, Tariq died leaving all his property to Vasha in his will.

For each of the events, explain whether or not the equitable joint tenancy has been severed and, if so, the effect of severance on the legal estate and equitable interest.

COMMENT

Initial purchase – the office was transferred to all the co-owners who all appear to be of full age. They are all trustees of the legal estate which must be held on a joint tenancy (LPA 1925, s 1(6)). The declaration in the transfer that they are to hold the beneficial interest as joint tenants is conclusive, despite the fact that the four appear to be business partners (*Goodman v Gallant*; see **4.2.4.2**).

Five years ago – the document signed by Ursula did not affect the legal estate (and in any event it is not possible to sever the legal joint tenancy) and so she remains as a trustee. The sale to Reena resulted in severance of Ursula's equitable interest (by alienation) if the document complied with s 53(1)(c) of the LPA 1925 – ie in writing and signed. If so, Reena now has a quarter share of the equitable interest held as a tenant in common (acquired from Ursula). The remaining three-quarters of the equitable interest is held as joint tenants by Reena, Simon and Tariq (they have done nothing to affect their existing joint tenancy). Note that Reena cannot 'add together' her equitable interests, as each is held in a different manner.

Last year – when Tariq dies, his interest in the legal estate passes automatically by survivorship to Reena, Simon and Ursula (who remains as a trustee as she only severed her equitable interest). His equitable interest in the three-quarter share held as a joint tenant passes automatically to Reena and Simon. His will is ineffective as severance can only be achieved *inter vivos*, so Vasha gets no share of the property.

The final position is that Reena, Simon and Ursula are the trustees, holding the office on trust for Reena and Simon as equitable joint tenants (holding three-quarters as equitable joint tenants) and Reena as a tenant in common (a quarter).

After co-owners sever the joint tenancy in equity, they should record this on the title to the property. How they do this depends on whether title to the land is unregistered or registered:

(a) *Unregistered titles.* When the joint tenancy is severed in equity, a memorandum of severance should be placed on the conveyance to the co-owners. This is just a note recording the fact that the joint tenancy has been severed in equity. The reason for doing this is to ensure that anyone who looks at the deeds can see that even though the co-owners may have originally bought as beneficial joint tenants, they now hold as equitable tenants in common. However, the fact that there is no notice of severance on the conveyance does not mean that the joint tenancy has not been severed and its absence does not affect the validity of the severance. The notice is to warn buyers that the co-owners are now tenants in common in equity.

(b) *Registered titles.* When the joint tenancy is severed in equity, a restriction should be placed on the register to indicate that the land is no longer held by the co-owners as joint tenants. Again, the purpose of the restriction is to warn buyers that the co-owners now hold the land as tenants in common in equity. See **Reading 4** in the **Appendix** for a reminder of the wording of the restriction that you looked at earlier.

So far we have looked at co-ownership from the point of view of the co-owners. In **4.4**, we will look at co-ownership from the point of view of buyers who want to buy land from co-owners.

4.3 Implied co-ownership

So far, you have concentrated on situations where anyone looking at the title could see that the land is co-owned. The legal estate has been conveyed or transferred into the joint names of the co-owners, and so there is express co-ownership. Now you will examine the much more complex issue of implied co-ownership.

Consider this example. Sundeep and Jaswinder are living together. They decide to buy a house together. The legal estate of the house is transferred into Sundeep's name. Sundeep and Jaswinder each contributed one-half of the deposit and they both contribute towards the mortgage. The title deeds to the land (or register of title if title to the land is registered) show that Sundeep is the sole legal owner. Whilst the relationship continues, this situation may not concern the parties. However, if the relationship breaks down, the title deeds show that Sundeep is the legal owner of the house. To claim a share in the house, Jaswinder must prove that she has acquired a share in the equitable interest in the land. To do this she must prove the existence of a trust.

We have seen that to establish the existence of an express trust of land, the creation of the trust must comply with certain formalities. Section 53(1)(b) of the LPA 1925 provides that a declaration of the trust must be evidenced in writing. The problem with proving an express trust in this context is that until their relationship broke down, it is unlikely that Jaswinder and Sundeep thought to record in writing anything about their ownership of the equitable interest in the house.

If Jaswinder cannot establish an express trust, she may be able to establish that she has an equitable interest in the property under an implied trust. An implied trust need not be evidenced in writing (LPA 1925, s 53(2)). If those arguments fail, it may be possible to establish a proprietary estoppel but this is beyond the scope of this textbook.

In this section, we will concentrate on how claimants in Jaswinder's position can claim a share in the equitable interest of their home by establishing the existence of an implied trust. We will begin by examining how the courts have applied the resulting trust in this context.

In particular, we will look at the effect that the parties' intention can have on the resulting trust. We will then move on to consider another implied trust - the constructive trust.

Where the court applies a resulting trust or imposes a constructive trust, remember that the trust exists over land and it takes the form of a trust of land. Any disputes between the parties will be dealt with under the provisions of the TLATA 1996.

4.3.1 Resulting trusts

The law presumes that a resulting trust has arisen where, for example, two people buy land together, both contributing to the purchase price, and yet the legal estate in the land is transferred into the sole name of one of them. In the absence of evidence that the non-legal owner's contribution was meant to be either a gift or a loan, a resulting trust will arise in their favour in proportion to the size of their direct contribution to the purchase of the property. The contribution must be of all or part of the purchase price at the date of the acquisition of the property and not subsequent to it. In these circumstances, the legal owner holds the legal estate on a trust of land for them both, as tenants in common of the equitable interest (*Bull v Bull* [1955] 1 QB 234).

We will now consider the sort of financial contributions non-legal owners need to make in order to acquire an interest under a resulting trust and how the court assesses the size of that share.

In the case of *Curley v Parkes* [2004] EWCA Civ 1515, the judge, Peter Gibson LJ, thought, first, that a contribution of all or part of the purchase money (including payment of all or part of a deposit) would suffice, unless it could be shown to be a gift or a loan. He did not consider that payment of legal fees or other ancillary expenses, such as removal costs at the time of the purchase, would give rise to a share under a resulting trust. Financial contributions to a joint account from which mortgage payments were subsequently made also would not be sufficient. The judge says that 'the resulting trust of a property purchased in the name of another, in the absence of contrary intention, arises once and for all at the date on which the property is acquired'. This means that later payments of mortgage instalments do not count as part of the purchase price already paid for the purposes of a resulting trust.

Example

Ken purchases a property for £300,000. The property was transferred into his sole name. Ken's partner, Saul, paid the deposit of £30,000 and Ken paid the remainder.

Ken holds the legal estate on trust for himself and Saul as a resulting trust has arisen. Saul made a financial contribution to the purchase price on the acquisition of the property (as long as the payment was not intended to be a gift or loan). His interest is proportionate to his contribution, ie 10%.

The use of mortgage finance to acquire property has had the effect of diminishing the importance of the resulting trust. Instead, reliance is generally placed on a constructive trust where an agreement or common intention can be found or inferred from the circumstances. As we shall see, many more factors can be taken into account to establish an interest under a constructive trust, including contributions to mortgage payments.

4.3.2 Constructive trusts

Constructive trusts are imposed in a number of situations involving land. In this chapter, we are studying the imposition of constructive trusts in the context of co-ownership.

In *Lloyds Bank plc v Rosset* [1991] 1 AC 107, Lord Bridge outlined two situations where the court could impose a constructive trust. The first situation involves showing that two elements are present:

(1) There must be an agreement, arrangement or understanding between the legal owners and the non-legal owners to share the equitable interest.

(2) The non-legal owners, relying on that agreement, arrangement or understanding, acted to their detriment or altered their position.

If both elements are present, the non-legal owners will acquire an equitable interest in the land under a constructive trust.

The second situation is where there is no evidence of an agreement between the legal and non-legal owners to share the equitable interest. In this situation, again, two elements must be present:

(1) The court considers the conduct of the parties and can use that conduct to infer a common intention to share the equitable interest. To make this inference of a common intention, the court needs to establish that the non-legal owners have made direct contributions towards the purchase price. These contributions could either be to the initial purchase price or be the payment of mortgage instalments. Lord Bridge stated that he doubted that anything falling short of direct contributions would suffice.

(2) Again, the non-legal owners acted to their detriment or altered their position. The court may consider all the conduct of the non-legal owners here, not just that of direct contribution.

To compare resulting and constructive trusts, in a resulting trust situation, a contribution towards the purchase price of property leads to a presumption that the non-legal owners acquire an equitable interest in the land in proportion to their contribution. This presumption of a resulting trust can be rebutted by proving that the non-legal owners made their contribution for a different reason - for example, they intended it to be a gift.

With constructive trusts, the court must either be satisfied that the parties expressly, but informally, intended that the non-legal owners should acquire an equitable interest in the land, or it must infer this intention from the parties' conduct. The parties' expressed or inferred intention forms the basis of the trust.

4.3.2.1 Agreement, arrangement or understanding

Now we will consider how the judiciary have imposed constructive trusts in the first situation outlined by Lord Bridge.

To establish the existence of an agreement, arrangement or understanding, sufficient to impose a constructive trust, the courts require that a specific statement about ownership must have been made. It does not matter that the statement is deceitful or a trick, or that the maker of the statement did not mean what was said. So, in *Eves v Eves* [1975] 1 WLR 1338, where the legal owner stated that the house would have been put into their joint names had his partner been aged 21, and in *Grant v Edwards* [1986] Ch 638, where the legal owner stated that the house had been put into his name only so as not to prejudice the other party's divorce proceedings, the court found that sufficient statements about the ownership of the property had been made to establish a constructive trust. It is important to note that there must be some statement about ownership; 'an assumed but unarticulated common assumption about ownership is not sufficient'.

4.3.2.2 Detriment or alteration of position

The non-legal owners must also act to their detriment or alter their position relying on the agreement. Without this, an oral agreement about the ownership of the equitable interest is an express trust of land that has failed for lack of written evidence. In *Grant v Edwards* [1986] Ch 638, Nourse LJ considered that the non-legal owners would not have done what they did if the agreement with the legal owners did not exist – 'the causal test'.

Examples of what can amount to an act to the detriment

- *Paying for improvements to the house out of their own money.*
- *Paying all of the household bills to allow the legal owner to pay the mortgage.*
- *Working unpaid in the legal owner's business.*
- *Paying one-third of the purchase price of the property.*

Nourse LJ in *Grant v Edwards* stressed that the act to the detriment must be strongly linked to, and dependent on, the common intention. So, a distinction has to be made between acts that arise from another motive, such as love and affection for the legal owner, and acts that arise from the agreement that the non-legal owner will acquire a share in the property.

Example

George is the sole owner of a property. At the time of the purchase eight years ago, George assured his girlfriend, Nicole, that the property would be their 'forever home'. Upon the purchase of the property, Nicole gave up her rented flat and since then has paid half of the mortgage payments for the property.

The agreement is George's statement that the property would be their 'forever home'. The detriment is that Nicole gave up her flat and has paid half the mortgage payments, provided that this was in reliance of the agreement (and not love and affection for George). Nicole is a beneficiary under a constructive trust.

4.3.2.3 Common intention

In the second situation where the courts can impose a constructive trust, the parties' conduct leads the courts to infer a common intention that the non-legal owners should acquire an equitable interest in the land.

With a common intention constructive trust, there is no evidence of an express informal agreement between the parties as to their ownership of the equitable interest. Instead, the courts look at the conduct of the parties and see if that conduct allows the courts to infer that the parties had a common intention to share the equitable interest.

The conduct of the parties is used to both infer the common intention and to show that the non-legal owners have acted to their detriment. As noted above, in *Lloyds Bank v Rosset* [1991] 1 AC 107, Lord Bridge made it very clear that the conduct that would be sufficient to allow the court to infer a common intention was 'direct contributions towards the purchase price by a person who is not the legal owner, whether initially or by payment of mortgage instalments'. He doubted 'whether anything less will do'.

With its emphasis on the direct financial contributions made by the non-legal owners, this kind of constructive trust appears to resemble closely the conventional resulting trust. In cases where cohabitants who have made a direct financial contribution are claiming a share, modern courts are more inclined to find a constructive trust (see **4.3.3** below). This form of constructive trust has developed to deal with the implications of the common method of funding the purchase of the family home. Most people acquiring the family home can fund only a small part of the purchase price. Most of the price is borrowed under a loan secured by a mortgage over the home. This means that most people will pay for the purchase of their house by making monthly mortgage payments over a long period of time (usually 25 years). Making mortgage payments will not trigger a resulting trust, as the payment of the mortgage instalments is viewed as the repayment of a debt incurred to finance a purchase that has already taken place. The mortgage payments will not lead to the presumption of a resulting trust, but can be used as conduct allowing the courts to infer the existence of a common intention constructive trust.

4.3.3 Comparison of resulting and constructive trusts

Now that we have considered resulting and constructive trusts, it would be useful to look at the relationship between them.

Under a resulting trust, the size of the non-legal owner's share is in proportion to the size of the contribution made towards the purchase of the property.

Under a constructive trust, once the courts have established an agreement, arrangement or understanding, or a common intention to share the equitable interest, together with acts to the detriment by the non-legal owner, they have discretion about the size of share they can award the non-legal owner. The Court of Appeal, in *Drake v Whipp* [1996] 1 FLR 826, confirmed that it is not necessary for the parties to the dispute to have a common intention about the value or size of their respective beneficial interests. Nor could the court go as far as to impute such an intention. If the court finds that there was no express agreement between the parties, the court can take a broad approach to quantifying the size of the parties' respective shares, taking into account the parties' conduct, the direct and non-direct financial contributions and any non-financial contributions, such as housework.

This was confirmed in *Stack v Dowden* [2007] 2 All ER 929, where Lord Walker and Baroness Hale referred to Chadwick LJ in *Oxley v Hiscock* [2004] EWCA Civ 546. He said that in determining the share of a beneficiary under a constructive trust, the court should consider the whole course of dealing between the parties in relation to the property and 'in that context, the whole course of dealing between them in relation to the property includes the arrangements which they make ... in order to meet the outgoings (for example, mortgage contributions, council tax and utilities, repairs, insurance and housekeeping) which have to be met if they are to live in the property as their home'.

The courts have been inconsistent in applying trust principles to situations. They have sometimes mixed up the requirements of the two trusts, thus creating confusion. Mixing up the two kinds of trust can have very important implications for the parties involved in the dispute. In *Drake v Whipp* [1996] 1 FLR 826, at first instance, the trial judge treated the matter as a resulting trust and Mrs Drake acquired a 19.4% share in the property. On appeal it was established that she had an interest under a constructive trust and was entitled to a 33.3% share. The courts have to assess each case very much on its facts. For example, in *Grant v Edwards*, Grant was awarded a 50% share; in *Eves v Eves*, 'Mrs' Eves received a 25% share; and in *Stack v Dowden*, Ms Dowden achieved a 65% share.

Because the finding of a constructive trust allows the consideration of all contributions, direct or indirect, the courts have recently been more inclined to find a constructive trust even where a direct financial contribution has been made. In *Stack v Dowden* [2007] 2 All ER 929, Baroness Hale of Richmond said that 'the doctrine of resulting trust has conceded much of its field of application to the constructive trust, which is nowadays fast becoming the primary phenomenon in the area of implied trusts'.

However, constructive trusts have not totally superseded resulting trusts. In commercial cases or where property has been bought as an investment, a finding of a resulting trust may be more appropriate. In *Laskar v Laskar* [2008] 7 EG 142, the Court of Appeal found a resulting trust rather than a constructive trust. In that case, a council house which had previously been rented by Z was bought in the joint names of Z and her adult daughter (as Z could not obtain a mortgage on her own). The adult daughter had made a small direct contribution to the purchase price. Neither Z nor her daughter lived in the house. They rented it to tenants and treated the house as an investment. Z took sole responsibility for making the mortgage payments and managing the property. The mother and daughter subsequently fell out and the daughter tried claiming a half share in the house. The Court of Appeal rejected the daughter's claim but awarded her a share proportionate to her contribution, applying resulting trust principles.

We have now examined the issue of implied co-ownership. Remember that co-ownership does not exist in isolation. Wherever there is co-ownership, there will be a trust of land. Therefore, the law relating to trusts of land will apply to co-ownership.

In the next section we will consider how co-owners can sell the land, and what the position of beneficiaries and co-owners will be in the event of a sale of the property, ie to what extent will their interest be enforceable against the buyer?

4.4 Sale by co-owners

Let us now look at what happens if co-owners decide that they wish to sell their land. Remember that whenever land is co-owned, there is a statutory trust of land. As trustees of land holding the legal estate, the trustees have the power to sell the trust land. To decide whether or not a third party (eg a purchaser/buyer or a mortgagee) will be bound by the beneficiaries' interests, you should consider the stages listed below.

4.4.1 Sale by two or more co-owners

Where there are two or more legal owners, the buyer pays the purchase price to all the legal owners to get the whole legal estate and, because they have bought from at least two trustees, the buyer overreaches any equitable interests arising under the trust of land. Whether the title to the land is registered or unregistered, a buyer who has overreached the equitable interest(s) will take the land free from them. The equitable interest(s) will then attach instead to the sale proceeds in the hands of the selling trustees.

Remember the conditions for overreaching from **Chapters 2** and **3** (LPA 1925, ss 2 and 27):

(a) the purchaser must acquire a legal estate (freehold or leasehold);

(b) the purchaser must pay all the trustees (remember, there can be a maximum of four under s 34 of the LPA 1925); and

(c) the trustees must be at least two in number (or a trust corporation).

4.4.2 Sale by sole surviving co-owner

If the co-owners held the equitable interest as joint tenants at the date of the death of one of the co-owners, the right of survivorship applies and both the legal estate and the equitable interest vest in the surviving co-owner. They are now the sole legal and equitable owner by survivorship and can sell alone. If, however, the co-owners were tenants in common, after the co-owner's death, the surviving co-owner will hold the land on trust for themselves and the beneficiaries under the deceased co-owner's will or intestacy, and the buyer needs to overreach by insisting that the surviving co-owner appoints a second trustee.

4.4.2.1 Unregistered title

The surviving co-owner will show the buyer a copy of the title deeds, ie basically a bundle of conveyances. The last conveyance in that bundle will show how the co-owners hold the equitable interest. If the equitable interest is held as joint tenants, the surviving co-owner shows the buyer a copy of the dead co-owner's death certificate. The legal estate must be held as joint tenants, so on the dead co-owner's death the legal estate vested in the surviving co-owner. The buyer will be concerned about whether the joint tenancy was severed in equity before the dead co-owner died. If the buyer can rely on s 1 of the Law of Property (Joint Tenants) Act 1964 ('1964 Act'), the buyer can assume that the joint tenancy was not severed in equity before the dead co-owner died. The buyer can then safely buy from the surviving co-owner alone without appointing a second trustee. The application of the 1964 Act is beyond the scope of this book.

If the transaction does not comply with the provisions of the 1964 Act or, in the case of any other sale where overreaching has failed, the buyer will be bound by the beneficial interests and rights of co-owners, unless they are equity's darling (see **Chapter 2**), ie a bona fide buyer for value of the legal estate without notice (actual, constructive or imputed) of the beneficiaries' interests.

4.4.2.2 Registered title

Where title to the land is registered, the surviving co-owner proves their ownership to a buyer by showing the buyer the copies of the entries on the register of title. If there is no restriction on the proprietorship register (Land Registration Act (LRA) 2002, s 40), the buyer is entitled to assume that the co-owners held the land for themselves as joint tenants in equity before the dead co-owner's death. If the surviving co-owner shows the buyer a copy of the death certificate, the buyer can assume that the surviving co-owner has taken the whole of the legal estate and equitable interest by survivorship, and so the buyer can buy safely from surviving co-owner alone.

However, if there is a restriction on the register, it will indicate to the buyer that the co-owners held the land as tenants in common in equity before the death. The surviving co-owner therefore holds the legal estate on trust for themselves and for the beneficiaries under the dead co-owner's will or intestacy. The buyer knows that they need to insist that the surviving co-owner appoints a second trustee to overreach the equitable interests of the beneficiaries under the dead co-owner's will or intestacy.

If the buyer fails to overreach the equitable interest, they will be bound by it only if the interest qualifies as an interest which overrides under Sch 3, para 2 to the LRA 2002 (assuming sale is on or after 13 October 2003) - see **Chapter 1**. The case of *William & Glyn's Bank v Boland* [1981] AC 487 covers the position under the old s 70(1)(g) of the Land Registration Act 1925, where a trust interest was seen to qualify as one that may be protected by 'actual occupation'.

If the interest is not overriding (eg the beneficiary is not in actual occupation of the land, or their occupation is not obvious and buyer did not know of the interest), the buyer will not be bound (LRA 2002, s 29). However, the buyer will be prevented from registering their purchase if the beneficiary has registered a restriction - see **3.3.1.3**.

You have now finished studying co-ownership. You will find two test your knowledge activities which cover this topic below. Use the following flowchart to help you analyse co-ownership problem questions.

4.5 Express co-ownership problems – summary

Co-ownership gives rise to statutory trust governed by the 1996 Act. Explain how legal and equitable interests are held when co-owners first acquire the land.

▼

- The legal estate can only be held by way of a joint tenancy (LPA 1925, s 1(6)).
- How is the equitable interest held?
  - are the four unities present? If so ...
  - an express statement (prevails over all else). If not ...
  - words of severance?
  - implied tenancy in common?

Explain and apply to facts.

▼

Go through the facts chronologically. Discuss the effect of subsequent events on *both* the legal estate and the equitable interest at each stage.

- The legal estate will pass by survivorship on death, but cannot be severed (LPA 1925, s 36(2)).
- The equitable interest can be severed by:
  - written notice (LPA 1925, s 36(2))
  - alienation (selling/giving away/mortgaging equitable interest and bankruptcy)
  - mutual agreement or a course of dealing
  - homicide

Where severance of equitable interest has occurred, try to work out shares as fractions.

▼

Conclude as to how legal and equitable interests are held.

If land is sold, you may need to apply enforceability rules (for registered/unregistered titles – see Unit 1) to work out whether buyer is bound by equitable interests.

Dispute, etc between beneficiaries/ trustees?

This may require detailed discussion of relevant provisions of TLATA 1996.

ACTIVITY 2 Test your knowledge: co-ownership, trusts of land and third party rights

There are strong links between co-ownership, trusts of land and third party rights in land. This consolidation exercise involves elements of all three topics.

Please read the case study below and then answer the questions based on it. Read the comment on each question before answering the next.

Last year Charles purchased the freehold estate of 9 Cotswold Terrace. One-third of the purchase money was provided by his mother, Liz, the rest by Charles. Liz moved into the property earlier this year with Charles and his new wife, Belinda.

Liz has come to you for advice because Charles has told her that 'the arrangement is not working' and Belinda has told her that 'I must have a share because I have decorated the house from top to bottom'. Charles and Belinda are now planning to sell the house.

(1) Advise Liz whether she has any rights in the house and whether she can prevent a sale by Charles.

COMMENT

Liz may have an equitable interest under a resulting (implied) trust, provided that her direct contribution towards the purchase of the house was not intended to be a loan or a gift to Charles (*Bull v Bull*). If so, Charles would hold the legal estate on trust for himself (two-thirds) and Liz (one-third) as tenants in common in equity as a trust of land under the 1996 Act. No formalities are required to create an implied trust (LPA 1925, s 53(2)).

As a beneficiary under a trust, Liz will have rights and Charles will have duties as a trustee, both under TLATA 1996. He must consult her, but only has to give effect to the wishes of the majority in value, so far as this is consistent with the interests of the trust (s 11). As a beneficiary with a two-thirds share, his wishes would seem to prevail. However, Liz could apply to the court under s 14 of TLATA 1996 to try to stop the sale; the court will consider the factors under s 15, including the purpose for which the house was bought and whether this still exists.

(2) Advise Liz whether Belinda is correct in what she says.

COMMENT

Belinda is claiming to have an equitable interest in the house, presumably on the basis of the first type of constructive trust set out in *Lloyds Bank v Rosset*. She has to show there has been an agreement or understanding between her and Charles that she should have an interest, and that she has acted to her detriment in reliance on this (she does not seem to have made any direct contributions, so it is unlikely that an agreement could be inferred from her conduct if all she has done is decorate the house). We do not know what, if anything, has been agreed between them, and it is not certain whether the court would accept even extensive decoration as sufficient detriment to give Belinda an interest. Similar work in *Rosset* was seen as *de minimis* by the court.

(3) Advise Liz whether a buyer of the house will be bound by any rights Liz and Belinda may have, assuming the title to the land is registered.

COMMENT

If the title is registered, Liz's equitable interest, combined with her actual occupation of the property, will give her an interest which will override any registered disposition under Sch 3, para 2 to the LRA 2002, unless inquiries are made and she fails to reveal her right. It seems that her occupation would be obvious on a reasonably careful inspection of the land as she lives in the house.

If so, her interest will bind a buyer unless it is overreached (LPA 1925, ss 2 and 27; and see *City of London Building Society v Flegg* [1988] AC 54). Any buyer would have to insist upon Charles appointing a second trustee in order to achieve this, and it is likely that a buyer would do so, having been alerted to Liz's interest by virtue of her occupation or the presence of a restriction on the register if she has registered one. If this occurs then Liz would no longer have an interest in the land but only in the proceeds of sale, which she would need to claim from Charles. If the buyer fails to overreach and Liz has registered a restriction, the restriction would merely prevent the buyer being registered.

If Belinda does have an equitable interest then she will be in the same position as Liz (above). However, this is unlikely to be a problem for a buyer as Belinda is in favour of the sale. She may even agree to be appointed as the second trustee.

Even if she does not have an equitable interest, Belinda will have a statutory right to occupy under s 30 of the Family Law Act (FLA) 1996, as she is a non-legal owning spouse and this is the matrimonial home.

If she wished to protect her right under the FLA 1996 against a buyer, Belinda would need to protect it by a notice on the register of Charles's title, as it is an interest affecting a registered estate. It cannot be protected by Sch 3, para 2 (FLA 1996, s 31(10)(b)) and cannot be overreached. However, again, she is unlikely to want to do this as it would hinder the sale.

(4) How would your answer to (3) above differ if title to the land was unregistered?

COMMENT

If the title is unregistered, whether Liz's equitable interest would bind a buyer will again hinge on whether the buyer overreaches. If so, the buyer is not bound and her interest attaches to the proceeds of sale.

If the buyer fails to overreach, they will be bound by her right unless they are a bona fide buyer for value of the legal estate without notice (equity's darling). They would be deemed to have constructive notice of Liz's right because her presence would be apparent from inspection (following the case of *Tizard* – see s 199(1)(ii) of the LPA 1925 and **Chapter 2**).

The same would apply to Belinda if she has an equitable interest, although this is unlikely to be an issue for the reasons stated above. If she had wanted to protect her FLA 1996 right, she would have had to register it as a Class F land charge under s 2 of the Land Charges Act 1972 against Charles's name (s 3) on the Land Charges Register before completion of the sale to the buyer in order to bind them (s 4).

ACTIVITY 3 Test your knowledge: co-ownership

Please read the second case study below and then answer the question based on it.

In January last year, five friends (Ann, Beata, Chloe, Dita and Eloise) bought a shop on a long lease, to run on a co-operative basis selling their own hand-crafted goods. Beata contributed slightly less than the other four, who all contributed equally to the lease premium. The grant of the registrable lease was to all of them as 'beneficial joint tenants'. The lease was subsequently registered at Land Registry.

A few weeks after the acquisition of the shop, Ann died of a heart attack. In April, finding herself short of money, Beata mortgaged her interest in the property to Chloe. She managed to repay the loan two months later.

In June, Dita finished an existing course she had been taking to become an acupuncturist and decided that she wanted to leave the business and release the money she had invested for her new career. Her solicitor drew up notices of severance which Dita handed to all of the other partners at one of their weekly meetings. Soon afterwards Dita was killed in a car accident. She left a will giving all of her assets to Eloise.

Beata is now disillusioned with the business and wants to sell it (including the premises), believing that the enterprise is jinxed. The others believe the worst is behind them and want to keep running the shop.

Explain to the partners what has happened to the legal estate and equitable interest, and what each will be entitled to if the shop were sold. Is it likely that Beata can force a sale?

COMMENT

When the shop was purchased, a trust of land under TLATA 1996 was created, with the legal estate being held by Ann, Beata, Chloe and Dita as joint tenants (LPA 1925, s 1(6)), as only the first four named may be trustees (LPA 1925, s 34(2)). The equitable interest was held by all five of them as joint tenants in equity, as the four unities appear to be present and the express declaration of trust rebuts the presumption of a tenancy in common arising from the fact that the shop was bought as partnership property (*Goodman v Gallant*).

When Ann died, both her legal and equitable interests passed to the other surviving co-owners by survivorship as she was a joint tenant in both. Thus the legal estate was held by Beata, Chloe and Dita, and the equitable interest by Beata, Chloe, Dita and Eloise.

In April, Beata's mortgage amounts to severance of her equitable share by alienation. It must have complied with s 53(1)(c) of the LPA Act 1925, ie have been in signed writing, to be valid. As at the date of severance there were four joint tenants in equity, Chloe receives Beata's now one-quarter share as a tenant in common, and Chloe, Dita and Eloise continue to hold the remaining three-quarters as joint tenants. The mortgage has no effect on the legal estate.

When Beata repays the loan, she gets back the one-quarter share from Chloe (again, provided the formalities in s 53(1)(c) of the LPA 1925 are complied with) but remains as a tenant in common. Again, this has no effect on the legal estate.

Dita's actions in June appear to have effected severance by notice under s 36(2) of the LPA 1925 as the notices were written, are likely to have shown an immediate intention to sever as they were drawn up by a solicitor and seem to have been correctly served by Dita handing them directly to her fellow joint tenants. Dita now holds her equitable share of one-quarter as a tenant in common, as does Beata, and Chloe and Eloise hold the remaining one-half as joint tenants. The notices have no effect on the legal estate, which remains vested in Beata, Chloe and Dita.

When Dita died, the legal estate vested in Beata and Chloe by survivorship. Dita's equitable share passed to Eloise under her will.

The end result is that Beata and Chloe hold the legal estate on trust for Eloise (one-quarter tenant in common), Beata (one-quarter tenant in common), and Chloe and Eloise (one-half as joint tenants).

This means that if the property were sold, Eloise would be entitled to half of the sale proceeds (at that point she could add her two interests together and would receive one-quarter from the joint tenancy aspect), Beata would receive one-quarter and Chloe one-quarter.

It is unlikely that Beata could force a sale. She and Chloe, as trustees, must consult the beneficiaries under s 11 of TLATA 1996, and give effect to the wishes of the majority by value so far as practicable. Chloe and Eloise together own three-quarters of the equitable interest and want to continue the business. Beata could apply to the court under s 14 for an order for sale, but the court will consider the factors in s 15 and may decide that the wishes of the majority, plus the purpose for which the trust was set up (to run a business, which remains), may be sufficient to reject her request.

Chloe and Eloise may seek to buy Beata out of the venture if they have sufficient funds to do so and continue running the shop together.

SUMMARY

- Co-ownership is a very important area of land law, in that it describes and regulates the relationship between multiple owners of land. As land ownership has become more widespread in England and Wales during the last century, recourse to these rules has become more common.
- In this chapter, you have studied the different forms that co-ownership can take and how these forms fit within the trust framework introduced in **Chapter 1**. You have also learned how changes to the beneficial ownership may occur via the various methods of severance. Implied co-ownership has remained of utmost importance to unmarried cohabitees, and you have seen how both resulting and constructive trusts can be created by the conduct of the parties to the trust. The existence of a trust interest may greatly affect a buyer of the land, and so you have also revisited the rules governing the enforceability of such interests in both the registered and unregistered systems.
- You now have sufficient background knowledge to identify and advise on the basic co-ownership issues that may arise in a standard conveyancing transaction. You could, for example, assist prospective buyers in deciding whether to choose a joint tenancy or a tenancy in common as the medium for their co-ownership, and advise them how this should be recorded to avoid a dispute in the future.
- You should use the test your knowledge activities contained in this chapter, either as a means of checking whether you have met the learning outcomes, or in order to reinforce what you have learned.

Part III Leases and Leasehold Covenants

5 Leases

LEARNING OUTCOMES

When you have completed this chapter, you should be able to:

- understand the different forms which a valid lease may take and how each may be determined;
- explain and apply the essential characteristics of a lease to a practical scenario and determine whether a lease or licence is present;
- understand the rules for creation of leases and appreciate that the rules rely on basic principles studied in **Part I**;
- assess the enforceability of a lease against a third party using the registered title and unregistered title rules.

5.1 Introduction

As you are aware, since 1925 there are only two estates in land that can exist as legal estates – a freehold estate (an estate in fee simple absolute in possession) and a leasehold estate (a term of years absolute). The freehold estate is an estate that endures for an uncertain length of time, whereas a leasehold estate is an estate of certain or fixed duration.

The parties to a lease will enter into an agreement and that agreement will constitute a contract between the parties. As seen in **Chapter 1**, it may not be a written agreement, but it will still constitute a contract. The contractual terms will be the terms of the lease as agreed between the parties, for example, the property that is to be let, the term of the lease, the payment of rent, responsibility for repairs, responsibility for insurance, and whether the tenant can sub-let the property. However, from the land law perspective, it must be remembered that as well as constituting a contract between two parties, a lease creates an estate in land and, as seen in **Chapters 2** and **3**, is capable of binding third parties.

A lease may be created for a number of reasons, for example so that the freehold owner may:

- obtain income;
- retain an interest in the property that can be sold; and/or
- enforce positive covenants against a successor in title to the original tenant (see **Chapter 6**).

5.2 Terminology

It is important to understand the terminology that is used in the study of leases. We will consider the variety of different terms you will come across in the context of an example.

Likhil owns the freehold estate in a house. Likhil does not want to live in the house himself at present, neither does he want to sell it. He would, however, like to obtain an income from the property, so he creates a *lease*. Another term is *tenancy*. However, this is usually applied to short-term lettings where land is let to someone, for example, on a weekly or monthly basis. The term *lease* tends to be used when referring to a fixed-term letting (eg, three years or 99 years). Section 1 of the Law of Property Act (LPA) 1925 refers to the expression *term of years*, and this means a lease. Lastly, a more technical term that can be used instead of 'lease' is *demise*. This is not used so frequently in modern lettings, but may be encountered in relation to older leases, where it may appear in the document creating the leasehold interest. The document will say, for example, that the landlord 'demises' the property to the tenant.

Were Likhil to create a lease, Likhil would be identified as the *lessor*, the original grantor of the lease. Alternatively, and more commonly, Likhil will be known as the *landlord*. It is usual to use the term 'lessor' only for the original party granting the lease, with 'landlord' being used for successors in title. When Likhil creates a lease, he still retains the freehold estate, but he has created a leasehold estate out of it. He therefore retains a freehold interest in the house, and this is known as the *freehold reversion*. As a consequence, Likhil will also be known as the *reversioner*.

Likhil is approached by Tina who wishes to rent the house. Likhil decides to grant a lease to Tina. Tina would then be identified as the *lessee*, the original grantee of the lease. She would also be known as the *tenant*, a more common term. If Likhil were to be referred to as the 'lessor', then use the corresponding term 'lessee' for Tina. Likewise, if Likhil were to be referred to as the 'landlord', then use the corresponding term 'tenant' to describe Tina.

Likhil granted a 10-year lease to Tina. She lives there for two years, then gets married and moves into the matrimonial home. She decides that she would like an income from the property, and so she *sub-lets* the house to Steve. There are now two leases affecting the house. The first lease, granted by Likhil to Tina, is known as the *head lease* and Likhil is known as the *head landlord*. The second lease, granted by Tina to Steve, is known as the *sublease*, *underlease* or *subtenancy*, and Steve is referred to as the *sublessee*, *underlessee* or *subtenant*. The sublease must be for a period of at least one day shorter than the lease out of which it is granted. Tina still retains a leasehold interest in the house, and this is known as the *leasehold reversion*. In the context of the lease granted to Steve, Tina will be referred to as the *sublessor* or *sublandlord*.

If Steve were to grant a lease, then the expression *subunderlease* would be used. After that there would be a *sub-subunderlease* and so on. This is shown in the diagram set out below.

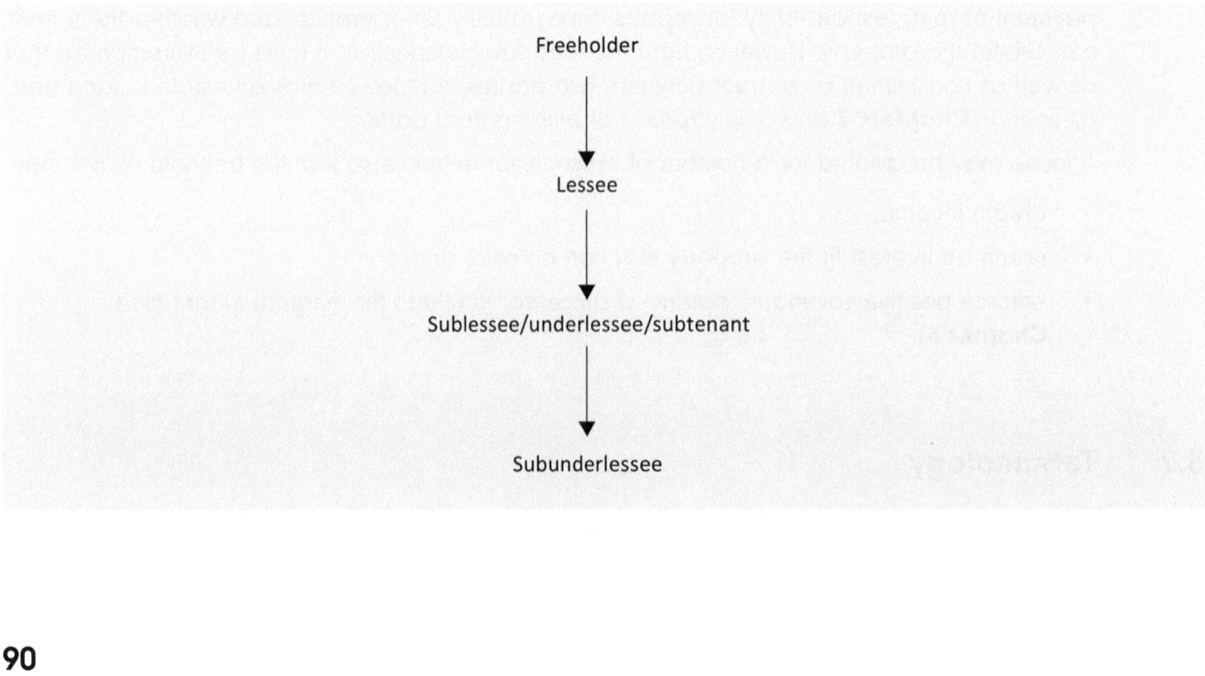

Lastly, in the context of terminology relating to leases, let us consider the terms used to describe the creation of leases, dealing with land that is subject to a lease and the parties involved. The original creation of the lease or sublease is known as the *grant*. Once the lease or sublease is in existence, it may then be sold. It is necessary to use a deed to transfer a legal estate (see **Chapter 1**). Likhil may decide to sell the freehold reversion in the house. The act of transferring the freehold reversion is referred to as an *assignment* of the freehold reversion, although the document used will still be a transfer. Likhil would assign the reversion. Likewise, if Tina decides to sell the remaining term of her 10-year lease to Ashie, this would also be referred to as an *assignment*. Tina would assign the lease. Again, the document used would still be a transfer. Tina would be described as an *assignor* and Ashie would be referred to as an *assignee*.

Below is an explanation of the practice adopted in illustrating the creation of a leasehold estate and the transfer of an existing estate.

Creation of a new estate

If a person is creating a new estate, that is a lease, out of their estate then that is illustrated vertically, as follows:

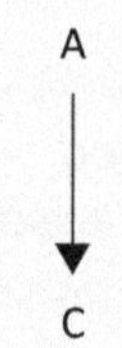

This means that A has granted C a lease.

If it is important to know the length of the term, this will be set out alongside the arrow. So

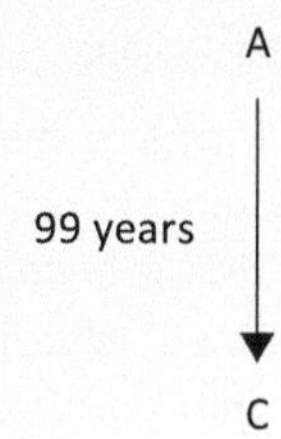

will mean that A has granted C a lease for 99 years.

Transfer of an existing estate

If a person is transferring (for example, by sale) their existing estate in land, this is represented horizontally in a diagram. So

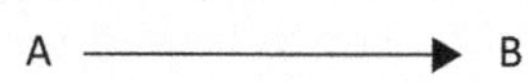

will mean that A has transferred the estate to B.

Example

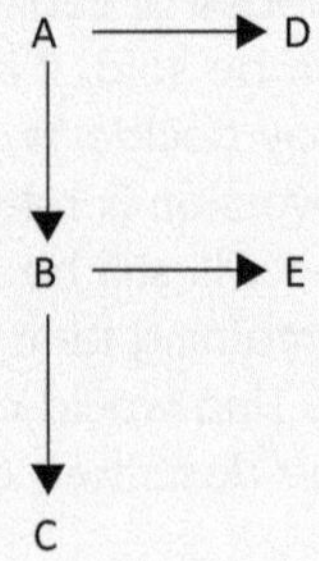

A (the freeholder/owner of the fee simple) has granted a lease to B. Alternatively, A has granted B a term of years or a tenancy, or A has demised property to B. A is the lessor or landlord. B is the lessee or tenant. A's interest after the granting of the lease is a freehold reversion.

B has granted an underlease, a sublease or a subtenancy to C. B, after the granting of the sublease, has a leasehold reversion. The lease between A and B is referred to as a head lease. (Note that A will therefore become the head landlord and B will be a sublandlord.)

A has also assigned the freehold reversion to D. This will have been done by deed (a conveyance if the title is unregistered or a transfer if the title is registered). D now becomes the head landlord or head lessor. B has assigned the head leasehold interest (a leasehold reversion) to E. E now replaces B as the sublandlord and is D's tenant and C's landlord.

5.3 Essential characteristics of a lease

Now that you are familiar with the terminology of leases, we will look at what essential characteristics are required for a lease to exist.

When a person is occupying premises that are owned by another, it is important to establish the nature of the occupation. Such a person is not automatically a tenant. If you allow a friend to stay at your house for the weekend, this is a completely informal and non-commercial arrangement. Neither you nor the friend would consider that you had created a landlord and tenant relationship. The friend is there with your permission, and you can withdraw permission and ask the friend to leave at any time. Such an arrangement is a licence (see **Chapter 1**).

However, there are occasions when a person will want to enter into an arrangement of a commercial kind but without giving the occupier the rights of a tenant. This would be so in the case of the owner of a hotel, for example, or someone who wants to take in a lodger purely on a temporary basis. There are other examples of situations where the parties might wish the arrangement to be regarded as a licence and not a tenancy. However, these arrangements can often have the appearance of a tenancy.

The law gives protection to certain kinds of tenant (see **5.6** below). Persons that the law classes as licensees do not enjoy the same protection (see **5.4** below). It is, therefore, important to be able to distinguish a licence from a tenancy.

What are the essential characteristics of a lease or tenancy? In the House of Lords decision in *Street v Mountford* [1985] AC 809, Lord Templeman determined that there should be exclusive possession for a term at a rent in order for there to be a lease.

5.3.1 Certainty of duration

Section 205(1)(xxvii) of the LPA 1925 defines a 'term of years absolute' as a term of years certain or liable to be determined by notice. A lease must be for a term. This can include either a lease granted for a fixed period of time - a fixed-term lease (see **5.5.1** below) or a lease granted for a basic period of time, either expressed, or implied by a regular payment of rent - a periodic lease (see **5.5.2** below).

For there to be certainty of duration, the date of commencement of the lease must be known to both parties at the start. In the absence of a date specified in the lease, it will be deemed to start immediately.

In *Lace v Chantler* [1944] KB 368, the Court of Appeal decided that a lease for the duration of the war was not valid, as it was not possible to say when the war would end. It was not sufficient to be able to say that at some future point in time its precise length would be known. A lease granted for an uncertain period of time is not a term certain and, therefore, not an estate in land.

Two subsequent cases have clarified the law concerning certainty of duration in relation to periodic tenancies and tenancies for life. In *Prudential Assurance Co Ltd v London Residuary Body* [1972] 2 AC 386, Lord Templeman confirmed that the ability of either party to end a periodic tenancy by notice was essential to meet the requirement of certainty. The case of *Berrisford v Mexfield Housing Co-operative* [2011] UKSC 52 clarified the position concerning a tenancy for life granted to an individual. The Supreme Court held that s 149(6) of the LPA 1925 operates to convert a tenancy for life into a 90-year lease, determinable either on the death of the tenant, or as provided in the agreement itself.

5.3.2 Exclusive possession

A grant of anything less than exclusive possession will not create a lease (it would only create a licence). Exclusive possession is the ability for the tenant to exercise control over the land:

(a) the tenant may exclude all (including the landlord) from the land; and

(b) exclusive possession extends beyond mere exclusive occupation. The latter is a characteristic of a licence. A tenant does not need to be in occupation to enjoy exclusive possession.

Lord Templeman in *Street v Mountford* decided that it was necessary to look at the effect of the agreement rather than at any labels given to the agreement. So, when the requirements are met, a lease is created even if it is labelled a licence. In *Street v Mountford* the circumstances and the conduct of the parties showed that what was intended was that Mrs Mountford should be granted exclusive possession at a rent for a term with a corresponding interest in the land which created a tenancy. Any express reservation of rights to the landlord to enter and view the premises for the purposes of repair emphasises the fact that the occupier is entitled to exclusive possession of the premises. Conversely, where the landlord provides attendance or services which require the landlord or their agents to have unrestricted access to the premises, there will not be exclusive possession by the occupier.

Lord Templeman decided that there could be circumstances in which there would not be a tenancy despite the occupier having exclusive possession, for example:

(a) where the parties clearly do not intend to enter into legal relationships at all;

(b) where occupation is required in connection with services provided or duties owed by the tenant to the landlord, for example pursuant to a contract of employment or the holding of an office;

(c) if the relationship between the parties is that of vendor and purchaser and occupancy takes place under a contract for the sale of the land;

(d) if the owner has no power to grant a tenancy.

Situations may also arise where it is not so clear whether or not an occupier has exclusive possession of premises. If several people, or a couple, occupy premises together, they may do so jointly where they live together and have joint responsibility for the property and the payment of rent. Alternatively, they may all be strangers to each other, for example, where students occupy student accommodation together, all being separately responsible for their rent. The House of Lords' decisions in *AG Securities v Vaughan* and *Antoniades v Villiers* were reported together at [1990] 1 AC 417. In both cases, each occupier had signed a simple agreement described as a licence.

In *AG Securities v Vaughan* the court held that, in this case, the agreements were independent of each other and did not confer a right of exclusive possession on any one party. The agreements had different dates and referred to different rents. The bedrooms were occupied on a rolling basis by incoming occupiers. The parties did not enjoy exclusive possession of the flat jointly under the terms of their agreements. As a result, the occupants only had licence agreements.

In *Antoniades v Villiers* the court held that the agreements were held to be interdependent and meant to be read together as a single agreement. Lord Templeman stated that '... the court must consider the surrounding circumstances including any relationship between the prospective occupiers, the course of negotiations and the nature and extent of the accommodation and the intended and actual mode of occupation of the accommodation.' As the agreements were in identical terms, signed on the same day and the intention was that Mr Villiers and Miss Bridger were to acquire joint and exclusive occupation of the flat, they therefore acquired a tenancy jointly. The clause allowing for the owner, his agents or invitees to share occupation of the flat was held to be a sham. Accordingly, a tenancy had been created.

5.3.3 Need for rent?

In *Street v Mountford*, Lord Templeman referred throughout his judgment to the need for 'exclusive possession for a term at a rent' in order to establish a tenancy. However, the Court of Appeal has since held in *Ashburn Anstalt v Arnold* [1989] Ch 1 that a tenancy may still arise even where no rent was payable. In particular, the Court of Appeal referred to s 205(1)(xxvii) of the LPA 1925, which defines 'term of years absolute' as meaning 'a term of years (... whether or not at a rent)'. Where rent is paid, this supports the view that the parties had intended a formal relationship of landlord and tenant to arise, rather than an informal/family relationship.

Where all three elements are present - certainty of duration, exclusive possession and payment of a rent - then a tenancy certainly exists. Lack of rent does not prevent a tenancy from existing, but it may have a bearing when determining whether it was the intention of the parties to grant a tenancy.

Examples - lease or licence

'The Haven'

Leilah owns a country cottage known as 'The Haven' and every year lets her aunt and uncle, Josephine and Steve, have the use of it for part of the summer, free of rent. Josephine and Steve are looking forward to spending another holiday there, but they have just learned that Leilah is planning to sell 'The Haven' and are worried about the effect this will have on their holiday arrangement.

In Street v Mountford, Lord Templeman set out the hallmarks of a tenancy. They are the grant of 'exclusive possession for a term at a rent'. The Court of Appeal in Ashburn Anstalt v Arnold made it clear, however, that a rent is not essential. In the case of 'The Haven', whilst Josephine and Steve may occupy it exclusively for a period, they cannot be said to have exclusive possession in the sense of having the right to exclude others from the cottage. If Leilah herself wanted to use it during the same period, or gave someone else the right to do so, Josephine and Steve could not prevent this.

Furthermore, it is clear that the arrangement is between members of a family. That, and the fact that no rent is charged, is a strong indication that there was no intention to create a legal relationship. Leilah is free to sell the cottage and the buyer will not be bound by any arrangement that Leilah had with Josephine and Steve. Josephine and Steve have only a licence.

'Elmgrove Villa'

When Leslie married his fiancée, Nell, six months ago, they moved into Nell's house. At the time, Frank, who was looking for somewhere to live, approached Leslie and asked him if he could move into Leslie's old house, Elmgrove Villa. Frank wanted to occupy the property on his own and to live there for only two years. He did not want to pay any rent, but he offered to pay Leslie £5,000. Leslie agreed to all these terms and signed a written contract with Frank to this effect. Frank moved in. Sylvia, a wealthy widow, has just made Leslie an offer to buy Elmgrove Villa. The offer is a very good one. Sylvia believes the property to be empty and wants to move in within six weeks. Leslie would like to accept the offer and wonders whether he can get Frank out a little earlier.

Frank is in sole occupation of Elmgrove Villa. He is not paying any rent, but a rent is not essential to a tenancy (Ashburn Anstalt v Arnold). He has, however, paid a capital sum for the right to occupy the property for two years and signed a written contract with Leslie, so the parties apparently intended to create a legal relationship. During the two-year period Frank can prevent anyone else occupying the property, including Leslie. He has, therefore, got exclusive possession of Elmgrove Villa for a term. This satisfies the test laid down by the House of Lords in Street v Mountford. Frank therefore has a tenancy. Sylvia wants to move in within six weeks. Whilst she can still buy the property from Leslie, it can only be bought subject to Frank's tenancy. (For an explanation of why Sylvia will be bound by Frank's tenancy, see ***Chapter 1*** *and* ***5.8*** *below.) Sylvia will have to wait until the tenancy ends before she can move in. Presumably, when she discovers this, she will withdraw her offer to purchase.*

5.4 Licences

In the absence of certainty of duration or exclusive possession, there cannot be a lease or a tenancy. However, there may be situations in which one party occupies premises with the permission of the lawful owner. This is merely a licence – a way in which someone may enjoy some right or privilege over the land of another. The essential thing about this type of licence is that it does not give the licensee an estate or an interest in the land, but it does make the licensee's presence on another's land authorised.

You have been introduced to bare licences and contractual licences in **Chapter 1**. A bare licence is automatically revoked by the death of the licensor or a transfer of their land. It can also be revoked by the licensor at will, ie by giving reasonable notice to a licensee.

A contractual licence will be enforceable against the original licensor in accordance with its terms, so cannot be revoked by the licensor until the contractual period has expired. However, as it is not a proprietary interest, it will not bind a successor to the licensor.

A licensor or a successor to a licensor cannot take possession of premises by criminal means (Criminal Law Act 1977, s 6); a court order for possession may be required against a licensee. In the case of dwelling houses, some further protection for certain licensees is provided under the Protection from Eviction Act (PEA) 1977.

5.5 Types of lease

5.5.1 Fixed term

5.5.1.1 Creation

A fixed-term lease is essentially a contract that gives the tenant the right to occupy the premises for a certain fixed period of time, usually in return for undertaking to pay the landlord a rent and to fulfil certain other obligations. Such a lease must be created expressly. An express grant of the lease is needed to identify the length of the term. The parties to the lease know from the outset the maximum duration of the agreement.

The formalities for the creation of a fixed-term lease are set out in **Chapter 1** (at **1.5.1**) and at **5.7** below.

5.5.1.2 Termination

Automatic

At the end of the period of the lease, the tenant loses their right to remain on the premises and the landlord once more can take possession of them, subject to statutory provisions that govern the procedure for taking possession in the case of dwelling houses (see **5.5.2.2** below) and security of tenure (see **5.6** below). This occurs automatically without the need for either party to serve notice on the other. This is often referred to as termination by 'effluxion of time'.

Forfeiture

The lease may include a provision that allows the landlord to end it prematurely if the tenant fails to meet their obligations, for example by failing to pay rent. This act is known as forfeiture, which will be discussed later (see **6.5.1.3**).

Surrender

Surrender occurs where the tenant yields up the lease to the landlord who accepts the surrender. Accordingly, surrender can only be achieved if both the landlord and the tenant agree to it. On surrender, the lease is said to merge in the landlord's reversion and is extinguished.

Merger

This occurs where the tenant acquires the immediate reversion to the lease (ie acquires the landlord's estate in land). It is the opposite of surrender. As with surrender, once the lease and the reversion are with the tenant or third party, the lease automatically merges with the reversion and is extinguished.

Break clause

There may be a clause included in the express grant of the lease providing for either party to serve a notice on the other to end the lease prematurely. A landlord, for example, might have the right to end the lease if they succeed in obtaining planning permission to redevelop the premises. On the other hand, a tenant setting up a new business might seek the right to bring a lease of commercial premises to an end after a certain number of years so that they can escape from their obligations should the business not prove to be as successful as anticipated. Such clauses are known as break clauses.

5.5.2 Periodic tenancies

5.5.2.1 Creation

Where the parties have not agreed a fixed term for the tenancy at the outset, the regular payment of rent will give rise to a periodic tenancy. Commonly for such tenancies, the landlord and tenant agree the basic period of the lease and that the lease shall continue to run from one period to another until it is determined by either party. As a periodic tenancy renews itself automatically at the end of each period of the tenancy and is certain to continue until either party decides to end it by serving a notice to quit, it does not offend the rule as to certainty of duration.

A periodic tenancy can be created expressly. Where an agreement contains terms such as 'weekly lease', 'weekly tenant', 'monthly tenancy' or 'from year to year', this determines the periodic term. In the absence of an express agreement, a periodic tenancy may be implied. Where, for example, a tenant goes into occupation with the landlord's consent and pays rent measured by reference to a period, such a tenancy may be implied (*Javad v Mohammed Aqil* [1991] 1 WLR 1007). In some circumstances, express reference to a period of notice required to terminate a lease will determine the periodic nature of the lease.

5.5.2.2 Termination

At common law a periodic tenancy will continue indefinitely from one period to the next until either party determines it by giving to the other a proper notice (a notice to quit). The length of notice required depends upon the periodic term of the tenancy. The general rule is that at least one full period's notice is required to terminate the tenancy. For example, a weekly tenancy would require a week's notice, a monthly tenancy a month's notice, a quarterly tenancy a quarter's notice. Such notice should expire at the end of a clear period. So, for example, a weekly tenancy that began on a Saturday can only be terminated by a week's notice that expires on a Friday. There are exceptions to this general rule. The most important of these is the relevant notice period for residential premises.

Where premises have been let as a dwelling, s 5 of the PEA 1977 provides that a notice served by either a landlord or a tenant will not be valid unless it is given in writing, contains certain prescribed information and is given at least four weeks before it is due to take effect. This requirement for four weeks' written notice applies to certain licensees of dwelling houses as well as tenants.

In addition, s 3 of the PEA 1977 requires the landlord to obtain a court order to recover possession of premises that have been let as a dwelling and where the occupier continues to reside there, or that are occupied as a dwelling under a licence.

It is clear, therefore, that even where a buyer of a freehold is bound by a leasehold interest (see **5.8** below), where the leasehold interest comprises a periodic tenancy, it is possible for the freehold owner to obtain vacant possession of the property by serving the appropriate notice. In the case of a dwelling, the freehold owner will need to obtain a court order for possession.

Example

Peter Anderson lives in a mews cottage that he moved into on a Monday nine months ago. He has been paying rent of £150 a week to Sheila Blackstone who owns several cottages in the same mews. Last Wednesday Sheila handed Peter a notice saying that she wanted Peter to leave by the following Wednesday. Peter claims that he has a tenancy and that Sheila has no right to end it in this way. Sheila maintains she can ask him to leave whenever she likes.

When Peter occupied the cottage, he began paying Sheila a weekly rent. In the absence of anything to suggest otherwise, Peter will be presumed to be a periodic weekly tenant (Javad v Mohammed Aqil). A weekly tenancy can be determined at common law by giving a week's notice. However, the notice must expire at the end of a period of the tenancy. As the tenancy began on a Monday, it cannot be made to end on a Wednesday as this would be during a period of the tenancy. The notice is not, therefore, a valid one. Moreover, as the mews cottage is a dwelling house, Sheila is obliged to give written notice in a prescribed form and the period of notice must be not less than four weeks (PEA 1977, s 5). She must also recover possession through the courts (PEA 1977, s 3).

5.6 Security of tenure

Although a tenancy may end at common law, many tenants may not have to leave the premises they are occupying because Parliament has decided that their occupation should be protected in some way. What follows is a very general summary, omitting a lot of detail and covering only the main statutes in this area, as security of tenure is a topic beyond the scope of this textbook.

5.6.1 Residential tenants

In the case of private sector residential tenancies, the two Acts that are relevant are the Rent Act (RA) 1977 and the Housing Act (HA) 1988. Both contain detailed provisions for identifying the tenancies to which they apply. A landlord wishing to remove the tenant will be able to do so only on certain grounds set out in these Acts. A landlord will find it far easier to remove a tenant if the tenancy falls within the HA 1988 than if it is protected by the RA 1977. In general, the RA 1977 applies to a tenancy granted before 15 January 1989, whereas the HA 1988 applies to one granted on or after 15 January 1989. There are also tight controls over the rent that a landlord may charge in the case of RA 1977 tenancies.

5.6.2 Business tenants

If a tenant is occupying premises and is doing so for the purpose of a business, then they may be protected under Part II of the Landlord and Tenant Act (LTA) 1954. A fixed-term tenancy will not terminate automatically at the end of the fixed term, and the landlord cannot end a periodic tenancy by serving an ordinary notice to quit. A tenancy protected by the LTA 1954 may be terminated only in accordance with the provisions of the Act. The tenant may also be able to claim a right to a new tenancy or to compensation if they lose their tenancy.

5.7 Formalities for creation of leases

You will recall from **Chapter 1** that the leasehold estate is capable of being legal as identified in s 1(1) of the LPA 1925. However, it must comply with certain formalities to be legal. If these formalities are not complied with, the lease may be void at law. However, it could still be valid in equity if certain requirements are satisfied. In the next part of this chapter, you will review the formalities required to create a legal lease and those required for an equitable lease.

Section 1(1)(b) of the LPA 1925 lists a term of years absolute in possession (the leasehold) as an estate which is capable of being a legal estate. Section 52(1) of the LPA 1925 sets out the general rule that a deed is required to create legal estates in land. Section 1 of the Law of Property (Miscellaneous Provisions) Act (LP(MP)A) 1989 specifies the current requirements for a valid deed. A deed must be clear on the face of the document that it is intended to be a deed, and it must be signed, witnessed and delivered.

Section 54(2) of the LPA 1925 allows for the creation by parol of leases (known as parol leases) taking effect in possession for a term not exceeding three years at the best rent which can be reasonably obtained without taking a fine. Effectively, short-term legal leases can be created in writing or orally. There is no need for a deed.

Section 27 of the Land Registration Act (LRA) 2002 classifies a leasehold estate for a term of more than seven years as a registrable disposition. Such a leasehold estate will require substantive registration and for a notice to be registered against the freehold title, if it too is registered, in order for the lease to be completed as a legal estate.

Where the correct formalities for the creation of a legal lease have not been followed, equity may intervene to recognise an equitable lease. This can occur where there is a contract to create or transfer a legal estate or where there is an attempt to use a deed, but the deed is not valid.

A valid contract complying with s 2 of the LP(MP)A 1989 is required. A contract disposing of an interest in land must:

- be made in writing;
- contain all the express terms expressly agreed between the parties; and
- be signed by or on behalf of the parties.

If these requirements are met then, because equity will normally enforce such a contract by granting the tenant an order for specific performance, the tenant will have an equitable lease under the doctrine in *Walsh v Lonsdale*. The decision in *Walsh v Lonsdale* (1882) 21 Ch D 9 was based upon the equitable maxim 'equity regards as done that which ought to be done'.

As specific performance is an equitable remedy, the courts will only grant it if the person seeking it has behaved justly and fairly (based on the equitable maxim 'he who seeks equity must do so with clean hands').

ACTIVITY 1 What kind of lease has been created?

Consider the scenarios set out below:

Sykes Properties own the freehold title of a building divided into three shops and two flats. On 1 November last year, Sykes Properties entered into the following arrangements:

(1) let one flat by deed to Akeena for 30 years;

(2) let one shop by an agreement in writing to Daisies Florists for 10 years; Daisies Florists pays a monthly market rent; no premium has been paid;

(3) let another shop by an agreement in writing to Lazytime on a yearly tenancy at the market rent; no premium has been paid by Lazytime; and

(4) let the second flat orally to Nadine until she finishes her degree course; Nadine paid a £15,000 premium to Sykes Properties.

Identify the possible types of tenancy that each occupier may have and explain the effect it will have on Sykes Properties' wish to sell with vacant possession.

COMMENT

(1) This is a term of years absolute and is capable of being a legal estate (LPA 1925, s 1(1)(b)). In order to create a legal estate, the parties must enter into a deed (LPA 1925, s 52(1)). Even though a deed has been used, if the title is registered, Akeena would need to ensure substantive registration of the lease for it to be legal (LRA 2002, s 27), as it is for a term of more than seven years. If she has done this, Akeena will have a legal lease for a fixed term of 30 years. If title to the land is unregistered, creation by deed is sufficient for Akeena to have a legal lease.

Akeena will have the right to remain in the flat until her lease expires at the end of the term. Sykes Properties will not have the right to recover possession any earlier than this.

(2) This arrangement is also a term of years absolute and is therefore capable of being a legal estate (LPA 1925, s 1(1)(b)). However, it has been created by an agreement in writing, which suggests that it is not a deed. If the document is not a deed, it may nevertheless amount to a contract if the formalities set out in s 2 of the LP(MP)A 1989 are complied with.

If these requirements are met then, because equity will normally enforce such a contract by granting Daisies Florists an order for specific performance, Daisies Florists will have an equitable lease under the doctrine in *Walsh v Lonsdale*. This will be an equitable lease for a fixed term of 10 years. Any attempt by Sykes Properties to remove Daisies Florists before the agreed term expires will amount to a breach of contract.

If the requirements in s 2 are not met, Daisies Florists may have a legal monthly tenancy instead as it is paying a regular rent. This will satisfy the requirements of s 54(2) of the LPA 1925. No formalities are required for a tenancy for a term that does not exceed three years (the term is monthly), takes effect in possession (Daisies Florists is in possession) and is at the best rent reasonably obtainable without taking a fine (a market rent is paid). However, as it is merely a monthly periodic tenancy, Sykes Properties would be able to end the tenancy by serving on Daisies Florists a notice to quit.

(3) Again, this is a term of years absolute, as it is a yearly tenancy. Although capable of being legal (LPA 1925, s 1(1)(b)), a deed has not been used to create it. However, it is short enough to qualify under the parol lease exception in s 54(2) of the LPA 1925. It also appears to fulfil the other conditions of s 54(2) in that: it is let at the market rent; no premium has been paid; and Lazytime is in possession of the shop.

(4) This arrangement cannot be a fixed-term lease as it is not a term of years absolute under s 1(1)(b) of the LPA 1925. There is no fixed and certain duration.

Nor is it possible for Nadine to rely upon s 54(2) of the LPA 1925, under which a periodic tenancy may arise (see (3) and (4) above), as she has paid a premium (a fine) to Sykes Properties. Sykes Properties can end the tenancy by serving on Nadine a notice to quit.

5.8 Enforceability of leases against third parties

Registered title

You have already looked at the enforceability rules relating to registered titles in **Chapter 3**. A legal lease for a term of more than seven years is recognised as a registrable disposition (LRA 2002, s 27). Such a leasehold estate will require substantive registration and for a notice to be registered against the freehold title. An example of how a leasehold interest is registered is provided in **Reading 6** in the **Appendix**. A legal lease of seven years and under will be an unregistered interest which overrides (LRA 2002, Sch 3, para 1).

If a registrable lease is not registered, the lease is only recognised by equity (see **5.7**). However, it may be an unregistered interest which overrides if the tenant is in actual occupation at the date of completion of the sale and their occupation is obvious on a reasonably careful inspection of the land or the buyer knows about the lease (LRA 2002, Sch 3, para 2).

An equitable lease created because of lack of formalities (ie one created under the doctrine of *Walsh v Lonsdale* - see **5.7**) is enforced as an interest affecting a registered estate and is protected by a notice on the register of the freehold title. If the equitable lease is not so protected, it may (as above) be an unregistered interest that overrides if the tenant is in actual occupation at the date of completion of the sale and their occupation is obvious on a reasonably careful inspection of the land or the buyer knows about the lease (LRA 2002, Sch 3 para 2).

Unregistered title

In the event that the property has unregistered title, it would be necessary to apply the enforceability rules that you looked at in **Chapter 2** to determine whether or not a buyer would be bound by each of the interests that exist in the building. Any legal lease (by deed or under s 54(2) of the LPA 1925) would be binding on a buyer, as legal interests affecting unregistered title bind the whole world irrespective of notice. An equitable lease (one which satisfies s 2 of the LP(MP)A 1989) must be registered as a Class C(iv) land charge on the Land Charges Register to bind a buyer.

ACTIVITY 2 Test your knowledge: leases

The aim of this activity is to give you some practice in applying your knowledge of leases to a problem. Set out below is a suggested approach to problem questions that you may find useful:

(1) Determine whether the right is a lease (rather than, say, a licence), unless the question tells you that it is a lease, by considering and applying to the facts the essential characteristics of a lease.

If you decide it is merely a licence, this is not a proprietary interest in the land and will not generally bind a purchaser - see **Part I**.

(2) Decide what type of lease it is. (This is important if, say, the landlord wants to terminate the lease or if the freehold has been sold, where the new freeholder wants to know if lease binds him.)

(a) Duration of lease:

(i) fixed term;

(ii) periodic - beware of leases which do not qualify as fixed-term leases due to uncertainty of duration but are capable of being converted into periodic tenancies.

(b) Lease may be legal or equitable - see formalities.

(3) Consider whether the lease binds a purchaser of the freehold - registered or unregistered title?

Now consider the following scenario:

Five years ago, Alex bought the freehold of Maple Lodge, a large Victorian house ('the Property'). The Property contained a small self-contained flat in the basement. Alex was duly registered as the proprietor of the Property.

Last year Alex allowed a young couple, Mark and Kathy, to occupy the flat until they were able to find a property to buy. He required them each to sign a separate agreement, one of the terms of which was that their right to occupy the flat was to be in common with others to whom Alex might grant similar rights. Mark and Kathy each agreed to be responsible for paying an occupation fee, which was payable by them quarterly, and to vacate the flat between 12 noon and 2 pm each day.

Discuss what rights Mark and Kathy may have to remain in the flat and whether Alex could end the arrangement?

COMMENT

Mark and Kathy signed a document under the terms of which they were allowed to occupy the flat until they were able to find a house to buy. This cannot be a fixed-term lease as it is for a period that is uncertain. A lease has to be for a term certain (*Lace v Chantler*).

However, as they are paying a quarterly sum to Rupert, their occupation may amount to a legal periodic tenancy. The document does not have to satisfy the formalities for a deed or a contract if the arrangement amounts to a lease granted for a term not exceeding three years and it takes effect in possession at the best rent that is reasonably obtainable without the taking of a fine (LPA 1925, s 54(2)).

The other essential requirement for a tenancy is that Mark and Kathy should enjoy exclusive possession (*Street v Mountford*). The flat is a small one and it seems that the term requiring them to share occupation with others, as well as the term that they should vacate it between 12 noon and 2 pm are not likely to be seen as genuine. Additionally, they are each liable for the whole of the quarterly payment. These all point to them having exclusive possession and to their occupation amounting to a joint tenancy of the flat and not a licence.

However, as they are periodic tenants, Alex will be able to end the tenancy by giving them a quarter's notice and obtaining a court order for possession.

SUMMARY

- You have now acquired the knowledge to recognise when a valid lease has been created and to identify different types of lease. You have developed your knowledge of the leasehold estate that you acquired in **Part I**, and you now have sufficient background knowledge to advise either a landlord or tenant on the effect of a lease where land is sold subject to that lease.

6 Leasehold Covenants

LEARNING OUTCOMES

When you have completed this chapter, you should be able to:

- identify the types of covenant that may be expressly included in or implied into a lease;
- assess whether and explain how covenants contained in leases may be enforced by successive owners of the freehold and leasehold estates in land;
- identify and explain suitable remedies for breach of covenant.

6.1 Introduction

As well as being an estate in land, a lease is a contract. The terms of that contract govern the obligations that parties have to each other.

A fixed-term lease can only be created expressly. A periodic tenancy may be created expressly, or it may be implied. Where a lease or a tenancy is expressly created, the parties can, of course, agree what obligations each is to undertake. An expressly created lease or tenancy, particularly one that is for a long fixed term, is, therefore, likely to contain promises made by the parties to each other. Such promises are known as covenants. Covenants may be either positive or negative. A positive covenant is one that requires a person to carry out work or spend money, for example a covenant to repair. A negative (or restrictive) covenant is one that places restrictions on what a person may do, for example a covenant not to use the property for business purposes. Lease covenants should be agreed through negotiations between the landlord and the tenant.

This is particularly so if you are concerned with a tenancy that is for a fixed term, especially if the term is a long one. However, what happens when the parties fail to include express provisions?

6.2 Landlord's implied covenants

In the absence of an express obligation, certain covenants will be implied on the part of the landlord.

6.2.1 Quiet enjoyment

When a landlord grants a lease to a tenant there is, in the absence of any express provision, an implied covenant by the landlord for quiet enjoyment. This means that the tenant's lawful possession of the land will not be substantially interfered with by the acts of the landlord.

Although a covenant that the tenant is to have quiet and peaceable enjoyment of the premises might suggest that the tenant can complain about any noise, that is not the aim of the covenant. The aim of the covenant is to protect the tenant against interference with the tenant's possession of the property by the landlord or persons who claim title through the landlord. If the landlord should threaten the tenant, such a threat may amount to a breach of the implied covenant for quiet enjoyment (*Kenny v Preen* [1963] 1 QB 499, CA).

A residential tenant is further protected by s 1(2) and (3) of the Protection from Eviction Act (PEA) 1977, which prevents a landlord from unlawfully depriving the tenant of their occupation. Any act likely to interfere with the residential tenant's peace or comfort that is done with the intention of causing them to give up occupation is an offence under the PEA 1977.

An implied covenant for quiet enjoyment does not therefore mean the absence of noise, although regular excessive noise may amount to a substantial interference (*Southwark LBC v Mills* [2001] 1 AC 1).

6.2.2 Repair

Another important area to consider concerns the responsibility for repairing the property that is comprised in the lease.

A tenant of a residential property where the lease is for less than seven years cannot be made responsible for any matter falling within s 11 of the Landlord and Tenant Act (LTA) 1985. The most that is expected of the tenant is that they use the property in a tenant-like manner. If the tenant has caused, for example, a sink to be blocked by their waste then this is a matter they must put right as it is 'one of the little jobs about the place which a reasonable tenant would do' (*Warren v Keen* [1954] 1 QB 15, per Denning LJ).

Instead, where there is no express repairing obligation imposed on the landlord to repair, certain obligations are implied, and the landlord is required under s 11 of the LTA 1985:

(a) to keep in repair the structure and exterior of the dwelling-house;

(b) to keep in repair and proper working order the installations for the supply of water, gas, electricity and for sanitation; and

(c) to keep in repair and proper working order the installations for space heating and heating water.

Where the landlord has the obligation to repair the structure, the landlord must repair and, if necessary in order to carry out the repair, will have to remedy any inherent defect in construction (*Ravenseft Properties Ltd v Davstone (Holdings) Ltd* [1980] QB 12). However, the landlord is not liable to carry out a repair until they have been notified of the need for repair (*O'Brien v Robinson* [1973] AC 912).

If there is no disrepair, the landlord cannot be made liable under their implied covenant to repair (*Quick v Taff Ely Borough Council* [1986] QB 809).

You now have some idea of the provisions that may be implied into a tenancy agreement. You also know that a tenancy may be created without any formality whatsoever if it takes effect in possession for a term not exceeding three years at the best rent reasonably obtainable without the taking of a fine (Law of Property Act (LPA) 1925, s 54(2)). Implied terms are, therefore, more likely to be encountered where the tenancy is either a periodic one or is for a short term and where there is little or no formality. If the parties have a formal written agreement or deed, the chances are that such a document will expressly deal with all the important areas that would concern a landlord and tenant. This will certainly be true in the case of a long lease or a lease of, for example, commercial property where the rent is likely to be high.

6.3 Tenant's express covenants

The lease will contain a considerable number of covenants by the tenant. The following are common express covenants which may appear in the lease.

6.3.1 Rent

There will be an implied covenant by the tenant to pay the rent agreed, but under the implied covenant the tenant pays the rent in arrears. Most landlords will want the rent to be paid before the tenant occupies the property, so most leases contain an express covenant by the tenant to pay the rent in advance.

6.3.2 User

The landlord will usually want to control the tenant's use of the property, so there will usually be a restriction on the use to which the property can be put. For example, in a lease of a residential property, there will probably be a covenant restricting the use to residential purposes and prohibiting any business or commercial use of the property. If the lease does not contain any restriction on user, the tenant may use the property for any purpose they wish, subject to obtaining planning permission.

6.3.3 Not to assign or sub-let (alienation)

Where the lease is for a long period, the tenant may want to sell the lease or create a sublease at some point during the term of the lease. If the lease does not contain any restriction on the tenant's right to deal with the lease in this way, the tenant may dispose of it as they wish. If the landlord wants to restrict the tenant's right to deal with the lease, the landlord will need to impose an alienation covenant on the tenant.

This covenant can take a number of forms. First, the landlord may impose an 'absolute covenant' against assignments or sub-lets. In this case, any attempt by the tenant to deal with the lease will be a breach of covenant.

It is more common to come across a 'qualified covenant' under which assignments and sub-lettings are prohibited *unless* the landlord's licence or consent is obtained first. In the case of a qualified covenant, s 19(1)(a) of the Landlord and Tenant Act (LTA) 1927 implies a proviso into the covenant that the landlord must not unreasonably withhold consent. Under s 1 of the Landlord and Tenant Act (LTA) 1988, the landlord must either consent or give the tenant reasonable grounds for refusing consent within a reasonable period of the tenant's request. Section 19(1A) of the LTA 1927, which applies to leases granted on or after 1 January 1996, allows the landlord to require the tenant who wishes to assign a lease to enter into an 'authorised guarantee agreement' ('AGA') - see **6.4.2.2** below.

6.4 Enforceability of covenants in leases

We now need to consider how covenants are enforced.

Example

Jamil is the freehold owner of a registered property acquired last year from Ian. The property comprises a greengrocer's shop with a flat above. In 1995 Ian leased the shop to Mary for a fixed term of 50 years. Mary duly registered her lease. Mary then assigned her lease to Fred in 2014. Two years ago, Ian leased the flat to Rebecca for a fixed term of six years. Last month, Rebecca assigned her lease to Sonia.

Both leases contain a covenant by the landlord to keep the structure and exterior in good repair. The shop lease contains a covenant by the tenant not to change the use of the shop. The flat lease contains a covenant by the tenant to keep the interior in good repair.

Jamil is now seeking advice about certain problems that have arisen in relation to the property. Fred has converted the shop into a computer repairs outlet and has complained that the back wall of the shop has cracks in it. In addition, a number of internal doors in Sonia's flat need repair.

In order to be able to advise Jamil, you need to understand the extent to which a successor in title to either the original landlord or the original tenant is able to enforce covenants entered into by those parties. Therefore, you will now consider the enforceability of covenants in leases between both the original parties and successors in title.

Before you do, you need to be aware that the Landlord and Tenant (Covenants) Act (LT(C)A) 1995 made some important changes to the law in this area. The LT(C)A 1995 applies to most tenancies granted on or after 1 January 1996. We refer to tenancies to which the LT(C)A 1995 applies as 'new' tenancies. The majority of the provisions in the LT(C)A 1995 do not apply to tenancies granted before 1 January 1996, nor to some tenancies granted after that date, for example where the tenancy was granted pursuant to a contract or a court order made before 1 January 1996. We call tenancies not affected by the principal provisions of the LT(C)A 1995 'old' tenancies.

As a result of the LT(C)A 1995, every time you consider the question of the enforceability of covenants, you must decide first of all whether the tenancy you are considering is an old tenancy or a new one. For this purpose, you must look at the date of the grant of the lease. The date of any subsequent assignment is irrelevant.

We need initially to see what the position is where the tenancy is an old one, as this will reveal the problem to which the LT(C)A 1995 sought to provide a solution.

6.4.1 Enforceability of covenants in 'old' leases

6.4.1.1 Liability of the original parties to the lease

A lease not only creates an estate in land but it is also a contract. Between the original parties, therefore, there is privity of contract. This is shown in **Diagram 1**.

Diagram 1

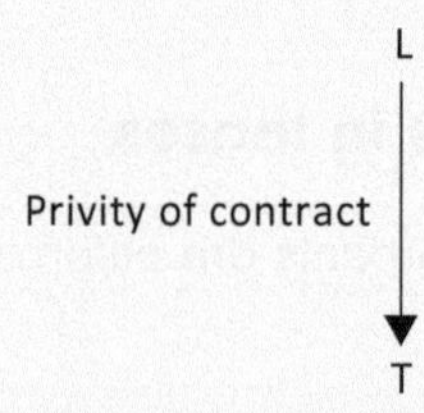

Whilst L and T remain respectively the landlord and the tenant, they can enforce each other's covenants.

However, if the original tenant assigns the lease, it does not end privity of contract between them and the original landlord. Privity of contract lasts for the duration of the lease, that is, for the life of the contract. This is shown in **Diagram 2**, in which L represents the original landlord, T the original tenant, and T^1 the assignee of the lease.

Diagram 2

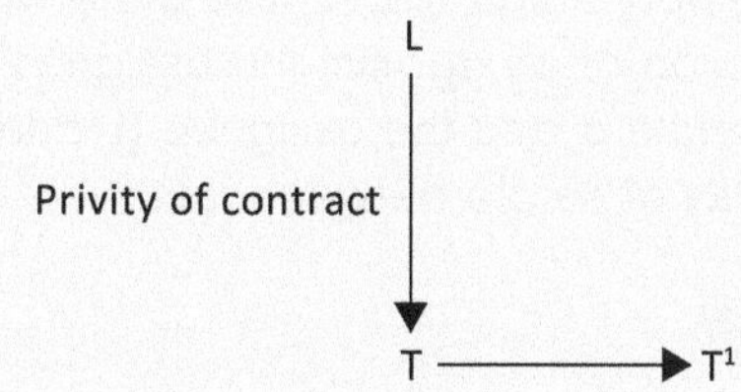

As there is still privity of contract between L and T, it means that if T¹ breaches any of the covenants in the lease, T remains liable to L. This is the position throughout the entire lease term, despite the fact that the lease may have been assigned many times. The fact that the tenant remains liable after assignment does not depend upon them covenanting both for themselves and their assignees in the lease. A similar situation will arise if the original landlord assigns the reversion. The assignee of the reversion is shown in **Diagram 3** as L¹.

Diagram 3

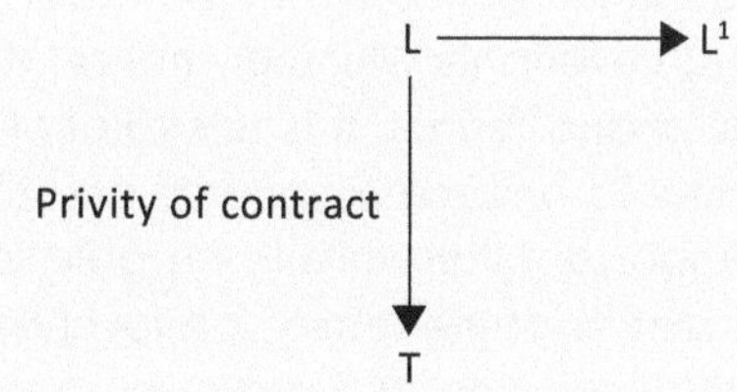

In this case, L remains liable for breaches of covenant by L¹, and L's liability continues throughout the whole term notwithstanding that the freehold reversion may have been assigned many times. As the covenants given by the landlord in the lease tend to be less onerous than those given by the tenant, the principle of continuing liability is less of an issue for the landlord.

6.4.1.2 Liability of successors to the original parties

You will now consider the position of successors in title to the original parties to the lease.

Please refer to **Diagrams 2** and **3** above.

The position of T¹ (Diagram 2)

When the original tenant covenants with the landlord, for example, to repair property, it is an obligation that passes with the land. The assignee of the original tenant (T¹ in Diagram 2 at **6.4.1.1** above) and all other successors in title to the original tenant will have the benefit of covenants entered into by the landlord with that tenant, but they must also accept the burden of the original tenant's covenants, provided that they are covenants that 'touch and concern' the land - *Spencer's Case* (1583) 5 Co Rep 16a (77 ER 72). There is a modern interpretation of *Spencer's Case* in the following extract from the judgment of Lord Templeman in *City of London Corporation v Fell* [1994] 1 AC 458:

> At common law, after an assignment, the benefit of a covenant by the original landlord which touches and concerns the land runs with the term granted by the lease. The burden of a covenant by the original tenant which touches and concerns the land also runs with the term: see *Spencer's Case* ...

Although there is clearly no contract between the landlord and the assignee of the original tenant (L and T^1 in Diagram 2 above), the assignee (T^1) has replaced the original tenant (T) as the tenant. It would be very unfair if, because there was no contract between them, the landlord (L) could take no action at all against the assignee (T^1) if the assignee (T^1) committed a breach of covenant. The landlord and the assignee (L and T^1) are in the position of landlord and tenant, and there is privity of estate between them.

The position of L^1 (Diagram 3)

Section 141 of the LPA 1925 says that entitlement to the rent and the benefit of all the tenant's covenants in the lease that have 'reference to the subject matter thereof' are annexed to the reversionary estate. They will pass to L^1 and any subsequent owner of the reversion, thus allowing L^1 to sue T.

Section 142 of the LPA 1925 says that obligations under any covenant entered into by the landlord 'with reference to the subject matter of the lease' are similarly annexed to the reversionary estate. These obligations will be binding on L^1 and subsequent owners of the reversion. There will thus be privity of estate between L^1 and T since L's estate is now vested in L^1.

You will note that ss 141 and 142 of the LPA 1925 say that the assignee of the reversion only acquires the benefit of the tenant's covenants, and is only liable on the landlord's covenants, if the covenants have 'reference to the subject matter of the lease'. *Spencer's Case* likewise only applies to covenants that 'touch and concern' the land. You can understand the rationale behind this if you consider that covenants which do not relate to the land have nothing to do with the relationship of landlord and tenant. It is this relationship that establishes the basis for the right of successors in title to enforce covenants and the liability of successors in title to comply with covenants. It is important therefore to be able to determine whether a covenant has 'reference to the subject matter of the lease', or 'touches and concerns' the land. These two expressions are identical in meaning and are also often referred to as 'real' covenants as opposed to 'personal' covenants, which you will look at in **6.4.1.3** below. In order to discover whether the benefit and burden of a covenant passes, you have first of all to establish whether it is covered by one of these expressions.

It is to that question that we turn to next. You need to be warned, however, that in *Grant v Edmondson* [1931] 1 Ch 1, Romer LJ had this to say:

> In connection with the subject of covenants running with the land, it is impossible to reason by analogy. The established rules concerning it are purely arbitrary and the distinctions for the most part quite illogical.

In *P & A Swift Investments v Combined English Stores Group plc* [1989] AC 632, Lord Oliver set out the following test:

> Formulations of definitive tests are always dangerous, but it seems to me that, without claiming to expound an exhaustive guide, the following provides a satisfactory working test for whether, in any given case, a covenant touches and concerns the land: (1) the covenant benefits only the reversioner for the time being, and if separated from the reversion ceases to be of benefit to the covenantee; (2) the covenant affects the nature, quality, mode of user or value of the land of the reversioner; (3) the covenant is not expressed to be personal (that is to say neither being given only to a specific reversioner nor in respect of the obligations only of a specific tenant); (4) the fact that a covenant is to pay a sum of money will not prevent it from touching and concerning the land so long as the three foregoing conditions are satisfied and the covenant is connected with something to be done on to or in relation to the land.

Examples of covenants that have reference to the subject matter of the lease and which touch and concern the land include:

- the tenant's covenant to pay rent to the landlord;
- the tenant's covenant to only use the demised premises for a specified purpose;
- the tenant's covenant to repair the demised premises;
- the landlord's covenant to insure the demised premises;
- the tenant's covenant not to assign without L's consent;
- the landlord's covenant to renew the lease.

Now that you have some idea of the covenants to which *Spencer's Case* and ss 141 and 142 of the LPA 1925 apply, consider again the example set out at the start of **6.4**. As the original lease of the shop was granted in 1995, it is an 'old' lease and therefore subject to the rules just considered.

Example – liability of the parties under the 'old' lease rules

The position is illustrated in the following diagram:

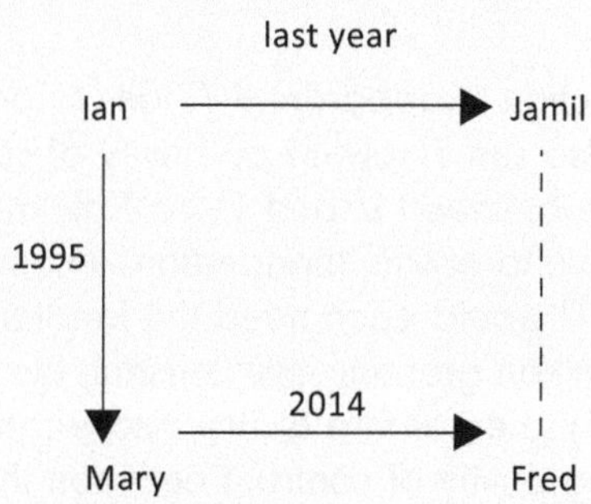

Fred has committed a breach of covenant by converting the shop into a computer repairs outlet. Jamil is the current landlord, and it is necessary to decide whether he has the benefit of the covenant. The covenant restricting the use of the shop is a covenant that has reference to the subject matter of the lease. The benefit of that covenant passed, therefore, to Jamil when Ian assigned the reversion to him (LPA 1925, s 141).

Mary, as the original tenant, is liable on the tenant's covenants throughout the entire term of the lease due to privity of contract. Jamil can sue Mary for Fred's breach as privity of contract passed under s 141 of the LPA 1925 to Jamil. He can also, of course, sue Fred for the breach of the covenant restricting the use of the shop, because such a user covenant touches and concerns the land, and the burden of the covenant will have passed to Fred (Spencer's Case). There is privity of estate between Jamil as current landlord and Fred as current tenant.

Jamil is also in breach of covenant himself, as the back wall of the shop has cracks in it and the lease contained a covenant by the landlord to keep the structure and exterior in good repair. (Note that ss 11 to 14 of the LTA 1985 are irrelevant as the lease relates to shop premises not a dwelling-house.) The covenant is one that touches and concerns the land, and the benefit of it passes to Fred (Spencer's Case). There is privity of estate between Fred and Jamil, to whom the burden of the covenant to keep the structure and exterior in good repair will have passed as it is a covenant that has reference to the subject matter of the lease (LPA 1925, s 142). Fred can therefore seek a remedy from Jamil (see ***6.5*** *below).*

You can see that it is important to ascertain, by applying these rules, whether the person seeking to enforce the covenant has the benefit of it and whether the person against whom they are seeking to enforce it has the burden of it.

Although the original parties to the lease will, in the case of an old tenancy, remain liable throughout the term, their successors in title are only liable for breaches committed whilst the lease or reversion is vested in them. Thus, in the following diagram, L^1 and T^1 are not liable for breaches committed by their successors, L^2 and T^2, nor those committed by their predecessors, L and T.

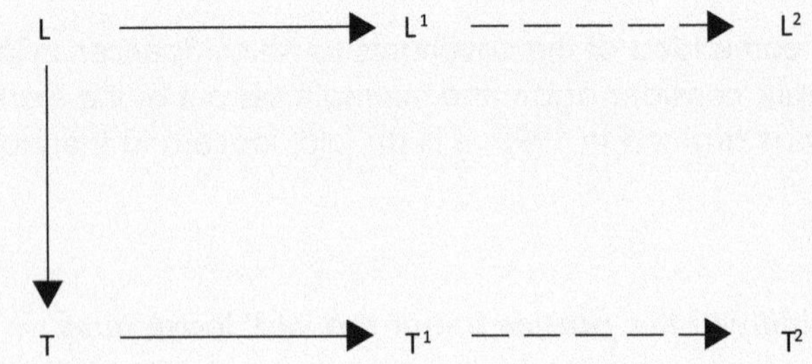

The importance of this distinction is apparent if T^2 fails to pay rent. As well as suing T^2, relying on privity of estate, L^2 can also sue T, relying on privity of contract. There is, however, privity neither of contract nor estate between L^2 and T^1, so T^1 is 'off the hook', so to speak. (Note that, in practice, a tenant may have to obtain the landlord's consent in order to assign the lease. If that were the case, T and T^1 would each need the landlord's prior permission, T to assign to T^1 and T^1 to assign to T^2. When granting this consent, the landlord may have required the assignee (first T^1 and then T^2) to enter into a direct covenant to observe the terms of the lease. This has the effect of creating privity of contract between the landlord and the assignee, and in those circumstances T^1 would remain liable, despite having assigned the lease to T^2, because of the contract between T^1 and L.)

The fact that the original tenant under an old lease remains liable for breaches of covenant throughout the entire term of the lease can result in considerable hardship. Although, in the main, the LT(C)A 1995 applies only to leases that are granted on or after 1 January 1996, some of its provisions also apply to old tenancies. Section 17 of the LT(C)A 1995 relates to the recovery of a fixed charge from a former tenant. (Note that a 'fixed charge' is defined as rent, a service charge or a liquidated sum payable by a tenant for breach of covenant and that these provisions apply to both old and new tenancies.) Before a landlord can pursue a former tenant for the payment of rent, they must serve a default notice on the former tenant within six calendar months beginning with the date when the fixed charge becomes due.

Example

In 1995, Arthur was granted a lease of a large shop for 50 years. The initial rent was £10,000 pa, payable by equal half-yearly payments in advance on 1 June and 1 December. The rent was to be reviewed every five years. In 2011, Arthur sold the business and the leasehold interest to Clarissa. A year later, Clarissa disposed of the business and the leasehold interest to Denzil. Following the last rent review, the rent was increased to £60,000 pa. This proved disastrous for Denzil's business and he was forced to cease trading. Shortly afterwards he was made bankrupt. The last two half-yearly payments under the lease were not made and the landlord, Doltice

Properties, is owed £60,000. Arthur has heard that Doltice Properties is trying to trace his whereabouts, as it wants Arthur to discharge the £60,000 arrears. Arthur wishes to know if he will be liable.

The lease was granted in 1995 and is, therefore, an old lease. Arthur will have covenanted to pay the rent and remains liable on this covenant throughout the entire lease term. Doltice Properties does, therefore, have the right to sue Arthur even though Arthur ceased to be the tenant in 2011. However, the rent is a fixed charge and, in order to succeed in claiming the arrears, Doltice Properties must first serve on Arthur a notice informing him that the charge is now due and specifying the amount. The notice must be served within six months beginning with the date when the charge becomes due (LT(C)A 1995, s 17). As Doltice Properties does not appear to have served a notice, it will be unable to recover the first of the half-yearly payments since that liability will have arisen more than six months ago. It may still, however, recover the latest instalment, as long as it serves notice on Arthur within six months of the date upon which it became due.

If the former tenant pays the arrears, then they may have the following rights:

Moule v Garrett

In *Moule v Garrett* (1872) LR 7 Ex 101, Cockburn CJ held:

> [T]he premises which are the subject of the lease being in the possession of the defendants as ultimate assignees, they were the parties whose duty it was to perform the covenants which were to be performed upon and in respect of those premises. It was their immediate duty to keep in repair, and by their default the lessee, though he had parted with the estate, became liable to make good to the lessor the conditions of the lease. The damage therefore arises through their default, and the general proposition applicable to such a case as the present is, that where one person is compelled to pay damages by the legal default of another, he is entitled to recover from the person by whose default the damage was occasioned the sum so paid.

Therefore, under *Moule v Garrett*, where one person discharges the liability of another, that person may seek to recover the amount they have paid from the person whose liability they have discharged. Thus, returning to the example, Arthur, having discharged Denzil's liability, may seek to recover the amount from Denzil.

Indemnity covenant

When a tenant assigns the lease on to an assignee, they may have obtained from the assignee an express covenant to indemnify them in the event of any breach of the covenants by the assignee. In the absence of an express indemnity covenant, such a covenant will be implied either under s 77 of the LPA 1925 (if the title is unregistered) or under Sch 12, para 20 to the Land Registration Act 2002 (if the title is registered).

Overriding lease

If a former tenant pays the sum demanded in accordance with a s17 default notice in full, s 19 of the LT(C)A 1995 allows the former tenant to request an overriding lease from the landlord. This is a topic that we mention only briefly, as it is beyond the scope of this textbook. The grant of an overriding lease would enable the former tenant to regain an interest in the premises. They would then be in a position to seek a remedy against the current tenant to recover some of the money they have had to pay to the landlord. This would include the remedy of forfeiture, which would end the current tenant's lease (see **6.5.3** below).

6.4.1.3 Personal covenants

You will now know that a successor in title to the landlord takes the benefit of the tenant's covenants and is liable on the landlord's covenants if the covenants have reference to the subject matter of the lease (LPA 1925, ss 141 and 142). Similarly, a successor in title to the tenant takes the benefit of the landlord's covenants and is liable on the tenant's covenants if the covenants touch and concern the land (*Spencer's Case*). What is the position if the covenants are personal in nature?

Consider, by way of example, two covenants entered into expressly in a lease. One covenant restricts the use of the property that is the subject of the lease to use as a restaurant. The other covenant provides that the tenant will give the landlord a free three-course meal every month. The first covenant clearly relates to the land. The second is a personal covenant. Would a successor in title to the landlord be able to insist upon a free meal? Would a successor to the tenant have to provide a free meal to the landlord?

The provisions in ss 141 and 142 of the LPA 1925 and the rule in *Spencer's Case* would not apply to the personal covenant as it does not have reference to the subject matter of the lease, neither does it touch and concern the land. The benefit and liability for this personal covenant will not pass to successors in title.

6.4.2 Enforceability of covenants in 'new' leases

A new tenancy is one that is granted on or after 1 January 1996. However, some tenancies granted after that date remain old ones. These are, for example, tenancies granted pursuant to a contract or a court order, where the contract or court order is made before 1 January 1996.

6.4.2.1 Liability of the original parties to the lease

The position of the original landlord and the original tenant whilst they each retain their interest in the property is the same as that of the original parties to an old lease. Each of them has entered into a contract and can enforce the covenants entered into by the other.

6.4.2.2 Liability of the original parties following assignment and liability of their successors

The position of the tenant when the lease is assigned

In the following diagram, T has assigned the lease to T^1:

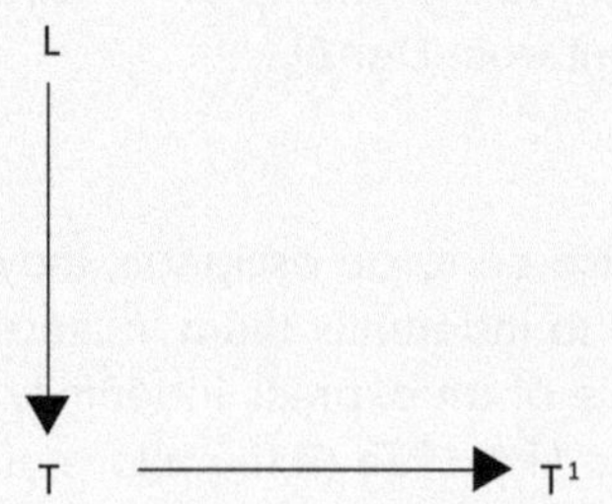

Where the lease is a new lease and T assigns the lease, T is released from the tenant covenants (LT(C)A 1995, s 5(2)(a)). (Note: we will be looking at an exception to this a little later.) T will not, therefore, be liable for the breach committed by T^1. T will also cease to have the benefit of the landlord covenants (s 5(2)(b)).

The position of the landlord when the reversion is assigned

In the following diagram, L assigns the reversion to L[1]:

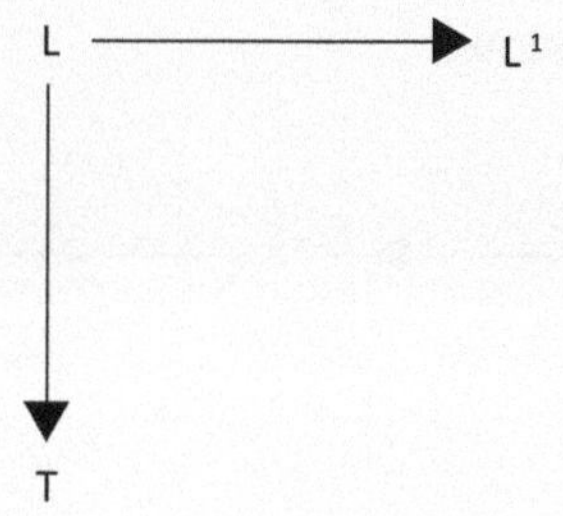

Unlike the landlord who is able to exercise some control over a tenant's assignment of a lease, the tenant has no control over the landlord's assignment of the reversion. If the landlord were therefore to be automatically released from the burden of its covenants on assigning the reversion, this could have serious consequences for the tenant if the assignee is an individual or company of no substance. Thus, the LT(C)A 1995 does not provide an automatic release for the landlord. Instead, the landlord has to apply to the tenant for release (s 6(2)(a)) using the procedure set out in s 8(1) and (2). It is therefore possible for L to remain liable after the reversion has been assigned to L[1].

If L is released, they lose the benefit of the tenant covenants (s 6(2)(b)).

This means that (if the outgoing landlord has not been released) the tenant will have a choice of pursuing the former landlord, the new landlord or both.

The decision in *Avonridge Property Co Ltd v Mashru* [2005] UKHL 70 provides an alternative exit route for landlords. The landlord can limit their liability by stating in the lease that their liability ends once they have disposed of the reversion. The landlord is, therefore, only responsible for the landlord's covenants whilst they hold the reversion.

The position of the successor landlord and tenant

In the following diagram L[1] and T[1] are the current landlord and tenant.

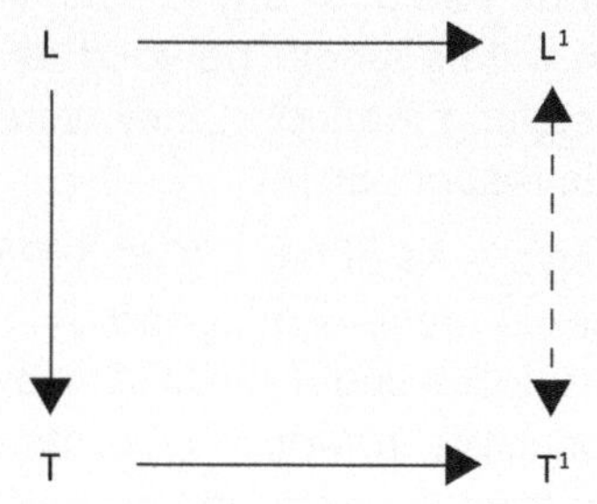

From the date of the assignment, T[1] takes the burden of the tenant covenants (s 3(2)(a)) and acquires the benefit of the landlord covenants (s 3(2)(b)) as long as the covenants are not covenants that were expressed to be personal (s 3(6)(a)).

Also, from the date of assignment of the reversion to L[1], L[1] takes the burden of the landlord covenants (s 3(3)(a)) and acquires the benefit of the tenant covenants (s 3(3)(b)) as long as the covenants are not covenants that were expressed to be personal (s 3(6)(a)). L[1] also acquires the benefit of the right of re-entry (that is, of forfeiture) (s 4).

Whether the covenants touch and concern the land or have reference to the subject matter of the lease is no longer of any relevance.

L^1 and T^1 may each therefore enforce breaches of covenant committed by the other.

What is the position if L^1 and T^1 then assign their interests to further successors in title as demonstrated in the diagram below?

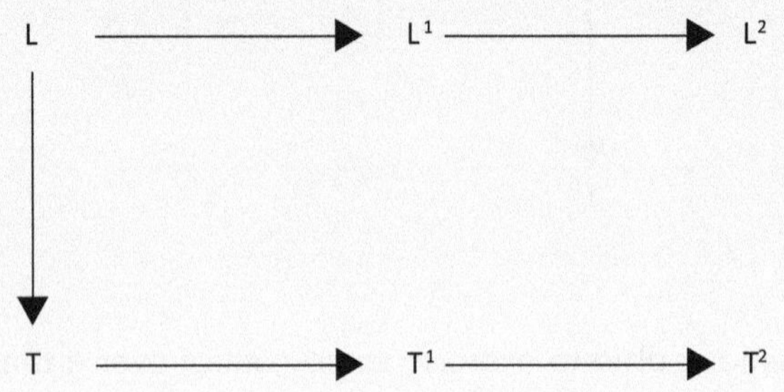

As you have seen above, L and L^1 are not automatically released following the assignment by each of them of the reversion (ss 6 and 8). Unless on the occasion of each assignment they were able to obtain a release from the landlord covenants, they will continue to be liable.

When a tenant assigns a lease, they are released from the tenant covenants (s 5(2)(a)). On the face of it, therefore, both T and T^1 can no longer be made liable. However, s 16 of the LT(C)A 1995 will apply where the lease contains either an absolute or a qualified covenant against assignment. In this case the landlord may, before giving consent, impose, where it is lawful (that is, reasonable or the lease expressly requires it) to do so, a condition that the tenant must agree to guarantee the performance of the tenant covenants by the assignee. This is known as an authorised guarantee agreement (an 'AGA'). However, a tenant can only be made to guarantee the liability of their immediate successor. The AGA will cease to operate once that successor assigns the lease. When that occurs, the successor can be called upon to enter into an AGA in respect of the person to whom they are assigning the lease. Therefore, only one former tenant can be liable under an AGA at any one time.

The landlord can, however, require a former tenant to enter a new lease if the assignee is declared bankrupt and the lease is disclaimed by the trustee in bankruptcy.

Thus, in the diagram, T will not be liable for any breach committed by T^2 as, even if they entered into an AGA, that AGA will no longer be valid as T^1 has assigned the lease. T^1 may, however, be liable if, when assigning the lease, they were called upon to enter into an AGA with the landlord at that time in respect of T^2.

Note: in relation to new tenancies, s 14 of the LT(C)A 1995 abolishes the indemnity covenants that are implied by statute when a lease is assigned. As the tenant is released, they are not required. If the tenant becomes liable under an AGA, they will be able to recover from the assignee on the basis of the principle in *Moule v Garrett* or, more commonly, on the basis of an express indemnity obtained from the assignee on assignment (see **6.4.1.2** above).

Example

*Returning again to the example set out at the start of **6.4**, Jamil is the freehold owner of a registered property acquired last year from Ian. The property comprises a greengrocer's shop with a flat above. Two years ago, Ian leased the flat to Rebecca for a fixed term of six years. Last month, Rebecca assigned her lease to Sonia. The lease contains a covenant by the tenant to keep the interior in good repair. Jamil is now seeking advice as a number of internal doors in Sonia's flat need repair.*

As the original lease of the flat was granted last year, it is a new tenancy.

The position is illustrated in the following diagram:

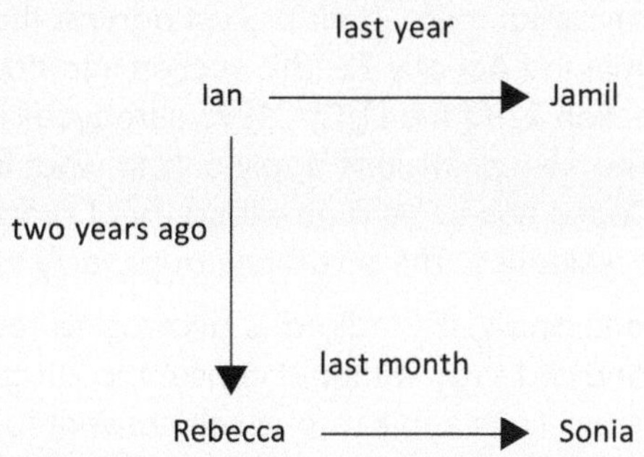

Sonia has committed a breach of covenant by allowing the internal doors in the flat to fall into disrepair. Jamil is the current landlord, and it is necessary to decide whether he has the benefit of the covenant. Under s 3(3)(b) of the LT(C)A 1995, Jamil acquires the benefit of the tenant's covenants. Sonia is the current tenant, and it is necessary to decide whether she has the burden of the covenant. Under s 3(2)(a) of the LT(C)A 1995, Sonia acquires the burden of the tenant's covenants. The covenant to keep the interior in good repair is not 'expressed to be personal'; therefore s 3(6) of the LT(C)A 1995 does not prevent the benefit and the burden of the covenant from passing to Jamil and Sonia respectively.

Rebecca cannot be sued as under s 5(2)(a) of the LT(C)A 1995 she is released from liability on assignment unless she entered into an AGA with Jamil at the time of the assignment to Sonia. This is unlikely as the lease relates to residential property (see the explanation of s 22 of the LT(C)A 1995 below).

Jamil can therefore sue Sonia but not Rebecca for Sonia's breach. (Note that ss 11 to 14 of the LTA 1985 would probably not cover internal doors in the flat.)

'Qualifying leases'

You now have an idea of the changes introduced by the LT(C)A 1995. When the Bill was going through Parliament, landlords of commercial premises expressed alarm at the basic provisions of the Act. Commercial premises are leased at much higher rents than residential premises, and the freehold interest in many developments, such as shopping centres, is often owned, for example, by a pension fund or an insurance company as a way of investing some of its money.

Such institutions will take great care in selecting an original tenant, as they will want as a tenant someone who they feel sure can fulfil all the obligations imposed by the lease. Under s 19(1)(a) of the LTA 1927, we have seen that a landlord may not unreasonably withhold consent to an assignment. To justify refusing consent, the landlord must therefore discover something about the proposed assignee that makes that assignee unsuitable in some way as a tenant and do so relatively quickly. If they are not able to do so, they will have to agree to the assignment or face a claim for damages from the tenant under the LTA 1988. As long as the old rules applied and the liability of the original tenant continued throughout the lease, the landlord was secure in the knowledge that, if the current tenant defaulted in any way, there was always a sound tenant to fall back on.

The effect of the LT(C)A 1995, as we have seen, is to deprive the landlord of the right to recover against the former tenant, except in the very limited circumstances of an AGA. Commercial landlords, therefore, feared that the investment value of their reversion would be significantly reduced because they could no longer claim against the original tenant and had only a limited right to refuse consent to an assignment. Their protest against the Bill did not go unheard, and the result was the inclusion in the Act of s 22. This section introduces some important amendments to s 19 of the LTA 1927. Section 22 of the LT(C)A 1995 introduces into s 19 of the LTA 1927 five new subsections: (1A) to (1E). The new provisions apply only to what is termed 'a qualifying lease'. To be a qualifying lease the lease has to be a new tenancy of property that is not used wholly or mainly as a single private residence. The provisions apply only where such a lease is assigned.

Where these new provisions apply, a landlord is allowed to reach an agreement with the tenant whereby the landlord may withhold consent to an assignment in specified circumstances and state conditions subject to which consent to assignment will be given. The landlord will usually seek such an agreement with the tenant when negotiating the lease, and the agreement will be included in the lease itself.

If the landlord has entered into an agreement of this kind with the tenant, then, if the landlord withholds consent because a specified circumstance exists or seeks to impose one of the stated conditions, the tenant will not be able to argue that the landlord is unreasonably withholding consent. You will appreciate that the unreasonableness provisions of s 19(1)(a) have, therefore, been considerably watered down and the landlord's control over the assignment of a new lease involving commercial premises correspondingly strengthened. Commonly, the landlord will specify in the lease that the tenant must enter into an AGA as a prerequisite to an assignment of the lease.

We have seen that some provisions of the LT(C)A 1995 apply both to new and to old tenancies. In the following activity you will consider the effect of these provisions where the tenancy is a new one.

ACTIVITY 1 Suing a former tenant

Consider the following situation:

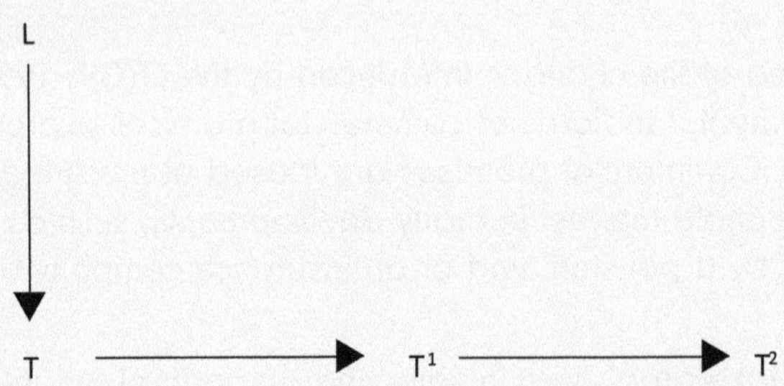

In the above situation, the lease is a new tenancy and T^2 has not paid the rent due three months ago. L has decided it is not worthwhile suing T^2 for the rent.

Are there any circumstances in which L may have a remedy against one of the former tenants? If so, what steps does L need to take and what are the possible consequences of taking them?

COMMENT

As the tenancy is a new one, T will have been released from the tenant covenants on assigning the lease to T^1. T^1, likewise, will have been released on the assignment to T^2. L will in no circumstances be able to sue T. However, L may be able to sue T^1, if T^1 (when T^1 asked for consent to assign) entered into an AGA. If that is the case, then the position is that a default notice must be served on T^1 within six months of the rent becoming due. L, therefore, has another three months within which to serve the notice. If T^1 discharges the arrears, they will be able to recover from T^2 if they obtained an express indemnity from T^2 on assignment or on the basis of *Moule v Garrett* (see **6.4.1.2** above). However, this may not be worth doing if T^2 does not have the resources to indemnify T^1. The landlord has chosen to pursue T^1 for precisely this reason.

6.5 Remedies for breach of covenant

When either the landlord or the tenant breaches a covenant, you need to know what remedies are available in respect of the breach. You will by now have realised that the law does not provide much in the way of help to parties to a lease if they have failed to agree its terms expressly. As many leases will last for considerable periods of time, a lease is therefore likely to contain many express covenants. Most of these covenants will be covenants by the tenant, but a lease may also contain important covenants on the part of the landlord. You will need to know what action a party may take when faced with a breach of covenant by the other. We are going to begin by looking at the tenant's obligation to pay rent.

6.5.1 Tenant's breach of a covenant to pay rent

Although rent is not essential to a lease, the vast majority of leases will be granted on the understanding that the tenant is to pay a rent to the landlord. If the landlord simply grants the tenant a lease at, for example, a rent of £600 a month, a covenant is implied on the part of the tenant to pay that rent. Nevertheless, the lease will almost certainly contain an express covenant for the payment of rent. What happens if the tenant fails to pay the rent?

6.5.1.1 Action for debt

The most obvious action a landlord can take is the same action that any other person would take when faced with the failure to fulfil a contractual promise to pay money: the landlord may sue the tenant for debt. However, the landlord is prevented by s 19 of the Limitation Act 1980 from bringing such a claim after the expiration of six years from the date on which the arrears became due.

Where the landlord is suing a former tenant on an AGA (new tenancies), or the original tenant under privity of contract (old leases) for arrears of rent, the landlord must serve a default notice in accordance with s 17 of the LT(C)A 1995.

6.5.1.2 Commercial rent arrears recovery ('CRAR')

The procedure for the recovery of rent arrears for commercial property was introduced by Sch 12 to the Tribunals, Courts and Enforcement Act 2007. The Act abolished the common law right to distrain for non-payment of rent and replaced it with a procedure which applies only to leases of commercial premises. It can be used to recover rent payable in advance or arrears and is subject to a minimum amount of arrears. This amount is prescribed by regulations and is currently seven days' rent.

To exercise CRAR, rent has to become due and payable, and at least seven days' notice of enforcement has to be served on the tenant. An enforcement agent is instructed to serve an enforcement notice on the tenant, and the notice binds the property in the tenant's goods from the time it is served. The goods remain bound until the arrears are paid or the goods are sold.

6.5.1.3 Forfeiture

Forfeiture is perhaps the most important weapon the landlord can use against the tenant since it means the lease will be brought to a premature end. As it is a remedy that is available for the breach of other covenants as well, we will look at the whole subject of forfeiture in **6.5.3** below.

6.5.2 Breaches of other covenants

The lease, as we have seen, will contain covenants other than the one to pay rent. These will be, for example, covenants to repair, not to assign without the landlord's consent, not to alter the premises, not to use them for certain purposes, to insure and so on. The majority of these covenants will be ones that are entered into by the tenant, but in certain cases a landlord may also enter into covenants, for example a covenant to repair or to insure. What is the position if either the tenant or the landlord breaches one of these covenants?

6.5.2.1 Damages

As in the case of other contracts, if a party fails to fulfil an obligation, the other party may bring a claim seeking damages. The rule in *Hadley v Baxendale* (1854) 9 Ex 341 applies where a claimant seeks damages for breach of a contract. That rule says that the damages are limited to:

(a) such as may fairly and reasonably be considered either arising naturally, ie according to the usual course of things, from such breach of contract itself; or

(b) such as may reasonably be supposed to have been in the contemplation of both parties at the time they made the contract, as the probable result of the breach of it.

That is the basic rule that will apply if a party to a lease brings a claim for damages for breach of covenant.

Damages may be claimed against the tenant in possession, a former tenant who remains liable (ie via privity of contract in an old lease or via an AGA in a new lease) or both. A default notice under s 17 of the LT(C)A 1995 is not required to be served on a former tenant, as damages are not included within the definition of a fixed charge.

Any claim for damages for disrepair is limited to the amount by which the reversionary interest has diminished in value as a consequence of the disrepair (LTA 1927, s 18). Where the lease has three or more years unexpired, the landlord must first serve on the tenant a s 146 LPA 1925 notice (see **6.5.3.2** below). Such notice must include a statement to the effect that the tenant is entitled to serve a counter notice claiming the benefit of the Leasehold Property (Repairs) Act 1938. The tenant has 28 days within which to serve a counter notice and, if served, the landlord cannot take further action without leave of the court.

6.5.2.2 Specific performance

A party to a lease may, of course, not be content with an award of damages but may wish the court to order the other party to perform the obligation. In the law of contract, at common law a party could only claim damages. A party who wanted to have the contract performed had to seek the help of equity. Equity, however, would intervene in a situation only where it considered damages to be an inadequate remedy and the claimant was not barred by any other rule of equity. Specific performance is, therefore, a discretionary equitable remedy that will be granted only where an award of damages is considered to be inadequate as a means of compensating the claimant for loss. This remedy is not usually available for breach of a tenant's covenant to repair but may be granted in exceptional cases.

6.5.2.3 Injunction

In the case of a restrictive covenant, for example not to use premises for the purposes of a business, an appropriate remedy might be an injunction ordering the defendant not to contravene the covenant. Again, this is a discretionary remedy.

6.5.2.4 Self-help by means of set-off

Seeking damages, an order for specific performance or an injunction therefore comprise steps that may be taken by a party (either landlord or tenant) wishing to obtain a remedy for the breach of a non-rent covenant depending upon the precise facts. The tenant may also have an additional remedy where it is the landlord who is in breach of a repairing covenant.

In *Lee-Parker v Izzet* [1971] 1 WLR 1688, Goff J held:

> First, the tenants say that in so far as the first defendant was, as landlord, liable to do repairs by the express or implied terms of the tenancy agreement ... they, having done them themselves, are entitled to treat the expenditure as a payment of rent, for which reliance is placed on *Taylor v Beal* (1591) Cro Eliz 222 ...
>
> [This] is an ancient common law right. I therefore declare that so far as the repairs are within the express or implied covenants of the landlord, the [tenants] are entitled to recoup themselves out of future rents and defend any action for payment thereof. It does not follow however that the full amount expended by the [tenants] on such repairs can properly be treated as payment of rent. It is a question of fact in every case whether and to what extent the expenditure was proper.
>
> For the sake of avoiding misunderstanding I must add that of course the *Taylor v Beal* right can only be exercised when and so far as the landlord is in breach and any necessary notice must have been given to him.

Therefore, the fact that a landlord fails to perform an obligation does not entitle the tenant to withhold payment of rent. A tenant who does so runs the risk of the landlord seeking to forfeit the lease. However, in certain circumstances, the tenant may have a right at common law to withhold payment of rent.

The case of *Taylor v Beal* (1591) Cro Eliz 222 (78 ER 478) established that there is the possibility of a set-off against rent. To succeed in claiming the right to set-off at common law, the tenant must notify the landlord that repairs are needed and that, unless they carry out the repair work in accordance with their covenant, the tenant will arrange to have the repairs done themselves. Having carried out the repairs, the tenant may then deduct the cost of the repairs from future payments of rent until the tenant has been reimbursed in full. It is essential that the amount the tenant is seeking to recover is a liquidated, or fixed, sum.

As an alternative, if the tenant does withhold payment of rent and the landlord sues them, equity may allow the tenant to have their unliquidated claim set off against the liability for rent. This will only occur, however, where the connection between the two claims is sufficiently direct so that it would be manifestly unjust not to allow set off. The tenant's claim must therefore be one that arises directly from the relationship of landlord and tenant created by the lease.

6.5.3 Forfeiture

Forfeiture is a remedy that enables the landlord to terminate a fixed-term lease before that term expires. The landlord will have a right to forfeit where:

(a) the lease contains a provision for the landlord to re-enter the property for a breach of covenant by the tenant (a forfeiture clause); or

(b) the lease is granted subject to a condition that the landlord may forfeit it on the happening of some event.

The first is by far the most common situation, and this is the one we will concentrate on. If the lease contains a forfeiture clause and the tenant is in breach of a covenant, the lease does not end automatically. The landlord must decide whether to forfeit the lease or to treat it as still continuing. If they adopt the latter course, the landlord is said to have waived the breach. Waiver may be express or implied. It will be implied if the landlord does some unequivocal act showing recognition of the continued existence of the lease and in full knowledge of the facts giving them the right to forfeit. Examples of implied waiver include exercising CRAR, demanding future rent or suing for or accepting rent after the breach. Waiver will not be implied by such conduct if the landlord has already shown that they no longer regard the lease as subsisting; for example, where the landlord has commenced possession proceedings.

It is important for a landlord faced with a breach of covenant by the tenant to consider carefully which course of action to take, as the decision, once made, is binding on the landlord.

A landlord signifies an intention to forfeit either by means of peaceable re-entry, that is, physically re-taking possession, or by the service of proceedings. There are some important limits on the right to forfeit by peaceable re-entry, as we shall shortly see. For historical reasons, the rules that apply where a landlord is seeking to forfeit for non-payment of rent are different from the rules that apply where the forfeiture is for breach of some other covenant. In each case, however, again subject to different rules, a tenant may apply to the court for relief from forfeiture.

6.5.3.1 Non-payment of rent

At common law, a landlord wishing to forfeit a lease because the tenant had not paid the rent had to show that the tenant had been given an opportunity to pay it. The landlord did this by making what is known as a formal demand. The landlord would attend at the premises on the last day for payment at a convenient hour before sunset and demand payment of the exact amount, such demand continuing until sunset (*Duppa v Mayo* (1669) 1 Wms Saund 275). Only if the rent had still not been paid by the end of the last day could the landlord proceed to forfeit the lease.

You can imagine that it would be highly inconvenient for a landlord to have to follow this procedure every time a tenant is late in paying rent. Not surprisingly, therefore, it is open to the parties to include a provision in the lease dispensing with the need for a formal demand. The forfeiture clause will almost invariably say that the landlord has a right to re-enter when payment of rent is overdue, whether the payment has been formally demanded or not.

An example of a standard form of forfeiture clause is set out below:

> PROVIDED ALWAYS and it is hereby agreed that if the said rent or any part thereof shall be unpaid for 21 days after becoming duly payable (whether or not the same shall have been formally demanded) or if the Tenant shall fail to perform their covenants or obligations hereunder then in any of the said cases it shall be lawful for the Landlord or any person duly authorised by the Landlord in that behalf to re-enter the Premises or any part thereof in the name of the whole and thereupon this demise shall absolutely determine but without prejudice to any right of action of the Landlord in respect of any breach of the Tenant's covenants herein contained.

Assuming the landlord does not have to make a formal demand, they next must decide whether to forfeit by means of peaceable re-entry or whether to commence forfeiture proceedings. If the lease is a lease of a dwelling-house, the landlord will not be able to use peaceable re-entry as a means of forfeiting the lease. Section 2 of the PEA 1977 states that it is not lawful to forfeit a lease of a dwelling otherwise than by court proceedings while a person is lawfully residing at the premises. If s 2 does not apply because, for example, the premises are business premises or, if a dwelling, because the tenant has left of their own accord, the landlord may re-enter peaceably and forfeit the lease, although it remains to be seen whether and, if so, to what extent the Human Rights Act 1998 applies.

If the landlord uses violence or threatens violence to obtain possession of the premises, whether they are commercial or residential premises, the landlord will commit a criminal offence under s 6 of the Criminal Law Act 1977. Even where the landlord has a lawful right to possession of the premises, they do not have lawful authority to take possession of the premises by criminal means. As a result, most landlords will obtain a court order to take possession of premises, unless it is clear that peaceable re-entry can be obtained.

If the landlord seeks to end the lease, the tenant may well seek relief from forfeiture. As long as the tenant acts reasonably swiftly and pays the arrears of rent and costs, relief will usually be granted.

Having considered forfeiture in a case where the tenant is in breach of a covenant to pay rent, we now need to look at situations involving the breach of some other covenant.

6.5.3.2 Breaches of other covenants

As in the case of forfeiture for non-payment of rent, the landlord, before proceeding to forfeit, must check that the lease contains a right to do so, usually in the form of a forfeiture clause. Having done this, the landlord must then serve on the tenant a notice under s 146 of the LPA 1925:

(a) specifying the breach;

(b) requiring it to be remedied within a reasonable time, if capable of remedy; and

(c) requiring compensation if desired.

Breach of a covenant against alienation, ie not to assign or underlet, is a once and for all breach and is not capable of remedy. The landlord, therefore, does not have to include a reasonable time within which to remedy the breach within their s 146 notice (however, relief against forfeiture may be available).

Assuming that the landlord has served a valid s 146 notice then, unless the tenant complies with the notice and remedies the breach, as in the case of forfeiture for non-payment of rent, the landlord may choose to forfeit either by serving proceedings on the tenant or by means of peaceable re-entry. Again the tenant may be entitled to relief from forfeiture.

If a head lease is forfeited, then any sublease ceases to exist. A subtenant can apply for relief against forfeiture of the head lease (LPA 1925, s 146(4)), even in cases where the tenant may not be able to obtain relief. The relief here consists of the court vesting the head lease in the sub-lessee and on such terms as to rent, costs and damages as the court thinks fit.

Where there is a mortgage affecting the tenant's leasehold interest, as the effect of forfeiting the lease will be to end the security for the mortgagee, it is open to the mortgagee to apply for relief against forfeiture under s 146(4) of the LPA 1925.

Example

*Using again the example set out at the start of **6.4**, the appropriate remedies for the various breaches of covenant that have occurred are:*

Shop premises

Fred has committed a breach of covenant by converting the shop into a computer repairs outlet. Jamil can sue Fred. The remedies available to Jamil against Fred are:

(1) to seek an injunction not to use the premises as a computer repairs outlet;

(2) to seek damages against Fred under the rule in Hadley v Baxendale; or

(3) to forfeit the lease, where the lease contains a right to do so, by serving on Fred a s 146 notice and then either serving possession proceedings on Fred or forfeiting by means of peaceable re-entry if Fred fails to comply with the notice.

Mary, as the original tenant, is also liable for the breach of the user covenant. Jamil can therefore sue Mary for Fred's breach. Jamil can only seek to recover damages from Mary. As she is not in possession of the premises, the remedies of an injunction or forfeiture are not available against Mary.

Jamil is in breach of the covenant to keep the structure and exterior in good repair. As the current tenant, Fred can seek damages against Jamil. Alternatively, Fred could seek an order for specific performance, but this is a discretionary remedy and will be granted only where an award of damages is considered to be inadequate. Fred could also exercise the remedy of self-help by means of set-off.

Flat

Sonia is in breach of covenant by allowing the internal doors in the flat to fall into disrepair. Jamil can sue Sonia. As the current tenant, Sonia risks forfeiture of the lease by Jamil. The lease must contain a right for the landlord to forfeit the lease, and as it is a dwelling-house, where Sonia currently resides, Jamil will need to obtain a court order to obtain possession against Sonia (PEA 1977, s 2).

Note that the remedies that are available for breach of covenant are the same whether the covenant is contained in an old lease or a new lease.

6.5.4 Breach of landlord's covenants

The tenant has the following remedies available:

- specific performance/injunction
- damages
- self-help.

6.5.4.1 Specific performance/injunction

This is an equitable and, therefore, discretionary remedy which is rarely ordered in respect of the repairing covenant as damages will usually be an adequate remedy.

6.5.4.2 Damages

The ordinary contractual principles apply (see **6.5.2.1** above).

6.5.4.3 Self-help

The landlord's failure to perform an obligation does not entitle the tenant to withhold the rent. However, in relation to a repair obligation, the tenant may notify the landlord that the repair is needed and that the tenant will carry out the repair if the landlord fails to do so. If the tenant then carries out the repairs, they may withhold rent until the ascertained cost of repair has been repaid. This is common law set off.

As an alternative, if the tenant does withhold payment of rent and the landlord sues the tenant, equity may allow the tenant to have their unliquidated claim set off against the liability for rent. This will only occur where the connection between the two claims is sufficiently direct so that it would be manifestly unjust not to allow set off. The tenant's claim must, therefore, be one that arises directly from the relationship of landlord and tenant created by the lease. This is equitable set off.

Most well drafted commercial leases will exclude the effect of both common law and equitable set off.

6.6 Summary of enforceability of covenants

6.6.1 Enforceability of covenants (leases granted before 1 January 1996)

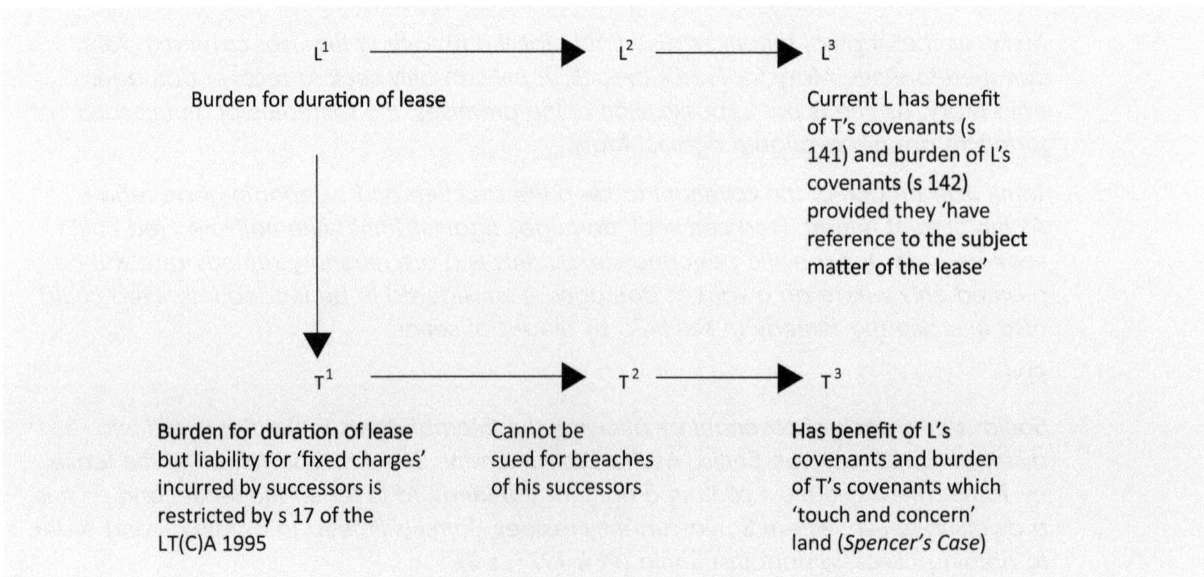

6.6.2 Enforceability of covenants (leases granted on or after 1 January 1996)

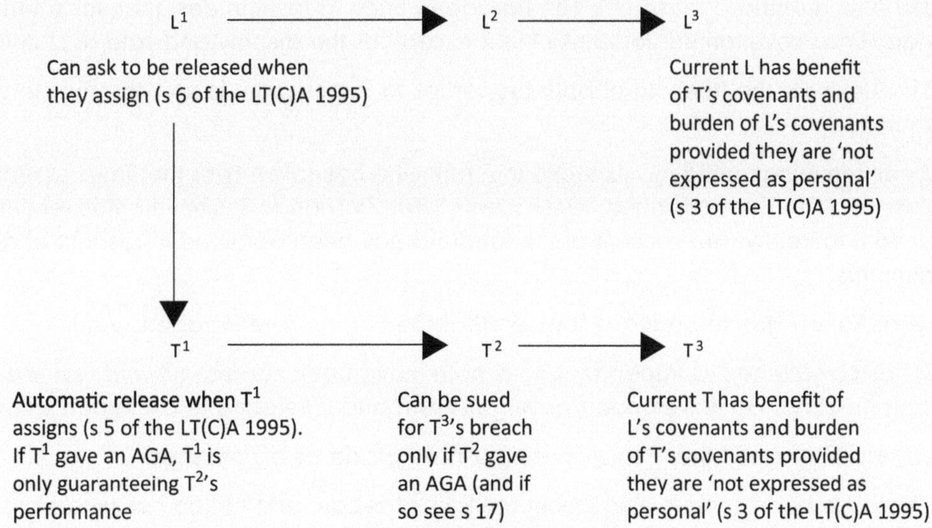

L^1
L^2
L^3
Can ask to be released when they assign (s 6 of the LT(C)A 1995)
Current L has benefit of T's covenants and burden of L's covenants provided they are 'not expressed as personal' (s 3 of the LT(C)A 1995)
T^1
T^2
T^3
Automatic release when T^1 assigns (s 5 of the LT(C)A 1995). If T^1 gave an AGA, T^1 is only guaranteeing T^2's performance
Can be sued for T^3's breach only if T^2 gave an AGA (and if so see s 17)
Current T has benefit of L's covenants and burden of T's covenants provided they are 'not expressed as personal' (s 3 of the LT(C)A 1995)

ACTIVITY 2 Test your knowledge: leasehold covenants

The aim of this activity is to give you some practice in applying your knowledge of leasehold covenants to a problem. Set out below is a suggested approach to problem questions on leasehold covenants that you may find useful.

(1) Determine whether lease is an *old* or a *new* lease (vital date is 1 January 1996). This means the date the lease was originally granted, *not* the date of any subsequent assignments. Be sure you know the difference between grant and assignment.

(2) Decide what the breaches of covenant are – by landlord or tenant. Be sure you could handle any party's breach. Questions could involve breaches of implied covenants.

(3) You will usually be asked to advise either the landlord or the tenant as to whom they could sue for those breaches. Consider every possible scenario and show for each that:

(a) the person wanting to sue has the benefit, giving the relevant authority;
(b) the person who is to be sued has the burden, giving the relevant authority.

(4) Unless the question excludes this, explain relevant remedies available to the claimant in each case and discuss any procedure involved (forfeiture only required in outline).

Now consider the following scenario:

In 1993 Alex bought two freehold properties, Nos 1 and 2 The Parade. Both properties are shops, but in the case of 1 The Parade there is a small self-contained flat immediately above the shop. Alex was duly registered as the proprietor of both properties.

In 1995 Alex granted a lease of the shop part of 1 The Parade by deed to Trimmings, a hairdressing business, for a term of 45 years. In the lease Trimmings entered into the following covenants:

(a) to pay the rent by equal half yearly instalments on 1 June and 1 December;

(b) to cut Alex's hair free of charge.

Alex covenanted to repair the structure and exterior of the shop.

In 2010 Alex granted a lease of 2 The Parade to Erica, a fashion designer, for a term of 25 years. Erica covenanted not to use No 2 except for the display and sale of clothing.

In 2012 Alex sold the freehold of both properties to Rupert, who is now the registered proprietor.

Last year Trimmings assigned its lease to Frank who has taken over the hairdressing business. In 2014 Erica assigned her lease of 2 The Parade to Josie, who has recently assigned it to Penny. The consent of the landlord has been obtained in respect of all the assignments.

Last year Rupert granted a lease (by deed) of the flat in 1 The Parade to Amir.

Frank has complained to Rupert that no repairs have been carried out and water is entering his shop. He has stopped paying his rent and is refusing to cut Rupert's hair.

Rupert has discovered that Penny is using 2 The Parade as a bookshop.

Amir has also been complaining about the lack of repair, and he too has water entering the flat due to a hole in the roof.

Discuss the following:

(1) What action can be taken by and against whom and what, if any, remedies are available in relation to the breaches of the tenant covenants in respect of both shops?

(2) What action can be taken and what, if any, remedies are available to Frank for breach of the landlord's covenant to repair the structure and exterior of the shop?

(3) What right has Amir to have the roof repaired?

COMMENT

(1) Breaches of the tenants' covenants

No 1 The Parade

Rupert may seek a remedy for breach of the covenants contained in the lease. The lease was granted in 1995. It therefore pre-dates the LT(C)A 1995, which came into force on 1 January 1996. The lease is thus an old tenancy.

Can Rupert take action against Frank for the breach of the rent and hair cutting covenants?

In order to decide whether Rupert can take action against Frank for a breach of covenant, it is necessary to determine whether Rupert has the benefit of each covenant and whether the burden of them have passed to Frank.

The benefit

On the freehold reversion being assigned to him, Rupert would have acquired the benefit of all the covenants that have reference to the subject matter of the lease (LPA 1925, s 141). This would include the covenant to pay rent but not the covenant to provide free haircuts.

The burden

On the lease being assigned to Frank, the burden of all the covenants that touch and concern the land will have passed to him (*Spencer's Case*). These include the covenant to pay rent but again not the covenant to provide free haircuts.

Rupert can only, therefore, take action against Frank to recover the rent arrears. He may simply sue Frank for debt, or he may take CRAR action against Frank's goods. If the lease contains a forfeiture clause, he may also seek to forfeit it, although Frank would have a right to apply to the court for relief against forfeiture.

Can Rupert take any action against Trimmings?

As the lease is an old tenancy, Trimmings remains liable on the tenant covenants due to privity of contract, and Alex's privity of contract will have passed to Rupert under s 141 of the LPA 1925. As Rupert now has the benefit of the covenant to pay rent, he may therefore sue Trimmings to recover the arrears. However, as a result of s 17 of the LT(C)A 1995, before doing so he must first serve a default notice on Trimmings within six months of the rent becoming due. As long as he does this, he can seek to recover the arrears from Trimmings. If he fails to serve notice within six months, he will lose the right to recover the arrears from Trimmings. (Note that he may still, however, recover the latest instalment, as long as he serves notice on Trimmings within six months of the date upon which it became due.)

Does Trimmings have any claim against Frank?

If Trimmings pays the arrears, it may seek an indemnity from Frank either under an express or implied indemnity covenant or under the rule in *Moule v Garrett.*

No 2 The Parade

This lease is a new tenancy for the purposes of the LT(C)A 1995, having been granted on or after 1 January 1996.

Can Rupert take action against Penny for breach of the user covenant?

The benefit of the tenant covenant will have passed to Rupert when he bought the freehold reversion (LT(C)A 1995, s 3). It is not a covenant which is expressed to be personal.

On any assignment of the lease, the tenant is released from the burden of the tenant covenants (s 5), which pass to the assignee, as long as the covenants are not expressed to be personal (s 3). Penny therefore now has the burden of the tenant covenants, and Rupert may therefore claim damages from her, seek an injunction or, if the lease contains a forfeiture clause, forfeit the lease, subject to Penny's right to seek relief from forfeiture.

Action against Erica or Josie

Rupert may not take any action against Erica, as Erica will have been released from her covenants on the assignment to Josie (s 5). Although Erica may have been required to enter into an AGA, guaranteeing the liability of Josie, any such agreement would end when Josie assigned the lease to Penny (s 16). Whether Rupert can seek damages from Josie will depend on whether or not Josie entered into an AGA when she assigned the lease to Penny. If Josie does have to pay damages, she can seek to recover them from Penny, as it is Penny's liability that she will have discharged.

(2) Breach of the landlord's covenant

No 1 The Parade

The burden of the landlord covenant to repair

Rupert has acquired the freehold and will have the burden of all the covenants entered into by the landlord that have reference to the subject matter of the lease (LPA 1925, s 142). The covenant to repair the structure and exterior of the shop is such a covenant.

The benefit of the landlord covenant to repair

As a successor to the original tenant, Frank will have the benefit of all the landlord covenants that touch and concern the land (*Spencer's Case*). This will include the landlord's repairing covenant.

The fact that Rupert has failed to carry out repairs does not entitle Frank to stop paying his rent. However, it is open to Frank to notify Rupert that unless he carries out the repairs, he will do them himself and recover the cost by withholding payment of rent (*Lee-Parker v Izzet*). He appears not to have done this. He will have a claim against Rupert for damages, and equity may therefore allow him to set off the claim against the liability for rent.

It is also possible for Frank to seek an order for specific performance against Rupert, although the courts are reluctant to grant this if it means the court has to supervise the carrying out of the order.

Can Frank take any action against Alex?

As the lease is an old tenancy, Alex remains liable on the landlord covenants due to privity of contract and so Frank may sue Alex for breach of contract (with a remedy of damages only). However, on these facts, the most effective action will be against Rupert.

(3) Right of repair

Amir has a five-year legal lease of the flat. On the basis that Amir is a tenant and as his tenancy is for less than seven years, ss 11–13 of the LTA 1985 will apply. This means that Rupert is under an implied obligation to repair the structure and exterior of the premises.

SUMMARY

- You are aware of some of the types of covenants that are commonly expressed in a lease as well as covenants that are implied at law. This enables you to understand the importance of comprehensive drafting of leases, something that will assist in your further study of conveyancing practice.
- You are now able to advise on the enforceability of leasehold covenants in relation to both old leases and new leases by applying complex rules to determine whether a claimant has the benefit and a defendant has the burden of a leasehold covenant. Your understanding of this approach will assist you in relation to your study of the enforceability of freehold covenants in **Chapter 7**.
- In a practical context, you will now have enough knowledge to advise a client who is acquiring either a freehold subject to a lease or an existing leasehold estate in the event that breaches of covenant occur, and you are also aware of the remedies that it may be appropriate to seek.

Part IV Third Party Rights Over Land

7 Freehold Covenants

LEARNING OUTCOMES

When you have completed this chapter, you should be able to:

- understand how covenants over freehold land are created;
- identify whether covenants are positive or restrictive, real or personal;
- assess the enforceability of freehold covenants at law and in equity and identify the appropriate remedies available;
- understand the options available for the modification or discharge of freehold covenants.

7.1 Introduction

In **Chapter 6** you encountered covenants within the context of a lease where they were promises that a landlord and tenant made to each other. However, it is also possible for persons to enter into a covenant even though the relationship between them is not that of landlord and tenant. These are freehold covenants, promises expressly made between neighbouring freeholders. In practice, they are often created when a seller sells part of their land but retains the rest of it.

In this chapter you will be looking at the issues raised in relation to freehold covenants in the context of the following example.

Example

Fifteen years ago, Bluebell Homes acquired six acres of land for development. The land contained a large, dilapidated country house. Soon afterwards, Bluebell Homes ran into financial difficulties and found a buyer for the house quickly, which enabled them to retain five acres of the land for future development. The purchaser was Daron Fischer, who owned and operated hostels and planned to refurbish the house for this purpose.

To preserve the development potential of the retained land, Bluebell Homes required Daron Fischer to give the following promises in the transfer:

(a) to allow the rooms in the hostel to be used for sole occupancy only;

(b) not to allow the grounds of the hostel to be used for public events.

Also, in the transfer, Bluebell Homes granted Daron Fischer a right of access over the driveway that crossed part of the land retained by it. This right of access comprised *an easement (see **Chapter 8**) and was conditional upon a covenant by Daron Fisher to contribute towards the cost of the maintenance of the driveway to the hostel that crossed part of the land retained by Bluebell Homes.*

The house was then refurbished and opened for business as Greybrick Hostel. Five years later Bluebell Homes were in a position to develop the remaining five acres of the land they held. The houses, comprising both two- and three-bedroom homes, sold quickly. All the houses had been sold within two years of the start of the development.

Two years ago, Daron Fischer retired and sold Greybrick Hostel to Broadland Ltd, a company that specialised in managing hostels for ex-prisoners. Within a year there were problems with the operation of the hostel which have caused difficulties for the owners of the houses on the retained land. The owners of the houses need to know whether they can enforce the covenants.

Later in this chapter you will see what the difficulties were, and you will also consider the legal advice that can be given to the parties involved.

7.2 Creation of covenants

7.2.1 Formalities

Strictly speaking a covenant is a promise contained in a deed, for example, a promise by one of the parties not to build on land. Such a promise amounts to a contract and is governed by the basic principles of contract law, although, as it is contained in a deed, consideration – though usually present – is not essential. The term 'covenant' may also be applied to any enforceable promise about the use of land even though it is not contained in a deed.

Covenants are not capable of being legal interests in land. They are not listed in s 1(2) of the Law of Property Act (LPA) 1925. They can therefore only be equitable (LPA 1925, s 1(3)). Invariably covenants are created expressly by deed. However, as an equitable interest, the minimum formality requirement is that the interest be created by signed writing (LPA 1925, s 53(1)(a)).

Covenants are usually imposed when a person sells part of the land that they own and are therefore contained in the transfer. For example, if you were to sell a part of your garden to a neighbour, you would probably want the neighbour to covenant to erect a fence along the new boundary and possibly also to covenant not to build on the land that they have bought. In this case it is the buyer who is entering into the covenants, but there is no reason why a person selling land may not also enter into covenants. Although a sale of part is the situation where you are most likely to encounter covenants, there is nothing to prevent a person approaching a neighbour and asking the neighbour to enter into a covenant in return for a payment of money. Here you will just have a deed containing the promise and there will be no transfer of ownership of land.

7.2.2 Covenants and easements

In the next chapter you will be looking at easements, and you will need to be able to distinguish a covenant from an easement. Set out below are some of the essential differences:

(a) An easement is capable of being legal, as long as it is granted for an interest that is equivalent to an estate in fee simple absolute in possession or a term of years absolute (LPA 1925, s 1(2)(a)). If it does not satisfy these requirements, it can only be equitable. In order to expressly create a legal easement, you have to use a deed; and in the case of land with a registered title, you also have to ensure that you apply for an entry to be made on the register. Failure to meet these requirements may mean that the easement is only equitable. An easement may thus be either legal or equitable.

As mentioned above, covenants can only be equitable (LPA 1925, s 1(3)).

(b) As you will see in the next chapter, the courts are reluctant to recognise all rights over land as capable of being easements. For example, you cannot have as an easement a right to a view. This is regarded as far too wide a right, and to recognise it would mean that the landowner claiming it would be able to prevent development taking place possibly over a wide area of surrounding land. On the other hand, if you were to sell to a neighbour a part of your garden, you could obtain a covenant from the neighbour not to build on it. This could serve to protect your view, but it is much more limited in its scope as it only affects the land that you have sold. Covenants are therefore more flexible than easements.

(c) The wording used in documents to create easements and covenants will also be different. To create an easement a person will either sell land 'together with the benefit of', for example, a right of way, or will grant a right of way. Where a covenant is imposed, the wording introducing it will be, for example, 'A covenants with B ...'.

7.2.3 Positive and restrictive covenants

You have already seen (in **Chapter 6**) that covenants may be either positive or restrictive (or negative). It is important to be able to distinguish them. A positive covenant requires some effort or expenditure to perform the obligation. A restrictive covenant requires no such effort or expense. It is the substance of the covenant and not its form that will define whether or not the covenant is positive or restrictive.

Example

Read through the list of covenants and decide whether or not they are positive or restrictive.

Covenant

(1) To keep the land as an open space.

(2) Not to divide the property into flats.

(3) Not to let the property fall into disrepair.

(4) To allow the rooms in the hostel to be used for sole occupancy only.

(5) Not to allow the grounds of the hostel to be used for public events.

(6) To contribute towards the cost of the maintenance of the driveway to the hostel that crosses part of the land retained by Bluebell Homes.

Covenants (1) and (4) are worded in such a way that they appear to be positive covenants but in substance they are restrictive. Covenant (1) is, in effect, prohibiting building on the land (ie, it is restrictive) and, likewise, covenant (4) is restricting the occupancy of the rooms in the hostel.

Covenant (3), on the other hand, appears to be a restrictive covenant, but what it is really saying is that the property has to be kept in repair. This is therefore a positive obligation. It will require the person entering into it to spend money. You can usually identify a positive covenant by asking yourself whether the person giving it will have to 'put their hand in their pocket'.

The wording of the remaining covenants, (6) (positive) and (2) and (5) (restrictive), matches their substance.

7.3 Terminology

It is important to understand the terminology that lawyers use in the context of freehold covenants:

Covenantor

The person who makes the promise is referred to as the covenantor, and the land in respect of which it is made is said to have the burden of the covenant.

Covenantee

The person to whom the promise is made is known as the covenantee, and that person's land is said to have the benefit of the covenant.

Annexation

Annexation is a term that denotes that the benefit of a covenant is attached to the land of the covenantee so that it passes automatically to successors of the covenantee.

Assignment

Assignment refers to the express transfer of the benefit of a covenant to a successor.

7.4 Enforcement of freehold covenants

7.4.1 General

Consider again the example at the beginning of this chapter. There are several covenants affecting Greybrick Hostel. What is the position if the Hostel starts to house occupants and their family members? What if the grounds around the Hostel are used for regular events open to guests of the occupants of the Hostel? What if maintenance costs for the driveway are not forthcoming? Will it be possible to take action against the owners of the Hostel? The answers to these questions can be found by looking at a combination of common law, equity and statute.

When dealing with the enforcement of a covenant, there are two questions to answer:

(a) Who has the benefit of the covenant?

(b) Who has the burden of the covenant?

Only if a party has the benefit of the covenant can they enforce it; and only if they have the burden of the covenant can action be taken against them. So it is always necessary to ascertain whether the present owner of the benefited land has any right to enforce the covenant and whether the present owner of the burdened land has any liability for the covenant. We are first going to consider the position of the original parties to the covenant.

7.4.2 The original parties to the covenant

7.4.2.1 The original covenantee

As you have seen, a freehold covenant is a promise given in a deed. This promise is effectively a contract and is therefore governed by the principles of contract law. The general contract rule is that only the parties to a contract may sue or be sued on it. This is the doctrine known as 'privity of contract', which you have already studied and which you saw existed between the original parties to a lease (**Chapter 6**).

The original covenantee is a party to the contract in which the covenant was created. As such, the original covenantee will get the benefit of all the express covenants, positive and restrictive, real and personal, in the contract. It is therefore possible for the original covenantee to enforce any express covenant against anyone who has the burden of the covenant, including successors in title in accordance with the principles considered in **7.4.3** below. However, the original covenantee cannot sue successors in title if the covenantee has parted with all the land for the benefit of which the covenant was taken.

7.4.2.2 The original covenantor

Although not always the case, covenants are very often imposed when a person sells part of their land, and it is usually the buyer (B) who is the covenantor and the seller (S) who is the covenantee. The original covenantor (B) and the original covenantee (S) are parties to a contract. Thus, if B, for example, has covenanted with S not to build on the land that they have bought, and subsequently breaches this covenant by beginning to construct a house, S will be able to obtain either an injunction or damages.

Under s 79 of the LPA 1925, the covenants relating to the land of the covenantor shall be deemed to have been made by the covenantor on behalf of their successors in title and persons deriving title under them, as well as on behalf of themselves. This will be so unless the deed contains a statement to the contrary.

Example

In the example set out at the beginning of this chapter, Daron Fischer gave covenants to Bluebell Homes when Greybrick Hostel was bought by him for refurbishment. Daron is the original covenantor, as he was party to the contract in which the covenant was contained, namely the transfer. Daron has sold Greybrick Hostel to Broadland Ltd. Bluebell Homes still own the remaining five acres of adjoining land. Recently, it has become apparent that there is a problem with overcrowding, with some families moving into the Hostel and rooms being shared. In addition, there have been several rowdy events in the grounds of the Hostel that have gone on until the early hours. To exacerbate matters, the driveway to the Hostel, which is also used in part by Bluebell Homes, is now in a state of disrepair and Broadland Ltd have refused to contribute toward the cost of maintenance. Can Daron Fischer be held liable for the actions of Broadland Ltd?

Comment

*Daron Fischer is the original covenantor. As seen in **Chapter 6**, where the lease is an old tenancy, an original tenant, despite having assigned the lease, remains liable throughout the entire term of the lease. In a similar way, Daron Fischer, as the original covenantor, will remain liable for breach of covenants relating to the land after selling his land to Broadland Ltd. The combined effect of privity of contract and s 79 of the LPA 1925 is that he has promised that not only will he observe the covenants, but that his successors will do so as well.*

Section 79 of the LPA 1925 does not apply to personal covenants. It is necessary for the covenant to relate to the land which means a covenant that affects the land. (Note: if there had been a personal covenant given by the covenantor in the original deed transferring the land from the covenantee to covenantor, and that personal covenant had been breached at a later date by one of the covenantor's successors in title, the covenantor would be liable on such a covenant but not by virtue of s 79. The covenantor would remain liable to the covenantee in contract law, despite the breach not being their own.)

For the purposes of s 79 of the LPA 1925, it does not matter whether the covenant is a positive one or a restrictive one.

As the estate is a freehold one, the liability of the original covenantor therefore has the potential to last forever. You will now consider whether there are any steps that the original covenantor may take to protect their position.

When the original covenantor sells the land, they should have been aware that the sale would not relieve them from liability under the covenants. Furthermore, by selling the land they would no longer be able to perform the covenants themselves. When the original covenantor sold the land to a buyer, they should have required the buyer to enter into a covenant with themselves in the transfer deed to perform the covenants and to indemnify them against any future breach. In this way, if the original covenantor is sued for a breach committed after they have sold the property and has to pay damages, they can seek to be reimbursed by the buyer. This potential claim on an indemnity acts as an incentive for the buyer to comply with the covenants.

Assuming now that the buyer were then to sell on the property to a further buyer, would the buyer require similar protection?

By entering into an indemnity covenant with the original covenantor, the buyer is now at risk of having to meet the liability, should the original covenantor be sued on the covenants. Therefore, should the buyer then sell on the land to a further buyer, they should seek an indemnity covenant from that further buyer and so on if the property is then sold on again. In this way a chain of indemnity covenants is built up.

Example

Daron Fischer has sold Greybrick Hostel to Broadland Ltd. Broadland Ltd then sell Greybrick Hostel on to Staywell Care Homes, and then Staywell Care Homes later sell it to Randals Hospice. Daron Fischer obtained an indemnity covenant from Broadland Ltd in the transfer. When Broadland Ltd then sold to Staywell Care Homes, it should seek a similar indemnity from Staywell Care Homes, and Staywell Care Homes, in its turn, should obtain an indemnity from Randals Hospice.

Comment

This is how a chain of indemnity covenants is built up. This is illustrated by way of the diagram below:

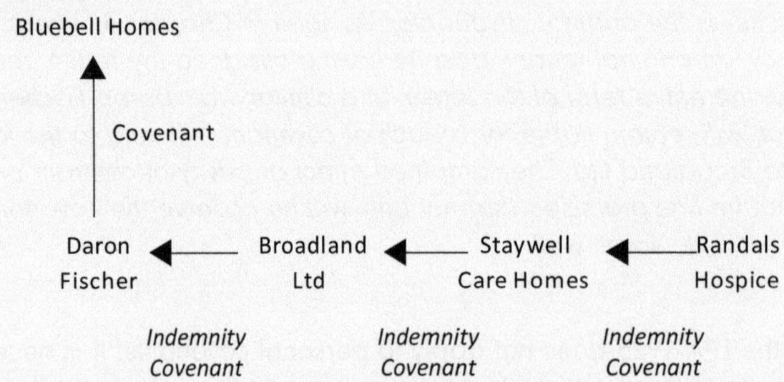

If Randals Hospice were to breach the covenants and Bluebell Homes successfully sued Daron Fischer, he could recover any damages he has to pay from Broadland Ltd. Broadland Ltd could then recover from Staywell Care Homes, who could in turn recover from Randals Hospice.

The following is a standard form of covenant that you would find in a transfer where a chain of indemnity exists. The covenants to which the indemnity applies will be noted in the Charges Register of the title affected.

> The Transferee [the Buyer] covenants with the Transferor [the Seller] to indemnify the Transferor against liability for any future breach of the covenants referred to in Entries 1 and 2 of the Charges Register and to perform the covenants from the date of this transfer.

However, the use of a chain of indemnity covenants is not always entirely satisfactory for a number of reasons. Using the diagram above as an example:

(1) Let us suppose that, when he sold his property, Daron Fischer obtained an indemnity covenant from Broadland Ltd but that Broadland Ltd omitted to obtain one from Staywell Care Homes. In this situation, Bluebell Homes may sue Daron for breach of covenant by Randals Hospice, and Daron may take advantage of the indemnity given by Broadland Ltd. Broadland Ltd, however, will not be able to pass the liability along the rest of the line of buyers, as there are no further indemnity covenants. It is only possible to rely fully on a chain of indemnity covenants if the original covenantor and each person giving an indemnity covenant obtains an indemnity covenant from the person to whom they sell. Failure to do this results in a break in the chain. In this situation, therefore, the buck stops with Broadland Ltd.

(2) However, despite the existence of an indemnity covenant from Broadland Ltd, Daron may still find that he is liable to pay damages to Bluebell Homes for breach of covenant by Randals Hospice. Broadland Ltd may no longer exist. The company may have gone into liquidation and therefore there is no entity to sue. The same may apply in relation to an individual who has given an indemnity. It may not be possible, for example, to trace that individual or, if they can be found, they may be bankrupt and not worth suing. Another possibility is that an individual may have died some years ago and their estate will have been distributed.

(3) Even where there is a complete chain of indemnity, there is still the possibility that the present owner - in this case, Randals Hospice - may not have sufficient money to pay any damages that are awarded. Thus, Bluebell Homes will have sued Daron for breach of covenant by Randals Hospice, and Daron will have sought to recover his losses through the indemnity given by Broadland Ltd. If Broadland Ltd have to indemnify Daron, they in turn will look to Staywell Care Homes for an indemnity. However, when it comes to Staywell Care Homes' turn to claim an indemnity, they will find that Randals Hospice's lack of money means that their claim is a worthless one. It is Staywell Care Homes, in this case, that will end up being out of pocket.

You can see from the above the shortcomings of a chain of indemnity covenants. The longer the chain, the more likely it is that there will be such shortcomings. Nevertheless, it is the usual practice of lawyers acting for a seller to require a buyer of land to enter into an indemnity covenant whenever the seller is a person who has entered into a covenant or given an indemnity covenant. It is a safety net, albeit a net that may develop rips.

So far we have been concentrating on the position of the original parties to the covenant. We now have to consider more fully what happens when land changes hands. Does the benefit of a covenant pass to a successor in title of the original covenantee? Does the burden of a covenant pass to a successor in title of the original covenantor? The position of successors in title is complicated by the fact that we need to consider two different sets of rules, one applied at common law and one applied in equity.

7.4.3 Successors in title to the original parties

We will start by considering the rules at common law.

7.4.3.1 The running of the benefit at common law

The benefit of both positive and restrictive covenants will pass to successors of the covenantee at common law in one of two ways:

(a) by express assignment; or

(b) automatically if certain conditions are met.

Express assignment

It is possible for the benefit of a covenant to pass to a successor by express assignment. Because a covenant confers a right to enforce it by way of action, it is 'a thing (or a chose) in action', and the assignment is an assignment of a thing in action. Such an assignment was recognised by equity and may also now be effective as a legal assignment under s 136 of the LPA 1925. The assignment must occur at the same time as the transfer of the land. It must be in writing signed by the assignor (eg the original covenantee), and written notice of the assignment must be given to the person with the burden of the covenant.

Automatically

The benefit of a covenant can pass automatically to a successor at common law. For the benefit of a covenant to pass automatically, the following requirements have to be met:

(1) The covenant must 'touch and concern' the land of the covenantee. In *Smith and Snipes Hall Farm Ltd v River Douglas Catchment Board* [1949] 2 KB 500, Tucker LJ said that it is necessary for the covenant to 'touch and concern' the land of the covenantee. By this he meant that the covenant must either affect the mode of occupation of the land or must by itself affect the value of the land. It is apparent from this requirement that the covenantee must, at the date of the deed, own land that is capable of benefiting from the covenant and that the land must be identifiable. (Note: this is the same test that you encountered in **Chapter 6** when looking at covenants in leases; see *P & A Swift Investments v Combined English Stores* referred to at **6.4.1.2**.)

(2) Both the original covenantee and the person now seeking to enforce the covenant must have a legal estate in the land. It was the position at common law that the person seeking to enforce the covenant had to have the same legal estate as the original covenantee. In *Smith and Snipes Hall Farm*, however, one of the claimants was a tenant and therefore did not have the same legal estate as the original covenantee, who was a freehold owner. Nevertheless, the Court of Appeal considered that s 78 of the LPA 1925 had now altered the position, because under it a covenant relating to land of the covenantee is deemed to be made not only with the covenantee's successors in title, but also with 'the persons deriving title under him or them'. A person having an equitable estate is not, of course, able to claim the benefit of a covenant at common law.

(3) The original parties must intend that the benefit of the covenant is to run with the land. It has to be shown that the parties to the deed intended the covenant to be enforceable not only by the original covenantee, but also by successors in title to the original covenantee. Such intention could be shown by express annexation of the benefit of the covenant to the land of the covenantee in the deed in which the covenant is created (see **Example** below) or deemed annexation under statute (s 78 of the LPA 1925 - see **7.4.3.3** below). However, deemed annexation will apply only to covenants created after 1925.

As long as these three conditions are satisfied, the benefit of the covenant will pass to any person who has the appropriate legal estate.

Example

*Consider the scenario set out at the beginning of this chapter, together with the additional facts given in **7.4.2.2**, but now reverting to the situation where the adjoining homeowners, as successors of Bluebell Homes, wish to take action, and state whether the homeowners are able to enforce the covenants. The covenants imposed by Bluebell Homes were:*

(1) to allow the rooms in the Hostel to be used for sole occupancy only;

(2) not to allow the grounds of the Hostel to be used for public events;

(3) to contribute towards the cost of the maintenance of the driveway to the Hostel that crosses part of the land retained by Bluebell Homes.

Comment

Each of the covenants can be seen to be of benefit to the retained land rather than simply of benefit to Bluebell Homes as a company. They are not like a covenant, for example, to provide Bluebell Homes with free printing, which is a purely personal benefit. They therefore 'touch and concern' the land.

The homeowners, in buying the houses from Bluebell Homes, acquire a legal estate. They are therefore persons who may claim the benefit of the covenants. If, instead of selling the houses, Bluebell Homes had granted legal leases of them, the homeowners would still be able to claim the benefit of the covenants by virtue of s 78 of the LPA 1925.

The final requirement is that the original parties, Bluebell Homes and Daron Fischer, must have intended that the benefit of the covenants was to 'run with the land', that is to say, was to pass to each successive owner of the retained land. This intention can be shown by looking at the wording of the deed in which Bluebell Homes transferred the country house to Daron. This deed contained the original covenants. The express annexation of the benefit of the covenants to the land can be shown by the following wording:

> *'The Buyer [Daron Fischer] covenants with the Seller [Bluebell Homes] for the benefit of each and every part of the land shown edged in green on the attached plan ("the Retained Land").'*

However, in the absence of such express annexation of the benefit to the land, the homeowners could in any event rely upon statutory annexation under s 78 of the LPA 1925.

We have seen, therefore, that the benefit of a covenant may pass at common law as long as certain requirements are met. It is important to note that under these rules, the benefit of a covenant may pass whether the covenant is positive or restrictive.

It is important to note that these rules are concerned solely with the benefit of the covenant: they do not clarify the person against whom the covenants can be enforced. In the next section, we shall consider whether the burden of a covenant may pass to successors in title at common law.

7.4.3.2 The running of the burden at common law

We have seen that when the original covenantor sells the burdened land, they will still be liable for the breach of a covenant relating to that land by their successor. However, will the buyer of the burdened land be bound by that covenant? The buyer was not a party to the original promise, so does the burden of the covenant attach to the land? In other words, does the burden of the covenant run with the land?

The common law gave a very simple answer to this question: it said that the burden does not run (*Austerberry v Oldham Corpn* (1885)). This follows the basic common law rule that a person cannot be made liable upon a contract unless they were a party to it. As the successor to the covenantor was not a party to the contract in which the covenant was created, the common law will not impose the burden of the covenant upon them.

As the burden of a covenant cannot run at common law, the only way to enforce covenants against the original covenantor's successors in title is generally in equity (see **7.4.3.4**).

Before looking at the rules in equity, however, it is worth looking at two mechanisms, both rather limited in scope, which can circumvent the rule at law that the burden of a covenant cannot run.

The first mechanism is the chain of indemnity covenants which you first saw in **7.4.2.2** in the context of the continuing liability of the original covenantor. The original covenantor should have protected themselves from this liability to some extent by requiring their buyer to enter into a covenant with them to perform the covenants and to indemnify them against any future breach. The buyer, in turn, might require any future buyer to enter into similar covenants with them. In time a chain of indemnity covenants may build up. In principle, although the original covenantor remains the only party against whom the covenants can be enforced directly by the person with the benefit of the covenants, the original covenantor would be able to seek reimbursement from their successor in title, and the successor in title in turn would be able to seek reimbursement from their buyer, and so on.

The chain of indemnity covenants does not act to pass the burden of the covenants on to successors in title and there is no direct liability owed by those successors to the person with the benefit of the covenant, but such a chain can work to pass financial liability indirectly back to the party which is actually in breach of the covenant.

The problems with such chains of indemnity covenants were covered in **7.4.2.2** and apply equally here.

The second mechanism is of limited application and is likely to be relevant only where the covenant in question is a positive one and is closely related to certain rights granted in the transfer deed, such as an easement. The principle in *Halsall v Brizell* [1957] Ch 169 is that a successor in title who takes the benefit of rights, eg easements, contained in a deed must accept the burden of covenants contained in the same deed. This is also often referred to as the 'principle of mutual benefit and burden'.

This principle can act as a way of enforcing the burden of a positive covenant against successors where this cannot otherwise be done at law. It can be seen, however, that the principle is of rather limited application. First, the covenant in *Halsall v Brizell* was a positive obligation, and so the principle does not apply to restrictive covenants, and secondly, there must be associated rights, such as easements, conferred as benefits in the deed on the covenantor and its successors. The principle in *Halsall v Brizell* is not, therefore, a means of making the burden of every positive covenant pass to successors in title, partly as there will not always be relevant easements in place.

The House of Lords in *Rhone v Stephens* [1994] 2 AC 310 interpreted the principle of benefit and burden rather more narrowly. Lord Templeman took the view that just because a deed conferred a benefit (easement) on a person, it did not mean that the burden of all the covenants imposed by that deed became enforceable. The burden must in some way be related to the exercise of the easement. This will be so where the covenantor can make a choice between accepting the benefit and burden together or rejecting the benefit and thereby being released from the burden.

In the case of *Wilkinson & Ors v Kerdene Ltd* [2013] EWCA Civ 44, the equitable principle of mutual benefit and burden was reaffirmed. The case concerned a number of privately owned bungalows situated in a Cornish holiday complex. The original transfer deeds for the bungalows granted the owners' rights to use the drains, roads, footpaths and leisure facilities on the retained land of the complex. The original transferees (the bungalow owners) covenanted to pay an annual sum in respect of the costs of maintaining the roads and recreational areas. Kerdene subsequently acquired the freehold and carried out a programme of repairs. Kerdene sought to recover the cost of these works under the positive covenant in the original transfers. The issue before the Court of Appeal was whether the positive covenant to pay for the upkeep of the facilities was enforceable against successors in title.

The Court emphasised that successors in title were not liable under the burden of a positive covenant unless that burden bore some 'real relation' to the right granted. The Court also noted that it was important to look beyond the express terms of the original transfer and consider what in substance the covenantor was paying for.

In the case of the bungalows, although the exercise of the rights on the retained land of the holiday village was not expressly conditional upon payment, and although not all owners made use of all the facilities, the Court held that payment was intended to ensure that the rights remained *capable* of being exercised. Accordingly, the principle of mutual benefit and burden applied, and the bungalow owners were obliged to pay for the works.

You will now understand that at common law the burden of a covenant cannot be enforced against a successor in title. However, it may be possible to achieve the desired result by indirect means, using a chain of indemnity covenants or adopting the principle of mutual benefit and burden, as happened in *Halsall v Brizell*. As *Rhone v Stephens* has shown, this second method will only be possible where there is a related benefit and burden.

Example

Looking again at the example set out at the beginning of this chapter, the owners of the driveway over which Bluebell Homes granted Daron Fisher a right of access could refuse to allow Broadland Ltd, the current owner of Greybrick Hostel, to use the right of access over the driveway unless Broadland Ltd paid the maintenance contribution. That is because the right to use the driveway is conditional upon a covenant to contribute towards the cost of maintenance of the driveway.

Having examined the rules at common law, we are now going to consider the approach that equity takes.

7.4.3.3 The running of the benefit in equity

Equity will recognise that the benefit of a covenant will pass to successors of the covenantee where:

(a) the covenant 'touches and concerns' the land of the covenantee; and

(b) the benefit of the covenant has passed to the successor of the covenantee either by express assignment or by annexation.

Express assignment

As is the case at common law, it is possible for the benefit of a covenant to run with the land in equity as a result of an express assignment of the benefit at the same time as the transfer of the land to a successor (see **7.4.3.1** above).

Annexation

As you saw when we considered the question of annexation in relation to the common law, this is a question of intention. Usually, the deed containing the covenant will contain an express annexation of the benefit of the covenants to the land, as shown in the **Comment** in **7.4.3.1** above.

But what if it does not contain express wording? As you have already seen in **7.4.3.1** above, s 78 of the LPA 1925 deems that the benefit of covenants relating to any land of the covenantee shall pass to successors in title. The effect of s 78 was considered by the Court of Appeal in the following case.

In *Federated Homes Ltd v Mill Lodge Properties Ltd* [1980] 1 WLR 594, a covenant had been made in 1971 over land in Newport Pagnell to restrict the overall density of the number of houses to be built on the land. The covenant was not worded expressly to annex the benefit of the covenant to the covenantee's land. The question before the Court of Appeal was whether the successor in title to the covenantee could enforce the covenant.

Brightman LJ considered the three ways in which s 78 might be interpreted, as put forward by counsel for the defendant.

The first interpretation - that it was simply a word-saving device aimed at reducing the length of legal documents - he rejected as being inconsistent with the wording of the section.

The second view was that the section only operated to annex a covenant if the document in some way showed that the land was intended to have the benefit of it.

The final way in which the section could be interpreted was by viewing the section as effecting annexation as long as the covenant touched and concerned the land of the covenantee, whether that was apparent from the document or from surrounding circumstances. Brightman LJ did not consider it necessary to distinguish between these two interpretations because they both produced the same result when applied to the facts of the case.

The reason Brightman LJ gave for regarding the section as effecting annexation was that it was differently worded from its predecessor (Conveyancing Act 1881, s 58(1)) and because it stated that a covenant was deemed to be made not only with the covenantee but with the covenantee's successors in title. If it was made with a successor in title, that meant that the successor in title was able to enforce the covenant. If the covenant was enforceable by a successor in title, then the covenant must run with the land.

Brightman LJ also rejected the argument that the benefit only ran with the land as a whole and was not annexed to part of it when that part was sold. He considered the proper interpretation to be that the benefit of a covenant is annexed to every part of the land, unless a contrary intention is expressed.

The effect of the *Federated Homes* case is that, to ensure annexation of a covenant, you need do no more than enter into a covenant with the covenantee and show that the covenantee had, at the time, land that was capable of benefiting from it.

There is always a risk, of course, that the Supreme Court may overrule the decision in *Federated Homes*. Where you want to be sure that the benefit of a covenant runs with the land, it is therefore preferable to annex it expressly. This is done, for example, by covenanting with 'the owners or owner for the time being of [named land]', or by stating that the covenant is taken 'for the benefit of [named land]'.

The issue of identifying the land that was intended to benefit was examined in *Crest Nicholson Residential (South) Ltd v McAllister* [2004] 1 WLR 2409. The Court of Appeal emphasised the importance of being able to identify the benefited land in order for s 78 to operate to annex the benefit. The Court of Appeal held that for s 78 to apply, the 'land intended to be benefited must be so defined that it is easily identifiable'. In addition, there must be sufficient definition within the conveyance itself.

However, this approach was not applied in *Mohammad Zadeh v Joseph* [2008] 1 P & CR 6, a case in which the court held that it was 'obvious' that the covenants were to protect and enhance the enjoyment, user and value of the retained land, although this land was not identifiable expressly or by implication from the conveyance itself.

The result of these two decisions is that where a conveyance does not expressly annex the benefit of a restrictive covenant to the retained land, all the elements of the transaction must be examined to establish whether the land intended to be benefited is sufficiently identified.

You have already seen that the burden of a covenant cannot be enforced against a successor in title at common law (**7.4.3.2** above). We will now consider whether equity will assist.

7.4.3.4 The running of the burden in equity

We can do no better than to begin our discussion in London's Leicester Square. At its centre there is an open square of land. Why is it there? Why not build upon it? To discover the answer to these questions we need to go back to the middle of the 19th century. A Mr Tulk had owned the land in Leicester Square. He sold it to a Mr Elms. Elms covenanted with Tulk that he would keep and maintain the land 'in its then form and in sufficient and proper repair, as a square garden and pleasure ground, in an open state and uncovered with any buildings, in a neat and ornamental order'. Subsequently, a Mr Moxhay acquired the land. His conveyance made no reference to the covenant although he knew about it. Moxhay proposed to build on the land, and Tulk, who still owned land in the area, sought to prevent him doing so. This gave rise to the case of *Tulk v Moxhay* (1848) 2 Ph 774.

Tulk v Moxhay was heard at a time when there was tension between the desire to keep land free from private covenants, so that it could be developed for profitable industrial use, and concern about inappropriate commercial and urban growth affecting residential amenity. The court considered the desire, recognised by equity, to prevent an unconscionable outcome. It was recognised by the court that there was no question about the liability of the original contracting parties, but there was an issue about a party being able to sell land free of a covenant affecting the land.

Lord Cottenham LC stated that:

> ... the question is, not whether the covenant runs with the land, but whether a party shall be permitted to use the land in a manner inconsistent with the contract entered into by his vendor, and with notice of which he purchased. Of course, the price would be affected by the covenant, and nothing could be more inequitable than the original purchaser should be able to sell the property the next day for a greater price, in consideration of the assignee being allowed to escape from the liability which he had himself undertaken.

Equity was prepared to enforce a covenant against a successor in title to the original covenantor where that successor had notice of that covenant.

After *Tulk v Moxhay*, the equitable principle was widely applied. However, over time, the principle has been refined, and there are now recognised conditions that have to be satisfied if the burden of a covenant is to run in equity. These may be summarised as follows:

(a) the covenant must be restrictive in nature;

(b) the covenantee owned land for the benefit of which the covenant was taken, ie the covenant must 'touch and concern' the land of the covenantee;

(c) the parties must have intended the burden to run with the covenantor's land. This may be done expressly in the deed creating the covenant. The following are examples of such express wording:

   (i) 'to the intent that the burden of the covenants will run with and bind the property and every part of it',

   (ii) 'so as to bind the property hereby transferred'.

   In the absence of express wording, such intention may be implied by s 79 of the LPA 1925. The effect of s 79 is that, unless a contrary intention is expressed in the deed, it will be implied by statute that the parties intended the burden to pass to successors in title. However, s 79 will only apply to the burden of covenants created after 1925;

(d) the covenant must be registered in the appropriate register. If the title to the covenantor's land is registered, then the restrictive covenant will be an interest affecting a registered estate. The method of protection is to enter a notice on the Charges Register before registration of the successor as the new proprietor. You will find an example of such a notice in entry 1 of the Charges Register at **Reading 4** in the **Appendix**.

   Where the title to the land is unregistered, the restrictive covenant will be protected by the entry of a Class D(ii) land charge against the name of the original covenantor on the Land Charges Register before the date of completion of a sale to a successor. See **Reading 5** in the **Appendix** for an example of the results of a Land Charges search showing a Class D(ii) land charge.

   Pre-1926 restrictive covenants cannot be registered as land charges and they will be enforceable against everyone, except equity's darling, ie a bona fide purchaser for value of the legal estate without notice (see **Chapter 2** at **2.3.4**).

7.4.4 Application of the rules

7.4.4.1 Application of the rules relating to benefit

In this section, you will look at how the rules are applied as to whether the benefit of a covenant passes to successors in title in the context of the example set out at the beginning of this chapter.

Example

*Consider again the example set out at the beginning of this chapter, together with the additional facts in **7.4.2.2**, but now reverting to the situation where the adjoining homeowners, as successors of Bluebell Homes, wish to take action. Identify whether the homeowners could take action for the various breaches of covenant.*

(1) To allow the rooms in the hostel to be used for sole occupancy only. This covenant has been breached as there are now families living in the Hostel and rooms are being shared.

(2) Not to allow the grounds of the Hostel to be used for public events. This covenant has been breached by the events that have taken place until the early hours in the grounds of the Hostel.

(3) *To contribute towards the cost of the maintenance of the driveway to the Hostel that crossed part of the land retained by Bluebell Homes and now owned by the homeowners.*

The homeowners are successors to the original covenantee - Bluebell Homes. It is necessary to ascertain whether the homeowners have the benefit of each of these covenants to determine whether they can take action for their breach.

Comment

Consider first the position at common law

The benefit of each of the covenants will have passed either by express assignment (LPA 1925, s 136) or automatically if the covenants touch and concern the land (which they do), both Bluebell Homes and the homeowners had/have the legal estate (both of them did/do), and the original parties intended the benefit to run (in the absence of express annexation, the benefit of each of the covenants would be annexed by statute pursuant to s 78 of the LPA 1925).

Consider the position in equity

Again, the benefit of each of the covenants will have passed to the homeowners in equity, provided that the covenants touch and concern the land (which they do) and the benefit of each of the covenants has passed by express assignment, or by express or statutory annexation (which they will under s 78).

It is therefore possible for the homeowners to show that they have the benefit of each of the covenants, even though they are successors to Bluebell Homes, the original covenantee. As a result, they would be able to take action against the party with the burden of the covenants.

7.4.4.2 Application of the rules relating to burden

In this section, you will look at how the rules are applied as to whether the burden of a covenant passes to successors in title in the context of the example set out at the beginning of this chapter.

Example

Consider again the example set out at the beginning of this chapter, together with the additional facts given in ***7.4.2.2*** *above, but now reverting to the situation where the adjoining homeowners, as successors of Bluebell Homes, wish to take action. The breaches of the covenants are set out in* ***7.4.4.1*** *above. Identify which of the covenants could be enforced by the homeowners.*

Comment

(1) Breach of the sole occupancy covenant

Common law

The burden of the covenant cannot run to Broadland Ltd as a successor in title at common law. It is therefore necessary to look to equity.

Equity

Equity will enforce the covenant against Broadland Ltd as successors in title if the four conditions from Tulk v Moxhay are satisfied.

(a) Although this covenant is positive in expression, it is restrictive in nature and therefore meets the first of the conditions.

(b) Bluebell Homes owned the retained land at the time that the covenant was entered into. As long as there is some ascertainable benefit for the land retained by Bluebell Homes, the second condition will be satisfied. It does not have to be a purely economic benefit for the land; it is sufficient if it is for the preservation of amenity or enjoyment of the retained land. As this covenant is aimed at avoiding overcrowding of Greybrick Hostel, it is likely that it would satisfy this condition.

(c) There is no indication that the parties expressly intended the burden of the covenant to run with the land. This would need to be clear from the wording in the transfer. Where there is no such wording, s 79 of the LPA 1925 will imply that the burden of the covenant runs with the land.

(d) It is likely that Broadland Ltd had notice of the covenant, as the covenant would almost certainly have been noted on the Charges Register of the title to Greybrick Hostel before Daron Fischer sold the land to Broadland Ltd.

In conclusion, the burden of this covenant would run with the land in equity so as to bind Broadland Ltd.

(2) Breach of the covenant regarding the use of the Hostel grounds

Common law

As with covenant (1) above, the burden of the covenant cannot pass to Broadland Ltd as a successor in title at common law. It is therefore necessary to look to equity.

Equity

Again, as with covenant (1) above, equity will enforce the covenant against Broadland Ltd as successors in title if the four conditions from Tulk v Moxhay are satisfied:

(a) This is a restrictive covenant and therefore meets the first of the conditions.

(b) Bluebell Homes owned the retained land at the time that the covenant was entered into. Also, it is likely that this covenant is capable of benefiting the land retained by Bluebell Homes.

(c) As with covenant (1) above, s 79 of the LPA 1925 could be relied upon to imply that there was an intention by the parties for the covenant to run with the land.

(d) For the reasons set out in relation to covenant (1) above, it is likely that Broadland Ltd had notice of the covenant.

Therefore, the burden of this covenant will also run with the land in equity so as to bind Broadland Ltd.

(3) Breach of the maintenance covenant

Common law

The burden of the covenant will not run with the land at common law. However, in this case, Bluebell Homes may be able to rely upon the rule in Halsall v Brizell. The transfer by which the covenant was created contained a benefit (the right of access over the driveway) that was conditional upon the performance of the covenant to contribute toward the maintenance of the driveway. If Broadland Ltd refuse to pay the contribution toward maintenance, they will lose the benefit of the right of access.

Equity

In relation to the breach of this covenant equity cannot assist. The covenant is positive in expression and nature; therefore it does not meet the first of the conditions derived from Tulk v Moxhay. The burden of the covenant does not run with the land in equity.

There are two parties liable on these covenants. Daron Fischer, as the original covenantor, is liable for breach of covenants relating to the land after selling his land to Broadland Ltd. Broadland Ltd are liable for breach of covenants (1) and (2) under the rule in Tulk v Moxhay, and for breach of covenant (3) under the rule in Halsall v Brizell.

7.4.5 Summary

In the following activity, you will use your knowledge of the rules you have just studied to complete a table indicating whether successors in title to the original parties are liable for or can take action for breaches of freehold covenants.

ACTIVITY 1 Freehold covenants

Complete Table 1 by indicating with a 'yes' or a 'no' whether the benefit of positive and restrictive covenants can run to successors in title at common law or in equity. Then complete Table 2 by indicating with a 'yes' or a 'no' whether the burden of positive and restrictive covenants can run to successors in title at common law or in equity. Give reasons for your decisions.

Table 7.1 The benefit of freehold covenants

	Common Law	**Equity**
Positive covenant		
Restrictive covenant		

Table 7.2 The burden of freehold covenants

	Common Law	Equity
Positive covenant		
Restrictive covenant		

COMMENT

Table 7.1 The benefit of freehold covenants

	Common Law	**Equity**
Positive covenant	Yes - The benefit may run by: • express assignment; or • automatically where: • covenant touches and concerns land of the covenantee, and • original covenantee and successor had/have a legal estate in the land, and • original parties intended the benefit to run - express annexation or statutory annexation under s 78 of the LPA 1925.	Yes - The benefit may run where the covenant touches and concerns land of the covenantee and the benefit has run to the successor by: • express assignment; • express annexation; or • statutory annexation under s 78 of the LPA 1925.
Restrictive covenant	Yes - The same rules apply for restrictive covenants.	Yes - The same rules apply for restrictive covenants.

Table 7.2 The burden of freehold covenants

	Common Law	**Equity**
Positive covenant	No - The burden of a freehold covenant cannot run at common law. This follows the basic common law rule that a person cannot be made liable upon a contract unless they were a party to it. [Liability of successors to previous covenantors is made possible by a chain of indemnity or the mutual benefit and burden rule (*Halsall v Brizell*).]	No - Equity will not assist in relation to positive covenants.
Restrictive covenant	No - The same rule applies for restrictive covenants - see *Austerberry*.	Yes - Where the conditions in *Tulk v Moxhay* apply.

Now that you know how covenants arise and how the benefit and burden of them may pass, our next task is to consider what the outcome of an attempt to enforce them might be.

7.5 Choice of rules

You will now appreciate that there are two sets of rules that can be applied when considering whether it is possible to take action for breach of covenant: the rules that apply at common law, and those that apply in equity. In each case it is necessary to use the same set of rules. So, if the party being sued has the burden of the covenant at common law, the party suing must show that they have the benefit of the covenant at common law. Similarly, if the party being sued has the burden of the covenant in equity, the party suing must show that they have the benefit in equity.

Example

Consider again the example at the start of this chapter. The homeowners are seeking to enforce the breaches of covenant. They are, however, successors in title to the original covenantee - Bluebell Homes. Should they enforce the covenants using the common law rules, or using the rules in equity?

Comment

*The common law rules will allow them to sue Daron Fischer, the original covenantor. The burden of the covenants does not run at common law (**7.4.3.2** above), but the original covenantor remains liable on the covenants. In order to sue Daron Fischer, the homeowners would need to show that the benefit of the covenants had passed to each of them at common law. This is illustrated by the diagram set out below.*

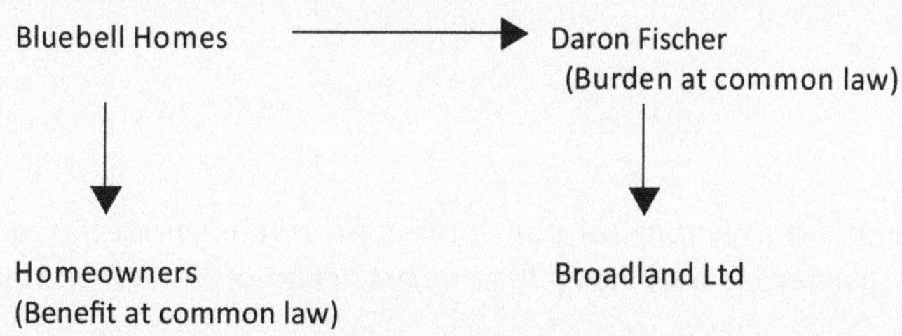

*However, as we will see in **7.6** below, the homeowners are likely to want to stop the breaches, and therefore they will want to sue the current freehold owners, Broadland Ltd. However, Broadland Ltd do not have the burden of the covenants at common law, only in equity, and only for the first two covenants (see **7.4.4.2** above and note the rule in Halsall v Brizell for the positive covenant). In order to sue Broadland Ltd, the homeowners would need to show that the benefit of the covenants had passed to each of them in equity. This is illustrated by the second diagram set out below.*

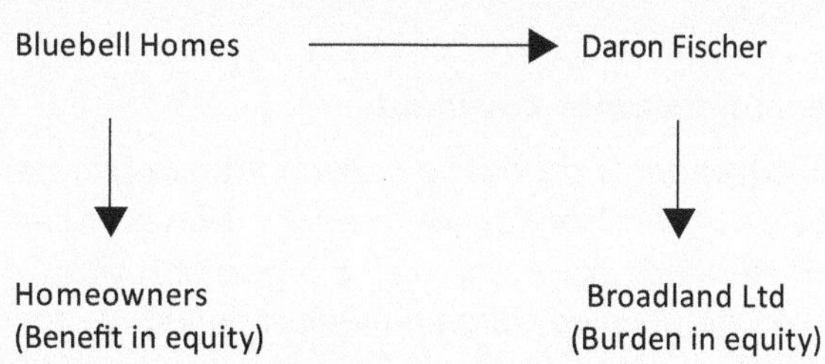

Now that you know which rules to use, we can consider the remedies that are available for breach of freehold covenants.

7.6 Remedies for breach of freehold covenants

7.6.1 Original covenantor

The original covenantor is liable for breach of covenant whilst they retain an interest in the land and also once the land has been sold. Whilst the original covenantor retains an interest in the land, in the event of a breach of covenant, the covenantee may obtain damages, or an injunction to restrain a breach of restrictive covenant, or, in the case of a breach of positive covenant, an order for specific performance.

However, once the land has been sold and the original covenantor no longer has an interest in the land, where there is a breach of covenant by a successor, an injunction or an order for specific performance would be unenforceable against the original covenantor. The only remedy available against the original covenantor for a breach of covenant by their successor would be damages.

7.6.2 Successor to the original covenantor

A successor to the original covenantor has liability for breach of a restrictive covenant under the rule in *Tulk v Moxhay*. Where there has been a breach of a restrictive covenant, the appropriate remedy would be an injunction restraining the breach of covenant. Therefore, if an injunction was obtained against a successor to the original covenantor, that successor would have to cease the activity that was in breach of the restrictive covenant. Alternatively, it is open to the court to award damages in lieu of the equitable remedy where it is considered that, in the particular circumstances, an injunction is not an appropriate remedy.

Example

Continuing with the example set out at the start of this chapter, the homeowners want to know what remedies they have for the breaches of the covenants.

Comment

(1) Breach of the sole occupancy covenant and breach of the covenant regarding the use of the Hostel grounds

*These are both restrictive covenants. The homeowners will have the benefit of these covenants in equity (see **7.4.4.1**) and Broadway Ltd will have the burden (see **7.4.4.2**). It is likely that the homeowners will be able to obtain an injunction against Broadland Ltd to stop the overcrowding from continuing and to prevent further parties being held in the Hostel grounds.*

(2) Breach of the maintenance covenant

*The maintenance covenant is a positive covenant and so the burden cannot pass to Broadland Ltd either at common law or in equity. However, the rule in Halsall v Brizell applies to the maintenance covenant, and if Broadland Ltd wish to continue to use the right of access over the driveway, then they must contribute towards the maintenance costs (see **7.4.4.2**). The homeowners will have the benefit of the covenant at common law (see **7.4.4.1**). They could seek an order from the court prohibiting the use of the right of access over the driveway unless Broadland Ltd contribute towards the maintenance costs.*

As an alternative to suing Broadland Ltd for breach of the covenants, the homeowners could consider suing Daron Fischer, the original covenantor, as Daron is the original contracting party and therefore retains the burden of the covenants. The homeowners have the benefit of the covenants at common law and therefore will be able to sue Daron at common law. If the homeowners can find Daron, they could sue him for damages, the appropriate contractual remedy. Daron may then be able to pursue Broadland Ltd if the transfer to Broadland Ltd contained an express indemnity upon which Daron could rely.

7.7 Discharge of freehold covenants

You will now be able to appreciate that as the burden of restrictive covenants can run in equity, effectively, restrictive covenants can affect the land to which they relate for all time. Clearly, this can cause problems if the covenant bears no relation to the modern use of the property or is totally unreasonable. It can blight land, possibly preventing development that is both needed and desired.

For example, development may be acceptable in planning terms, and indeed planning permission may have been granted by the local planning authority. However, if there is a restrictive covenant in existence which prevents that development and there is land that benefits from that covenant, then despite the fact that planning permission has been granted, the development can be thwarted by the enforcement of the restrictive covenant. You will now consider the various means by which a restrictive covenant can be dealt with.

7.7.1 Express release

The covenantee of the restrictive covenant can agree to the modification or release of the covenant. This will involve entering into a deed with the owner of the burdened land to that effect. Invariably, the covenantee will seek a payment for release of the covenant, and obviously such modification or release is voluntary. It cannot be forced upon the covenantee.

7.7.2 Common ownership

Where the burdened and benefited land come into the same ownership, the covenant will be extinguished. This is similar to the extinguishment of an easement, as you will see in **Chapter 8**.

7.7.3 Section 84 of the LPA 1925

It may be that the covenantee cannot be located in order to seek an express release from a covenant, or the covenantee may not be prepared to release or modify a covenant. Section 84 of the LPA 1925 provides an alternative means by which a restrictive covenant that burdens land can be released or modified. An application can be made to the Lands Chamber of the Upper Tribunal, and, if certain grounds can be made out, the Tribunal has power to release or modify restrictive covenants. These grounds are specified in s 84 and are limited. For example, to satisfy one of the grounds, the person seeking to have the restrictive covenant removed or modified would need to show that it is obsolete due to changes in the character of the property or the neighbourhood. It is also quite a lengthy process to make an application to the Tribunal, and it can be expensive.

7.7.4 Breach insurance

In some cases, the best option for a covenantor is to take out breach insurance. Payment of a premium will ensure that, should a restrictive covenant be breached, the covenantor will be able to recover insurance for any loss incurred by the enforcement of that breach. If, for example, there is an old covenant preventing the development of land without the consent of the covenantee and, due to changes that have taken place over the years, it is not possible to locate the covenantee, breach insurance may be obtained, which would then mean that if the development were to proceed, the risks would be taken by the insurance company.

7.8 Law reform

It has been recognised that many aspects of the law relating to freehold covenants are now outdated and a cause of difficulty. The Law Commission Report 'Making Land Work: Easements, Covenants and Profits à Prendre' (Law Com No 327) proposes a more coherent scheme of covenants, together with easements that you will study in **Chapter 8**. This scheme would also ensure compatibility with the system of registration introduced by the LRA 2002.

7.9 Freehold covenant problem questions

Set out below is a suggested approach to problem questions:

(1) It is often useful to draw a simple diagram to identify the various events and the benefited and burdened land, to help you structure your answer.

(2) You will need to analyse the types of covenants that exist and identify them as positive or restrictive. You may also need to consider whether the covenant is one that is likely to touch and concern the land or is personal only. Identify any breaches of these covenants to ensure you deal with each one in full.

(3) Identify which parties the claimant can sue (usually you are advising an aggrieved owner of the benefited land, but this is not always the case).

(4) In each case you need to explain how the claimant has the benefit of each covenant breached, using the common law or equitable rules depending upon who they are suing, *and* how the defendant has the burden of that covenant using that same set of rules. Remember a claim will succeed only if both are clearly shown.

(5) Consider appropriate remedies for the claimant, on the facts given.

(6) A reminder of some important points:

  (a) The common law is generally used when suing on a positive covenant:

    (i) where the original covenantee is suing the original covenantor;

    (ii) where the successor of the original covenantee is suing the original covenantor. (This may then lead to indirect enforcement against the successor of the original covenantor by an indemnity covenant.)

  (b) Equity is generally used when suing a successor of the original covenantor on a restrictive covenant.

  (c) Remedies – think about who the claimant is suing – does the defendant still control the land or not? What outcome would the claimant like to achieve?

    (i) Damages only against an original covenantor if they no longer own the land.

(ii) Injunction or specific performance against the current owner of the land (but remember that equity may award damages in lieu).

(iii) For a positive covenant the only option is to sue the original covenantor for damages (but see possible indirect enforcement by an indemnity covenant above).

ACTIVITY 2 Test your knowledge: covenants

The aim of this activity is to give you some practice in applying the rules that you have been studying in this chapter.

Anne Lovell was the registered proprietor of Bridgend. In December, 10 years ago, Anne sold part of her garden to Tariq. In the transfer Anne granted Tariq a right of access over her driveway conditional upon a covenant by Tariq to contribute towards the cost of maintenance of the driveway. Tariq also covenanted that the land he had bought would not be used for business purposes, and he covenanted to wash Anne's car every Monday.

Four years later, Tariq sold the land to Oliver, and in the following year Oliver sold the land to Samir. Last month Anne sold the remaining part of her land to Beth.

Beth seeks your advice because Samir is running a business from the land and is refusing to contribute towards the cost of maintaining Beth's driveway. He also refuses to wash Beth's car.

Advise Beth whether:

(1) she can sue Samir in respect of the user covenant and, if so, what remedy or remedies might she obtain;

(2) she can sue Samir for the cost of maintaining her driveway;

(3) there might be any indirect means of enforcing the maintenance covenant; and

(4) she can force Samir to wash her car.

COMMENT

(1) Beth is a successor of the original covenantee. Has she got the benefit of the covenant at common law? It will have passed either by express assignment (LPA 1925, s 136) or automatically if the covenant touches and concerns the land (it does), both Anne and Beth had/have legal estate (they do), and the original parties had intended benefit to run (they did - see s 78). Does Samir have the burden? The burden does not pass at common law, so consider equity.

Does Beth have the benefit of the covenant in equity? Yes, provided the covenant touches and concerns the land (it does) and the benefit has passed by express assignment, or by express or statutory annexation (it has - see s 78). Has Samir got the burden in equity? See whether the four conditions in *Tulk v Moxhay* have been satisfied:

(a) Restrictive covenant (it is).
(b) Beth owns land for the benefit of which the covenant was taken (yes).
(c) Burden intended to run - evidenced either by express wording in the transfer or implied under s 79 of the LPA 1925.
(d) Covenant is protected by a notice in the charges register.

If the restrictive covenant is registered, Samir is bound, and Beth can ask the court for an injunction (but might get damages in lieu).

(2) This is a positive covenant. Although Beth has the benefit of this covenant (see above), the burden does not pass either at common law or in equity (*Tulk v Moxhay*). Thus, Beth cannot sue Samir (but see below).

(3) As the positive covenant is linked to an express easement over the driveway, it could be argued that under the doctrine of 'benefit and burden' (see *Halsall v Brizell*), if Samir wants to continue to exercise right of way over Beth's driveway, he must accept the burden of contributing towards the cost of maintenance.

In addition, Beth could consider suing Tariq on the positive covenant, as Tariq is the original contracting party and thus retains the burden. (Beth has the benefit at common law (see (1) above).) If Beth can find Tariq and sues him (for damages), Tariq may be able to pursue Oliver (if the transfer to Oliver contained an express indemnity). If so, Oliver may be able to pursue Samir (if the transfer to Samir contained an express indemnity).

(4) The car wash covenant is almost certainly personal, ie does not touch and concern the land (see *Swift Investments* etc). Therefore, the benefit will not have passed to Beth, and the burden will not have passed to Samir.

SUMMARY

- You now have the knowledge to recognise whether a valid covenant exists that affects freehold land. You are able to identify whether that covenant is positive or restrictive, and whether it is real or personal in nature. You will now appreciate that this has a direct relevance when considering the enforceability of a freehold covenant against successors in title.
- Having examined the complex rules relating to the enforceability of freehold covenants, you now have sufficient knowledge to advise a client seeking to enforce a freehold covenant as to whether they are able to do so at common law or in equity. You will appreciate the different remedies available for these alternatives and therefore will be able to advise on the most appropriate solution for your client.
- Equally, you will have sufficient background knowledge to advise a client where land is adversely affected by freehold covenants. It may be that as a result of your advice, your client decides not to proceed with a transaction where it would not be possible for them to achieve their aims as a result of an adverse covenant. You would also be in a position to offer a solution to a client in that position through your knowledge of the methods by which covenants can be modified or discharged.
- You should use the test your knowledge activity contained in this chapter, either as a means of checking whether you have met the learning outcomes, or in order to reinforce what you have learned.

8 Easements

LEARNING OUTCOMES

When you have completed this chapter, you should be able to:

- understand the essential characteristics of an easement and how these may be used to differentiate easements from other third party rights such as covenants and leases;
- explain how and when easements may be created;
- identify and distinguish between types of easements and their methods of creation in order to solve multi-issue problems;
- predict whether an easement is likely to be enforceable against a new owner of the burdened land, developing your understanding of this area from the principles studied in **Part I**.

8.1 Introduction

An easement is a right that is attached to one piece of land and imposes a corresponding burden on another piece of land. Easements, like covenants, can be positive or negative. A positive easement is one that allows the owner of land to use the land of another in a particular way. A very common easement of this type is a right of way. The majority of easements are positive. A negative easement is one that restricts the use of another person's land in some way. An example of a negative easement is a right to light, since this can prevent the other person erecting a building on their land if this might significantly reduce the amount of light enjoyed through the windows of a building that benefits from the right. Negative easements are limited in practice.

You cannot simply go on to your neighbours' land without having a right, or the neighbours' permission, to do so. To enter upon a person's land without having any authority amounts to trespass to land. Your neighbours would be able to sue you. If your child kicks a football over the fence into the neighbours' garden, you cannot insist that you have a legal right to enter the garden to retrieve the ball. You have to go and ask your neighbours for permission to do so. Such permission is known as a licence, which we briefly encountered in **Chapters 1** and **5**. Although there are different kinds of licence, a licence of this sort allows only temporary access on to the land. The neighbours do not have to give you permission and they can withdraw the permission at any time. There is no question of them granting you and your successors in title a right of access at all times. Clearly a licence is all that you need if you merely wish to retrieve a ball from the neighbours' garden. You do not want a proprietary right. You hope that the ball is not going to be kicked over the fence that often; but if it is, and the neighbours refuse permission, all is not lost – you simply go out and buy a new ball.

However, there may be situations where you are going to need much more than a licence. You may need to take away some of your neighbours' freedom of control over their property by acquiring a proprietary right over it. For example, you want to build a garage at the bottom of your garden, but the only way you can obtain vehicular access to it is if your neighbours allow you to cross the bottom of their garden. You know that you cannot simply drive across the neighbours' land as to do so without their agreement amounts to trespass. However, if you obtain their permission each time, you will have a licence and will not be a trespasser. Asking your neighbours for permission each time you want to cross their land would be very inconvenient for all concerned. You could, of course, get them to grant you a licence that allows you to cross the land without seeking permission each time. However, as all a licence does is to confer permission, such permission may be revoked. If you quarreled with your neighbours, they would be very likely to revoke it. If your neighbours were to move, you have seen that a licence gives you no proprietary interest in the land. The new owners, therefore, come to the property with all their rights over it intact. You will have to ask them if they will give you the same permission that the previous owners gave you. You have no guarantee that they will. When you come to sell your house, the buyers are going to ask if you have a permanent right of access to your garage. They will not be happy with a licence that may be terminated at any time. The effect of ending the licence is that you have a garage that you can no longer use as a garage because you cannot gain access to it.

Before you incur costs in building the garage, you will want to be sure that your land enjoys a permanent right over your neighbours' land for you to gain such access. You will want to be able to exercise this right over your neighbours' land no matter to whom they sell it. You will also want to pass the benefit of the right to any person who buys your house. You will, in short, want your neighbours to grant you an easement.

We have now looked at two very simple situations involving access over land: one involving a licence, the other an easement. We now need to look at the essential characteristics of an easement.

8.2 Essential characteristics of an easement

You will need to distinguish an easement from other rights such as covenants and licences. What are the characteristics that the law considers essential to the existence of an easement? In *Re Ellenborough Park* [1956] Ch 131, the purchasers of plots of land surrounding Ellenborough Park were given a right to use the park for recreational purposes. A subsequent owner of the park wished to build on it, and the surrounding owners brought the case to assert that their rights were easements which would prevent the proposed development.

The Court of Appeal accepted that the rights to use the park were legal easements and set out four characteristics necessary for a valid easement:

(a) There must be a dominant and a servient tenement, that is to say, you must have two parcels of land, one of which has the benefit of the easement and the other of which has the burden of it.

(b) An easement must 'accommodate' the dominant tenement.

(c) The dominant and servient tenements must not be owned and occupied by the same person.

(d) A right over land cannot amount to an easement unless it is capable of forming the subject matter of a grant.

We will now look in more detail at these characteristics, taking each one in turn.

8.2.1 The need for a dominant and servient tenement

An easement can only exist if it is attached to (or appurtenant to) the dominant land. It is therefore essential that there is an identifiable dominant and servient tenement in existence at the time of the grant. Land having the benefit of the easement is referred to as the dominant tenement, and land having the burden of the easement is referred to as the servient tenement.

Example

A owns Redacre and B owns Blueacre. B grants to A, by deed, a permanent right to cross Blueacre, using a defined route. This is, therefore, more than just a temporary permission that would be given by a licence. A and A's successors in title have a right of way at all times over Blueacre as shown in the diagram below.

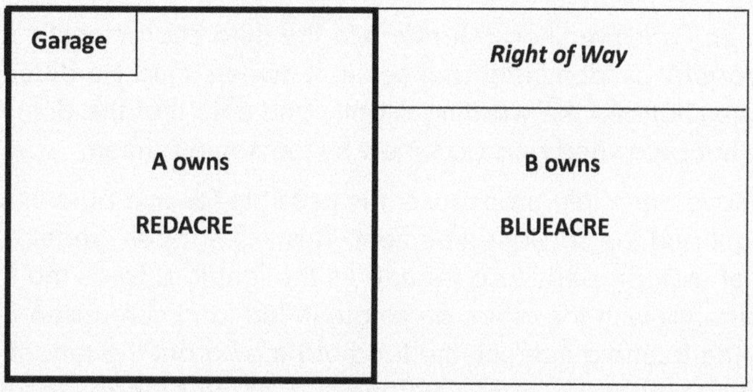

Does the right granted by B to A satisfy the first of the four requirements?

There are two separate pieces of land. Redacre has the benefit of a right of way over Blueacre. Redacre is, therefore, the dominant tenement. Blueacre is subject to a right of way. Blueacre is a servient tenement. The first requirement is therefore satisfied.

Another way of expressing the need for a dominant and a servient tenement is to say that you cannot have an easement in gross, that is without owning any land which is capable of benefiting from the right. Lord Cairns made it clear in *Rangeley v Midland Railway Co* (1868) 3 Ch App 306, that 'there can be no easement properly so called unless there be both a servient and a dominant tenement'. He went on to say that 'there can be no such thing according to our law ... as an easement in gross'. Any attempt to create an easement without an identifiable dominant tenement will create a licence only.

Example

Using the same facts as above, if the right had been granted by B not to A, but to C who was not the owner of any land, then this requirement would not have been satisfied as, because C owns no land, there can be no dominant tenement. C can only claim to have permission to cross B's land. This means that as long as the permission lasts, C may cross the land without being regarded as a trespasser. C therefore has a licence.

8.2.2 The easement must accommodate, or benefit, the dominant tenement

What amounts to a benefit to land? In *Re Ellenborough Park*, Mr Cross (counsel for the appellant) submitted it was not enough to show that the right enhanced the value of the dominant tenement. The person claiming the right had to show that it was connected with the normal enjoyment of the property. The Court agreed with his submission. Whether there is a connection between a right and the normal enjoyment of property is a question of fact.

Thus, as well as having a dominant and a servient tenement, you can see that the right enjoyed by the dominant tenement has to be one which you can say not only enhances the owner's enjoyment of their land, but also is sufficiently connected with that land. As Byles J remarked in *Bailey v Stephens* (1862) 12 CB (NS) 91 at 115: 'A right of way over land in Northumberland cannot accommodate land in Kent.'

8.2.3 The dominant and servient tenements must not be both owned and occupied by the same person

In *Re Ellenborough Park*, Evershed MR refers to the third characteristic taken from *Cheshire's Modern Real Property* as 'dominant and servient owners must be different persons'. You will note that we have changed the wording slightly and said that the dominant and servient tenements must not be owned and occupied by the same person.

The reason we have done this is because it is possible for one person to own an estate in both the dominant and the servient tenement. This will happen where a landlord grants a lease of part of their property to a tenant. As the landlord owns the freehold reversion, each has, concurrently with the other, an estate in the land comprised in the lease. However, despite owning the freehold interest, the landlord may grant the tenant an easement, for a term not exceeding that of the lease, over the part of the property the landlord retains.

For example, a tenant has a lease of office premises on the top floor of an office block. The only way to reach the offices is by using a lift or stairs. The tenant will, therefore, require an easement. Although the landlord owns the whole block, it is not owned and occupied in its entirety by the same person. Thus, the third requirement is met and it is possible for the landlord to grant the tenant an easement over a part of the building that is not comprised in the tenancy.

At this stage, it is helpful to look at the practical application of the first three characteristics.

Example

Look at the following diagram and the explanation that follows.

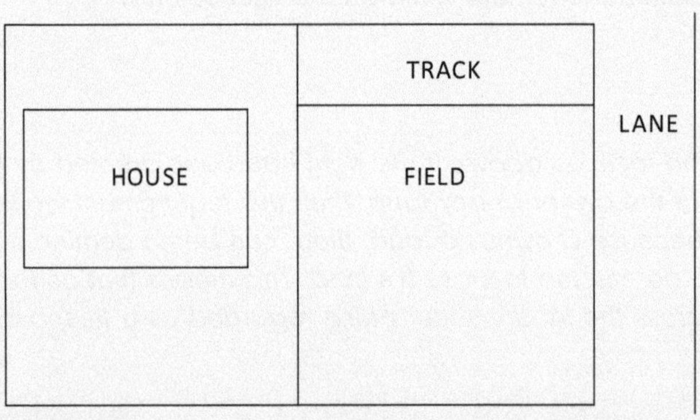

Adam owns a house and buys an adjoining field. There is a track running across the field leading to a lane. Adam uses the track as a shortcut to the lane. Is this right to cross the field capable of being an easement?

The first requirement is that there are two pieces of land: a dominant tenement benefiting from the right and a servient tenement which is subject to the right. That situation exists here.

The second requirement is for the right to accommodate or benefit the dominant tenement. Clearly it does so here.

Moving to the third requirement, Adam owns and occupies both pieces of land. There can, therefore, be no easement.

Any acts Adam does on the one which are of benefit to the other, Adam does because he is the owner of both. He cannot give himself a right of way over his own land; he already has all the rights he needs because he is the owner.

The nature of the right in this example is such that, if someone else owned the field, it could be an easement. This is known as a quasi-easement. Quasi-easements, as you will discover later (see **8.3.2.2**), become important if (in this example) Adam should sell his house but retain ownership of the field, though not vice versa.

And so, to the fourth and final characteristic.

8.2.4 The right must be capable of forming the subject matter of a grant

The fourth characteristic is that the right must be one capable of being granted by deed. To answer this question, the first consideration is if there is a capable grantor and a capable grantee. For there to be a capable grantor, the person who grants the right must have the power to do so. If the grantor is, for example, a company that by its constitution has not been given any power to grant easements, it cannot be a capable grantor and any rights it purports to grant cannot be easements.

The requirement that there must be a capable grantee means that the person to whom the right is granted must be capable of receiving it. You cannot grant a right to the inhabitants of a village, since they are a vague and fluctuating body. The inhabitants of a village may have rights such as the right to use the village green, but these are customary rights and not easements.

However, there are other features of the fourth characteristic that need to considered in more detail. Three further questions were set out in *Re Ellenborough Park* as being relevant to determine this issue:

(i) whether the rights are expressed in language which is too wide and vague;

(ii) whether such rights would amount to rights of joint occupation, or substantially deprive the park owners of proprietorship or legal possession; and

(iii) whether such rights would constitute mere rights of recreation, possessing no quality of utility or benefit.

Each of these questions is considered at **8.2.4.1–8.2.4.3** below.

8.2.4.1 When does a right become too vague to constitute an easement?

Is it possible to have a right to a view? When does a right become too vague? Where do you draw the line?

Lord Brougham LC, in the case of *Keppel v Bailey* [1834] 2 My & K 517, voiced his opposition to the law recognising 'incidents of a novel kind'. However, other judges were not as opposed to change. In *Dyce v Lady James Hay* (1852) 1 Macq 305, Lord St Leonards remarked that 'the category of ... easements must alter and expand with the changes that take place in the circumstances of mankind'.

Today, many people have a television set and a car. Whether a picture is received on the television screen may depend on signals reaching it from a transmitter. The signals have to cross other people's land. Do you have a right to stop a person putting up a building on their land if that would interfere with your reception? If they do erect a building, can you claim damages for interference with an 'easement'? When you get home in the evening, you need to have somewhere to park your car. Is it possible to be granted an easement to park? Let us now look at these practical questions.

The House of Lords in *Hunter v Canary Wharf Ltd* [1997] 2 WLR 684 referred to the distinction, drawn by Lord Blackburn in *Dalton v Angus* (1881) 6 App Cas 740, between a right to a view and rights such as those of light, air and support. Lord Blackburn considered that a right to a view imposed a burden on 'a very large and indefinite area'. Imagine that you live in a mansion that has been owned by your family for centuries. It is set in the heart of unspoilt countryside and you enjoy a splendid view for miles around. If the law were to allow you to claim a right to the view, then the effect would be to sterilise the use of the surrounding land because you could prevent a building being erected that might spoil the view.

(Note: When you looked at restrictive covenants, you saw that if you sell part of your land, it may be possible to protect a view by the indirect method of imposing a restrictive covenant on the buyer not to build on the land that you have sold.)

However, if you have a house with windows overlooking your neighbours' land, the law does recognise that you may have a right to the passage of light to the windows. An easement of light may be acquired via a defined channel or aperture because you have enjoyed the passage of light for a long period. If your neighbours build so close to your house that the degree of light you receive through the windows is adversely affected, you may have a claim against the neighbours for interference with that easement. Unlike a view, access of light to a window can be defined with some precision. Furthermore, the effect of the claim is far more limited in that access of light to a window will only be affected by erecting a building in very close proximity to the window. Claiming an easement of light will, therefore, affect only your immediate neighbour, and the neighbour is able to appreciate that the building may diminish the amount of light coming through your windows. A person building some distance away may well fail to appreciate that they are interfering with someone's view. To allow a person to claim a right to a view would lead to far greater difficulty in assessing the extent of the right than is the case with a right to light.

In *Hunter v Canary Wharf*, the court decided that a person erecting a building has no means of knowing precisely what its effect will be on television reception. Not only that, but the effect is not simply confined to buildings in the immediate neighbourhood. This would impose an immense burden on a person wishing to build on their land. They could be sued by 'an indeterminate number of [claimants], each claiming compensation in a relatively modest amount'. In addition, there are usually safeguards in the planning system that give people likely to be affected by the development of land an opportunity to raise objections. In this case, the problem was also a temporary one as the BBC brought a relay transmitter into service and aerials were aligned to the new transmitter.

It is clear from *Hunter v Canary Wharf* that the courts will not allow an unlimited number of rights to exist as easements. However, the decision of *Regency Villas v Diamond Resorts* (see **8.2.4.3** below) demonstrates that the categories of rights capable of constituting easements remain open to further expansion, but, as far as negative easements are concerned, the list may well be closed. In the case of *Phipps v Pears* [1965] 1 QB 76, the court refused to recognise as an easement the right for a wall of a detached house to enjoy protection from the weather from the wall of an adjoining house. Such an easement would have been a negative one because it would have prevented the neighbour from demolishing their own house. Lord Denning considered that negative easements had to be viewed with caution, as they could prevent a neighbour from enjoying their land to the full and would mean they would not be free to carry out legitimate development. An example of a negative easement which the courts have accepted is a right to light. However, such a right must be through a specific aperture, eg window, and cannot be a general right to light (*Colls v Home & Colonial Stores Ltd* [1904] AC 179).

8.2.4.2 When does a right amount to possession?

Another limitation that is placed on what can amount to an easement concerns the question of the extent to which the owner of land is excluded from using the land themselves.

In *Copeland v Greenhalf* [1952] Ch 488, the claimant owned an orchard and a strip of land leading to the orchard from the road. The defendant and his father before him, who were wheelwrights, had used part of the claimant's strip of land for more than 50 years to store their customers' vehicles. The defendant claimed that he had acquired an easement by long use, ie prescription (see **8.3.3** below). The court held that, as there was no limit placed on the number of vehicles that could be stored on the strip of land nor on the length of time for which they could be stored, the effect was to exclude the claimant owner. This was not a claim for an easement, therefore, but for possession of the land.

The question of the degree of exclusion of the owner is very relevant in the case of a claim to a right to park a motor vehicle.

In *London & Blenheim Estates Ltd v Ladbroke Retail Parks Ltd* [1992] 1 WLR 1278, the claimant asserted that the right for its customers to park in a car park was a valid easement.

Judge Paul Baker QC (at p 1287) said:

> ... That leaves the main point under this head, whether the right to park cars can exist at all as an easement. I would not regard it as a valid objection that charges are made, whether for the parking itself or for the general upkeep of the park. The essential question is one of degree. If the right granted in relation to the area over which it is to be exercisable is such that it would leave the servient owner without any reasonable use of his land, whether for parking or anything else, it could not be an easement though it might be some larger or different grant. The rights sought in the present case do not appear to approach anywhere near that degree of invasion of the servient land. If that is so – and I emphasise that I have not gone into the facts – I would regard the right claimed as a valid easement ...

The main issue in arriving at the decision that the right was a valid easement was that the court considered it to be a question of degree. The right would not be an easement if the effect of it was to leave the servient owner without any reasonable use of his land.

In *Bachelor v Marlow* [2003] 1 WLR 764, the defendants, who serviced and repaired cars at nearby garage premises, parked cars on a strip of land which was later acquired by the claimant. The defendants claimed a right to park as an easement.

Tuckey LJ stated:

> ... I return to the question which has to be answered in this case. Does an exclusive right to park six cars for 9½ hours every day of the working week leave the plaintiff without any reasonable use of his land, whether for parking or anything else?

> Miss Williamson emphasised the fact that the right asserted is exclusive of all others, including the plaintiff. Car parking over the whole of the land is highly intrusive because no other use can be made of it when cars are parked on it. In practice it prevents the plaintiff from making any use of his land and makes his ownership of it illusory.
>
> Not so, said Mr West. Mathematically the defendants only have use of the land for 47½ hours per week, whereas the plaintiff has 120½ hours. He suggested various uses which the plaintiff could make of the land. He could sell it to the defendants or charge them for using it outside business hours, if that is what they wanted. Outside those hours he could park on the land himself or charge others for doing so. He would be able to concrete over the surface of the land without interfering with the right.
>
> ... The plaintiff could of course park himself at night or the weekends but the commercial scope for getting others to pay for doing so must be very limited indeed. I cannot see how the plaintiff would benefit from concreting over the land, although this would certainly enhance the defendants' right.
>
> If one asks the simple question: 'Would the plaintiff have any reasonable use of the land for parking?' the answer, I think, must be 'No'. He has no use at all during the whole of the time that parking space is likely to be needed. But if one asks the question whether the plaintiff has any reasonable use of the land for any other purpose, the answer is even clearer. His right to use his land is curtailed altogether for intermittent periods throughout the week. Such a restriction would, I think, make his ownership of the land illusory ...

Tuckey LJ considered that the exclusive right to park six cars for nine and a half hours every day was so extensive a right as to leave the appellants without any reasonable use of their land. It was, therefore, too extensive a right to amount to an easement.

Qualifications to the test in Bachelor v Marlow

The test established in *Bachelor v Marlow* was criticised by Lord Scott in *Moncrieff v Jamieson* [2007] UKHL 42. Lord Scott expressed the view that the question of whether a right would leave the servient owner with no 'reasonable use' needed some qualification.

Lord Scott noted that where rights to park were granted, the servient owner still retained the ability to build above or under the parking area, or to place advertising hoardings on the walls. Lord Scott went on to state: 'I do not see why a landowner should not grant rights of a servitudal character over his land to any extent that he wishes.'

Rejecting the test in *Bachelor v Marlow*, Lord Scott suggested it be substituted with a test which asks whether the servient owner retains possession and, subject to the reasonable exercise of the right in question, control of the servient land.

Lord Neuberger concurred with the views expressed by Lord Scott, stating that 'a right can be an easement notwithstanding that the dominant owner effectively enjoys exclusive occupation, on the basis that the essential requirement is that the servient owner retains possession and control'.

8.2.4.3 When is a right a 'mere right of recreation', and when is it capable of being an easement?

The decision of the Supreme Court in *Regency Villas Title Ltd v Diamond Resorts (Europe) Ltd* [2018] UKSC 57 reaffirmed that the class of potential easements is not closed. This case established that an easement could exist to use a golf course, swimming pool or a tennis court.

In *Regency Villas Title Ltd v Diamond Resorts (Europe) Ltd*, Regency Villas was the freehold proprietor of land. Regency's predecessor in title had purchased the land and constructed 26 timeshare apartments. In the transfer to Regency's predecessor in title, an entry was made on the property register stating that the land had the right to use the swimming pool, golf course, squash courts, tennis courts, gardens and any other sporting or recreational facilities on the transferor's adjoining estate.

There was no issue with elements (i) and (ii) of *Re Ellenborough Park*: there was a dominant and servient tenement and the land was in separate ownership. Turning to limb (iii), the court was satisfied that the right to use the facilities was connected with, and part of, the normal enjoyment of the dominant land and should therefore be regarded as 'accommodating' that land.

The key issue, therefore, concerned the question of whether the rights were capable of forming the subject matter of a grant. At first instance, Judge Purle concluded that the rights were not excessively wide or vague; they clearly extended to all recreational and sporting facilities on the adjoining land. All that remained was the question of whether the rights failed as easements because they amounted to 'mere rights of recreation'.

On this point, it was noted that *Re Ellenborough Park* was authority for the proposition that an easement allowing the dominant owner to walk over all parts of the servient tenement purely for pleasure could exist in law. That being the case, it was held to be 'a relatively small step' to extend such rights to the enjoyment of sporting and other recreational facilities.

Judge Purle noted that there was no precedent determining whether or not an easement could exist to use a golf course, swimming pool or tennis court. However, he concluded that there was 'no legal impediment to the grant of such an easement, provided the intention to grant an easement, as opposed to a merely personal right, is evident on the proper construction of the grant construed in the light of the material surrounding circumstances'.

In the context of the rights granted to the timeshare apartments, there was:

- no reason why an easement could not be granted for recreational purposes;
- no compelling reason to construe the rights as personal; and
- very good reason for construing them as easements.

On appeal to the Supreme Court, the majority (Lord Carnwarth dissenting) held that the trial judge's interpretation of the law and facts had been correct. The Court concluded (per Lord Briggs):

> Whatever may have been the attitude in the past to 'mere recreation or amusement', recreational and sporting activity of the type exemplified by the facilities at Broome Park is so clearly a beneficial part of modern life that the common law should support structures which promote and encourage it, rather than treat it as devoid of practical utility or benefit.

Lord Briggs added that '[w]here the actual or intended use of the dominant [land] is itself recreational, as will generally be the case for holiday timeshare developments, the accommodation condition [in *Ellenborough Park*] will generally be satisfied'. He also commented that '[i]t is to my mind plain beyond a doubt ... that the grant of rights to use an immediately adjacent leisure development with all its recreational and sporting facilities is of service, utility and benefit to the timeshare apartments ...'.

Accordingly, following this case, the use of leisure facilities can amount to a binding property right and is not restricted to existing as personal contractual rights.

Now that you are aware of the characteristics of an easement, we need to discover how easements are created.

8.3 Methods of creation of easements

8.3.1 Acquisition of an easement by express grant or reservation

This is where the owners of two neighbouring pieces of land agree that one of them is to have an easement over the land of the other. They have clearly expressed their wish to create the easement and, provided they follow the correct procedure, the easement has been *expressly* granted. You have already encountered the procedures necessary to create a legal easement in **Chapter 1** and we will be considering them again later in this chapter.

The most usual situation in which the express grant of an easement is encountered is where a person sells part of the land they own. In this situation that person may also wish to retain rights over the land that they are selling. Where this occurs, we speak of the reservation and not the granting of an easement. There is no reason, however, why an easement cannot be granted independently of a sale of land.

8.3.2 Acquisition of easements by implied grant or reservation

In an ideal world, all easements would be expressly granted or reserved. By looking at a deed (unregistered title) or entries on the register of title (registered title), you should be able to establish what easements benefit a property and to what easements a property is subject. However, unfortunately, this is not always the case and implied easements may be created, without any formality, on a sale of part. They are deemed legal easements, as they are implied into the deed used to transfer the legal estate on the sale of part.

The rules on implied easements provide that, after a *sale of part* of their land, a *seller* will have the right to exercise, over the land sold to the buyer:

(a) easements of strict necessity; and

(b) easements implied due to the common intention of the buyer and seller at the time of the sale.

The *buyer*, on the other hand, will have the right to exercise, over the land retained by the seller:

(a) easements of strict necessity;

(b) easements implied due to the common intention of the buyer and seller at the time of the sale;

(c) easements created under the rule in *Wheeldon v Burrows* (1879) 12 ChD 31; and

(d) easements created under s 62 of the Law of Property Act (LPA) 1925.

We are going to look at all these methods by which implied easements can be created.

8.3.2.1 Easements of strict necessity and common intention

As mentioned, these apply to grants and reservations of easements.

Easements implied by necessity would arise on the sale of a landlocked parcel of land. The circumstances in which the law is willing to imply the grant/reservation of an easement of necessity are extremely limited:

> In my opinion, an easement of necessity means an easement without which the property retained cannot be used at all, and not merely necessary to the reasonable enjoyment of the property. (*Union Lighterage v London Graving Dock Company* [1902] 2 Ch 557)

A claim for an easement of necessity would, therefore, be defeated if there was an alternative means of access, even if that alternative access was dangerous.

An easement of necessity can only be used for those purposes for which the dominant tenement was being used at the necessity arose, ie at the date of the grant/transfer (*London Corporation v Riggs* [1880] 13 Ch D 798).

Easements by common intention arise if the parties intend that the land is to be used in a particular way; then any easements that are required to enable it to be used in that way will be implied into the sale of part deed.

Example

A client comes to see you about their business. They run a successful restaurant from the basement of a large building in the centre of the local town. As the business has expanded, they have encountered serious problems in ventilating the kitchen area and now need to put up an air duct on the rear of the building to carry used air away.

The premises are held under a lease, which was assigned to the client two years ago. The lease contains tenant covenants not to cause a nuisance, to control and eliminate all food smells and to comply with all relevant food hygiene regulations. Your client has approached their landlord for permission to erect the duct on the back wall of the building, as required by the local hygiene inspector, but the landlord has refused.

These are essentially the facts in the case of *Wong v Beaumont Property Trust Ltd* [1965] 1 QB 173. In this case, Lord Denning MR stated:

> The question is: Has the plaintiff a right to put up this duct without the landlord's consent? If he is to have any right at all, it must be by way of easement and not merely by way of implied contract. He is not the original lessee, nor are the defendants the original lessors. Each is a successor in title. As between them, a right of this kind, if it exists at all, must be by way of an easement. In particular, an easement of necessity.
>
> ... It was not realised by the parties, at the time of the lease, that this duct would be necessary. But it was in fact necessary from the very beginning. That seems to me sufficient to bring the principle into play. In order to use this place as a restaurant, there must be implied an easement, by the necessity of the case, to carry a duct up this wall. The county court judge so held. He granted a declaration. I agree with him.

The right to erect the duct on the side of the building is capable of being an easement. As there appears to be no express easement in the lease itself, your client must look elsewhere for a remedy. As their lease is for part only of the building (the basement), this qualifies as a sale of part and so the implied methods of creating an easement may apply.

They have derived title from an earlier tenant under the lease (the 'buyer' on the original lease of part) and so you can consider all four possible implied methods of creation. Reading Lord Denning's comments in the *Wong* case, it seems that an implied easement by strict necessity is the most likely option. An easement of *strict necessity* arises where, without it, no use can be made of the land. This is the case here, as to comply with the terms of the lease your client must ensure proper ventilation. They cannot run the restaurant without an easement allowing them to erect the duct on the landlord's wall.

You could also argue that the original parties to the lease had the shared intention that the basement be used as a restaurant and so an easement by *common intention* (an 'intended' easement) was also implied.

8.3.2.2 The rule in *Wheeldon v Burrows*

This applies only to the grant of an easement and not a reservation.

In the case of *Wheeldon v Burrows*, Thesiger LJ identified an important general rule, allowing a buyer on a sale of part to acquire an implied easement over the retained land of a seller where no express provision has been made. He said that the buyer would get such an easement if the right was:

(a) continuous;

(b) apparent;

(c) necessary for the reasonable enjoyment of the land; and

(d) being used as a 'quasi-easement' by the seller for the benefit of the part of the land being sold at the time of the sale of part.

Taking each of these elements in turn:

Continuous and apparent

This denotes some form of habitual enjoyment obvious from an inspection of the land. Ungoed-Thomas J in *Ward v Kirkland* [1967] Ch 194 considered that the words 'continuous and apparent' required some feature to be present on the servient tenement which would be apparent on an inspection. The feature must be one that has a degree of permanence, such as drains or a path.

Necessary for the reasonable enjoyment of the land sold

The standard of necessity in *Wheeldon v Burrows* is less stringent than for an easement of necessity. The presence of an alternative right may not, necessarily, defeat a claim.

Wheeler v Saunders [1996] Ch 20

A right of way was claimed, although there was in existence an alternative means of access. The claim failed as the alternative access was just as convenient as the right claimed. Therefore, the right claimed could not be said to be necessary to the reasonable enjoyment of the land.

Millman v Ellis (1996) 71 P & CR 158

A right of way was claimed, although (as in the case above) there was in existence an alternative means of access. The alternative route was dangerous and, therefore, the claim succeeded as the right of way claimed was necessary for the reasonable enjoyment of the land in order to avoid the dangerous route.

Quasi-easement

An easement can only exist if there is a dominant and a servient tenement (see **8.2.3** above). Therefore, rights exercised by a landowner over their own land cannot be an easement. However, such rights can be described as a quasi-easement. They have the characteristics of an easement save for the fact that there is no diversity of ownership.

The rule in *Wheeldon v Burrows* will only be effective if the quasi-easement was in use at the time of the sale of the land.

Provided all of the above conditions are satisfied, the rule in *Wheeldon v Burrows* has the effect of converting a quasi-easement into a full, legal easement.

Example

Andrew owns a large house with extensive grounds ('the Property'). Several years ago, he built a cottage in the grounds ('the Cottage') which he has used to accommodate his guests. He and his guests have regularly used a track that runs across the Property in order to access the Cottage. This avoids use of a busy main road. Andrew sells the Cottage to Helen together with a right of way over the main drive. The transfer made no mention of the use of the track in the transfer deed.

Would Wheeldon v Burrows apply? Applying the criteria to the facts:

(a) The use of the track has been continuous and apparent in that it has been used regularly, and presumably the track would be visible on an inspection of the land.

(b) The right is necessary for the reasonable enjoyment of the land as it avoids a busy main road.

(c) Andrew and his guests' use of the track amounts to a quasi-easement. It has all the characteristics of an easement except a dominant and servient tenement owned or occupied by separate people.

(d) The facts suggest that the right of way over the track may have been in use at the time of the sale to Helen.

On this basis the rule in Wheeldon v Burrows would apply and the Cottage would have the benefit of a legal easement over the track running over the Property.

Note that, when a landowner sells part of their land and fails to expressly reserve any rights over the land they have sold, the landowner will not be able to claim an implied easement under the rule in *Wheeldon v Burrows* because they are not the buyer on the sale of part, ie they cannot rely on the rules in *Wheeldon v Burrows* or under s 62 of the LPA 1925 to claim an easement by implied reservation. The only methods of creation of an implied reservation of an easement are necessity and common intention (see **8.3.2.1**). Thesiger LJ stated that the rules were founded on the maxim that 'a grantor shall not derogate from his grant'. In other words, 'a grantor having given a thing with one hand is not to take away the means of enjoying it with the other' (*Birmingham, Dudley & District Banking Co v Ross* (1888) 38 Ch D 295, per Bowen LJ).

We now want to turn to s 62 of the LPA 1925, under which implied easements may also arise in favour of a buyer.

8.3.2.3 Section 62 of the Law of Property Act 1925

You may remember from **Part I** that, when dealing with land, there may be problems in defining what exactly is being transferred. This resulted in the practice of including in a conveyance a list of general words designed to ensure that everything on the land or enjoyed with it passed to the buyer. This no doubt suited the lawyers, who were paid according to the time spent preparing documents – the wordier the document, the more they were paid. However, it was not in the best interests of the client who had to pay for it. Section 62 therefore implies general words into a conveyance of land. It is not necessary to state in the conveyance that you are conveying with the land, for example, all the buildings that are on it or, indeed, any easements that exist already.

Although the purpose behind s 62 seems clear, it has been interpreted in a rather surprising way.

Section 62 clearly enables existing rights of a permanent nature, such as easements, to be passed on automatically in a conveyance of land. However, the way the section has been interpreted has meant that a person who merely has permission to use land in some way may acquire, as the result of a conveyance, an easement. In the case of *Wright v Macadam* [1949] 2 All ER 565, Mrs Wright, a tenant of property, had a mere licence to use a coal shed. However, when she was granted a new tenancy, this amounted to a conveyance of land and the general words were implied into it. As the Court of Appeal considered the right to use the shed to be one capable of being an easement, its implied inclusion in a deed effected the grant and so transformed it from being a licence into a legal easement.

In most cases where s 62 applies, there is diversity of occupation at the time of the conveyance. Remember that under s 205(1)(ii) of the LPA 1925, 'conveyance' includes the grant of a lease as well as the sale of freehold. So, the land enjoying the relevant right will usually be tenanted initially, and then either the lease is renewed, or the tenant acquires the freehold estate of that part of the land. However, there have been several recent qualifications to this rule, which are summarised at (c) below.

For the new easement to be created under s 62, the following three requirements must be considered:

(a) There must be a conveyance of part (sale of freehold of part, or legal lease of part).

(b) Prior to the conveyance of part, the 'dominant' land must have enjoyed the benefit of a licence or permission capable of being an easement. Note that the right need not be in use at the time of the conveyance, provided it was being used shortly before. So, a right to use a road to a farm that had been used up until 11 months before the conveyance still fell within s 62 (*Costagliola v English* (1969) 210 EG 1425).

(c) There was diversity of occupation at the time of the conveyance of part.

There has been considerable academic debate as to whether diversity of occupation is an essential requirement for the creation of easements under s 62.

The Court of Appeal in *Payne v Inwood* (1996) 74 P & CR 42 held that s 62 cannot operate to convert a licence into an easement unless there is diversity of occupation prior to the sale. However, the Court also recognised an exception to the rule in the earlier case of *Broomfield v Williams* [1897] 1 Ch 602, which concerned a right of light.

While diversity of occupation is required to convert a licence into an easement, it is not essential to convert continuous and apparent quasi-easements.

In *Wood v Waddington* [2014] EWHC 1358 (Ch), the High Court looked at the conflicting authorities on this question and concluded that diversity of occupation was not essential. The Court of Appeal upheld the decision of the judge at first instance that '[t]here is no absolute rule that a right of way cannot be claimed under section 62 where there has not been diversity of occupation before the relevant conveyance'.

The judge went on to state that the ultimate question was whether the right in question was 'enjoyed with' the land conveyed in such a way that the right was appurtenant to the conveyed land, as opposed to the whole of the land in common ownership.

In deciding whether the right in question was enjoyed *with* the conveyed land, 'a consideration of how the advantage was actually used and whether it was apparently for the benefit of the land conveyed and apparently a burden on the land retained' was held to be 'of great importance'.

In summary, remember that the implied methods of creation of an easement (necessity, common intention, under *Wheeldon v Burrows*, or under s 62 of the LPA 1925) only apply where a sale of part of the land has occurred.

There is one more way in which you can acquire an easement, and we now move on to it.

8.3.3 Acquisition of an easement by prescription

An easement may be acquired by what is known as prescription. In this situation there is no grant, either express or implied, and there need not be a sale of part.

Example

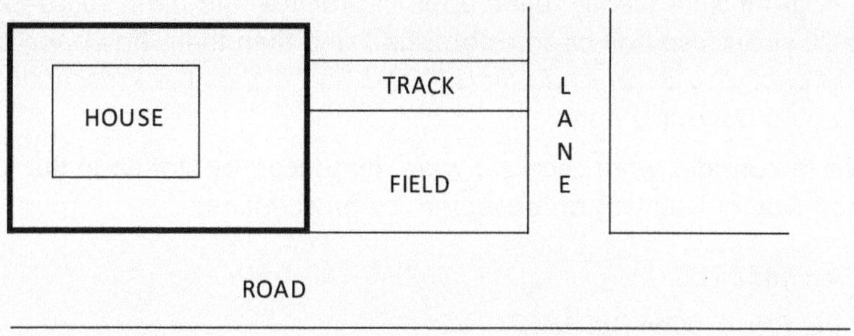

Talia owns the piece of land surrounded by the thick black line and the house on it as shown in the diagram above. Cyril owns the adjoining field. Talia begins to use a track across the field as a shortcut. If Talia is crossing Cyril's land without having any right to do so, and Cyril knows Talia is doing this and he is able to prevent it but fails to do so for a sufficiently long period, the courts will say that Cyril no longer has the right to prevent it. Cyril will be taken to have acquiesced in Talia's user and Cyril will have acquired an easement.

Generally certain conditions have to be satisfied in order for the use to qualify as an easement. These are known as the *common law conditions.*

(1) Because prescription is based on the notion of acquiescence on the part of the landowner, it is essential that the user is:

  (a) unchallenged by them (or *nec vi*, that is, without force);

  (b) exercised openly (*nec clam*, without secrecy); and

  (c) without permission (*nec precario*).

  The user must therefore be unauthorised, capable of being discovered and of a kind that can be prevented.

  The requirements that the user must be without force, without secrecy and without permission are what is meant when judges refer to the user being 'as of right'.

(2) The user must also be by a fee simple owner against a fee simple owner.

(3) It must be continuous for the requisite period of time.

Having established that if I purport to exercise a right over your land and you fail to take any steps to stop me, I will, after a period of time, become entitled to a right, you now need to know what the period of time is.

8.3.3.1 Common law and lost modern grant

In the judgment of Fox LJ in *Simmons v Dobson* [1991] 1 WLR 720, at pp 722–3, the two methods of creation of prescriptive easements are common law prescription and the doctrine of lost modern grant. At common law, where a person claimed a right by long user, the claim had to be based on the presumption that such a right had been granted and exercised since time immemorial (1189). Clearly it was virtually impossible to establish this. As a result, the courts were prepared to presume, where user had been 'as of right' for 20 years, that the use had been a continuous one since 1189. This was only a presumption, however, and it could easily be rebutted if it could be shown that the right could only have arisen some time after 1189.

Because of the difficulty with the common law, the judges developed the doctrine of lost modern grant. This was based on a pure fiction. Where user had been made for 20 years, it was assumed that there had been a deed granting the right but that the deed had been lost.

Although the basic common law claim is not often successful, the claim based on the doctrine of lost modern grant is frequently relied upon in practice and often succeeds. It is particularly useful where 20 years' use has been established and then there has been a break in the use (see *Mills and another v Silver and others* [1991] Ch 271), as the Prescription Act (PA) 1832 (see below) would not apply here.

We now need to consider what changes were introduced by statute in the 19th century. These provide a third way of claiming an easement by prescription.

8.3.3.2 Prescription Act 1832

Section 2 of the Prescription Act 1832

At common law, it was quite easy to defeat a claim to have acquired a right by prescription. All that had to be done was to show that enjoyment must have begun at some time after 1189. Section 2 of the PA 1832 prevents a common law claim to a non-light easement by prescription being defeated in this way where the easement has been enjoyed without interruption for a full period of 20 years. The section does not, however, prevent the claim to an easement being defeated in some other way, for example by showing that oral or written consent to the use was given at any time, as the common law conditions must still be satisfied (see **8.3.3** above).

Where the right claimed is one that has been enjoyed for a full period of 40 years then it becomes 'absolute and indefeasible' unless it can be shown that its enjoyment depends on some express written consent.

Section 4 of the Prescription Act 1832

Section 4 of the PA 1832 qualifies s 2 in two respects:

(1) It requires the 20- and 40-year periods to be 'next before some suit or action'. This means that, first, no right to an easement arises until a court action is brought to claim it and, secondly, the 20 or 40 years' use must be continuous right up to the date of that court action.

(2) This section also states that any interruption to the enjoyment of the right being claimed is ignored, unless the person making the claim allows it to continue for a year after becoming aware of both the interruption and of the person who is responsible for the interruption. (An interruption is any action which interferes with the right being claimed.)

So you now see that there are three ways in which you can claim an easement by prescription. First, you may use the PA 1832. In order to succeed you must show that your user was for at least 20 years immediately prior to the commencement of the court action. Secondly, you may still use the common law method and claim user from time immemorial. However, the weakness with this method is that if it can be shown that the right could not have existed before 1189, you will fail. The final method is to claim you have enjoyed the right for more than 20 years and that the doctrine of lost modern grant applies.

The PA 1832 has been described as 'a classic example of an incompetent attempt to reform the law', as it was intended to replace the common law and lost modern grant methods but has not.

So far, the easements we have looked at have all involved making some use of another person's land, such as using it as a means of access. The type of easement acquired in this way is a positive easement. As you saw in **8.1**, however, it is also possible for an easement to be negative. We gave you as an example of a negative easement the right to light. We will now consider how a right to light is acquired by prescription.

Section 3 of the Prescription Act 1832

As we saw above, s 2 of the PA 1832 lays down two periods for the acquisition of an easement other than an easement of light: a 20-year period and a 40-year period. It is only where the right has been enjoyed for 40 years without written consent that it is deemed absolute and indefeasible. Under s 3, however, in the case of an easement of light, there is only one period, that of 20 years. If the access and use of light has been enjoyed for this period without interruption and without written consent, it becomes absolute and indefeasible. Rights of light can be acquired only in respect of buildings.

To establish a claim to a right of light under the PA 1832, the claimant must show not only that there is access of light, but also that there is use being made of it. Unlike other easements, the user does not have to be as of right. All that need be shown is that the use has been enjoyed for 20 years without interruption next before action (see s 4 above) and without written consent. The statute gives no guidance, however, as to the amount of light to which the dominant tenement is entitled. This is a matter for the courts to decide, and they have held that the entitlement is to 'sufficient light according to the ordinary notions of mankind for the comfortable use and enjoyment ... or for the beneficial use and occupation of [the building]' (*Colls v Home & Colonial Stores Ltd* [1904] AC 179 per Lord Lindley, citing the doctrine as stated in *City of London Brewery Co v Tennant* (1873) LR 9 Ch App 212). Each case will be decided on its own facts, as there is no rule of law that a window must receive a certain amount of light. An important factor to take into account is the extent of the burden on the servient land.

(A right to light may also be claimed using the common law or lost modern grant methods, but, for both, the common law conditions must *all* be satisfied.)

In 2014 the Law Commission ('Rights to Light', Law Com No 356) made recommendations to make it easier to prevent rights to light from being created by prescription and to give power to the Lands Chamber of the Upper Tribunal to discharge or modify obsolete or unused rights to light. However, the Law Commission did not recommend that rights to light gained by prescription should be abolished.

8.4 Enforceability against third parties

Where the dominant tenement is sold after creation of the easement, the benefit of the easement will pass automatically to the new owner by virtue of s 62 of the LPA 1925 and its 'word-saving' effect (see **8.3.2.3**). Where the servient land has been sold since the date of creation of the easement, it is necessary to consider whether the easement is enforceable against the new owner.

In order to assess enforceability, the starting point is to consider the type of easement involved.

Legal easements

As you will recall, first, to be capable of being a legal easement, the right must comply with s 1(2)(a) of the LPA 1925. Section 1(2)(a) states that the easement can be legal only if it is for a duration equivalent to an estate in fee simple absolute in possession or a term of years absolute. This means that the duration of the easement must be forever (corresponding to a freehold estate) or for a fixed period of time (corresponding to a leasehold estate).

Secondly, to be a legal easement, the right must be created by the correct formalities. Section 52 of the LPA 1925 states that a legal interest must be created by deed. A deed is defined in s 1 of the Law of Property (Miscellaneous Provisions) Act (LP(MP)A) 1989 as a document which describes itself as a deed and is correctly signed, witnessed and delivered.

If both of these requirements are satisfied, the right is capable of being a valid expressly created legal easement (subject to one further condition if title to the land in question is registered - see below).

Note: All easements created by implication on a sale of part or by prescription are deemed to be legal as well. They are treated differently from expressly created easements in the registered system.

Equitable easements

It is important to distinguish between the formalities required to create an equitable easement and those required for equity to recognise an easement as an estate contract.

Express creation of an equitable easement

An expressly created equitable easement may arise if s 1(2)(a) of the LPA 1925 is not satisfied, for example if an easement is granted for an uncertain period, say 'until the servient land is sold'. An easement for an uncertain duration can only ever be equitable. The formalities for the creation of an equitable easement are that it must be in writing, signed by the party creating it (the grantor) in accordance with s 53(1)(a) of the LPA 1925.

An easement that takes effect as an estate contract

An expressly created easement may satisfy the duration requirements in s 1(2)(a) of the LPA 1925 (being granted forever, or for a defined period), but if such an easement fails to be created by a valid deed, then it cannot take effect as an expressly created legal easement. However, if this is the case, equity will recognise the easement so long as it satisfies the formalities for a valid estate contract in s 2 of the LP(MP)A 1989. This is another application of the doctrine in *Walsh v Lonsdale* where a specifically enforceable contract will give rise to rights of an equitable character. This principle was considered in the context of leases in **Chapter 5** at **5.7**.

8.4.1 Unregistered title

Now we need to consider the differences between unregistered and registered conveyancing when it comes to creating and enforcing a legal easement.

When land is conveyed under the unregistered system, the legal estate passes immediately on completion of the transaction. If the conveyance is by deed and contains the grant of an easement, the easement takes effect immediately as a legal easement. As a legal interest, a legal easement binds the whole world irrespective of notice. This rule applies to legal easements created by implication or prescription as well. There is no distinction between the different 'types' of legal easement in the unregistered system.

Remember that an expressly created equitable easement must be registered as a Class D(iii) land charge against the name of the servient owner on the Land Charges Register. As long as this is done before the date of completion of the sale, the easement will bind the purchaser. If it is not then the easement will be void against a purchaser of the legal estate (Land Charges Act 1972, s 4).

8.4.2 Registered title

Section 27(1) of the LRA 2002 says that a disposition of a registered estate required to be completed by registration does not operate at law until the registration requirements have been met. Amongst the dispositions that are required to be completed by registration are the express grant or reservation of an interest that falls within s 1(2)(a) of the LPA 1925 (s 27(2)(d)). The express grant of an easement for an interest equivalent to a fee simple absolute in possession or a term of years absolute is, therefore, a disposition that has to be registered. Once it is registered, it will bind successive owners of the servient land. However, until completion by registration, the easement does not operate at law: there is not, as yet, a *legal* easement.

The entry relating to the burden of the easement will appear in the charges register of the title to the servient tenement (burdened land). Look at entry 2 in **Reading 4** in the **Appendix** for an example of an entry. The entry relating to the benefit of the easement will be made in the property register of title of the dominant land (benefited land).

If the easement is not registered, there is a failure to comply with an essential formality. In this situation, the easement, pending registration, is an equitable one, which itself requires registration via a notice, as an interest affecting a registered estate, to bind a purchaser.

8.4.2.1 Summary - expressly created legal easements in registered title

You now know that, in the case of registered land, for an expressly granted easement to be a legal easement, the right must be:

(a) for an estate equivalent to a fee simple absolute in possession or a term of years absolute;

(b) granted by deed; and

(c) protected by registration.

If you have complied with those requirements, your legal easement is secure. This now includes easements contained in leases, even if the leases themselves are too short in duration to require substantive registration (ie, for a term of seven years or less).

An equitable easement must be protected by a notice against the servient title in order to bind a buyer of the land, as it is an interest affecting a registered estate.

8.4.2.2 Implied and prescriptive legal easements in registered title

We have seen, however, that not all easements are created by express grant. A legal easement may be acquired by implication or by prescription. It is important to bear in mind that easements that are implied into a deed and those that are acquired by prescription (as prescription operates on the basis of a presumed grant in a deed) are, in fact, legal easements.

Easements created in this way are protected as an overriding interest under Sch 3, para 3 to the LRA 2002 as long as:

(a) the buyer has actual knowledge of the easement on the date of the transfer in their favour; or

(b) the existence of the right would have been apparent on a reasonably careful inspection of the land over which the easement is exercisable; or

(c) the person with the benefit of the easement can prove that they have exercised the right in the year prior to the sale to the buyer of the servient land.

The conditions above have been effective only since 13 October 2006, under the LRA Act 2002.

Even if an easement is protected under Sch 3, para 3, Land Registry now has powers to require disclosure of the easement on a disposition of land so that it may be entered on the register. Over time, this will act to reduce the number of implied and prescriptive easements which exist 'off the register'.

ACTIVITY 1 Implied and prescriptive easements

Lucy, the registered proprietor of an outdoor activity centre (the Centre), sold it last week to Tom. The deed made no mention of the property being subject to any easement. However, several months prior to the sale to Tom, Lucy granted by deed to her neighbour, Graham, a drainage easement across the grounds of the Centre. At the same time, she sold to another neighbour, Judith, a part of the grounds so that Judith could build a garage on it. Unfortunately, in the deed transferring the land to Judith, no mention was made of an easement, and Judith cannot gain access to it except by crossing part of the driveway to the Centre, which she has been doing since the sale.

Tom has just discovered that Graham and Judith are claiming rights over the Centre and that Roger, another neighbour, has been regularly using a pathway across the end of the grounds as a short cut to the local pub for the last 20 years.

Explain to Tom whether these interests are binding on him.

COMMENT

In each case, there is a dominant and servient tenement, the rights accommodate the dominant tenement, the dominant and servient tenements are not owned and occupied by the same persons, and the rights are capable of forming the subject matter of a grant. All the rights are therefore capable of being easements under the rules in *Re Ellenborough Park*.

Graham

Lucy has granted Graham a drainage easement. Assuming that it is for an interest equivalent to a fee simple absolute in possession or a term of years absolute, it is capable of being a legal easement (LPA 1925, s 1(2)(a)). It is an express grant made by deed, so it complies with s 52 of the LPA 1925. However, the title to the land is registered, and s 27 of the LRA 2002 states that a disposition of a registered estate, which includes the express grant of an easement (s 27(2)(d)), must be completed by registration. If it is not then it is not a legal easement and Tom will take free from it (LRA 2002, s 29).

Judith

Judith can claim an implied easement of strict necessity which arose on the sale of part (the sale of the garage land). This is a legal easement and, as it is not an express grant, it does not have to appear on the register. It will be an overriding interest under Sch 3, para 3 to the LRA 2002 as long as either:

(a) it would have been obvious to Tom on a reasonably careful inspection of the land; or

(b) Tom actually knew about it; or

(c) Judith can prove that she has exercised the right in the year prior to the sale to Tom.

Judith, therefore, is likely to be protected, as she will undoubtedly be making regular use of the driveway for access and will be able to prove this.

Roger

Assuming that Roger can establish a valid claim to a prescriptive easement, this again will be a legal easement and be overriding in the same way as Judith's easement.

If an easement has already been acquired by implication or by prescription before 13 October 2003 then this would have been overriding under the old Land Registration Act 1925. This protection will continue under the transitional provisions in Sch 12, para 9 to the LRA 2002.

Note that Sch 3, para 3 to the LRA 2002 does not protect an expressly created legal easement that has failed to be registered.

8.4.2.3 Equitable easements in registered title

An equitable easement will be created in the following circumstances:

(a) the easement complies with s 1(2) of the LPA 1925 and is not created by deed, but does satisfy the s 2 LP(MP)A 1989 formalities for contracts relating to land; or
(b) the easement is created by deed but it does not comply with s 1(2) of the LPA 1925, for example it was created for the life of the grantee; or
(c) if title to the servient land is registered, the easement should have been registered at the Land Registry as a registrable disposition but this has not been done.

In all cases, equitable easements must be created in writing. It is not possible to create an equitable easement orally.

Where the title is a registered one, an equitable easement will be an interest affecting a registered estate. It must, therefore, be protected by an entry (a notice) on the register of the servient title before the purchaser is registered as the new owner.

Note that it is not possible for a person with the benefit of an easement to claim protection as an overriding interest under Sch 3, para 2 of the LRA 2002 as the exercise of an easement is a mere user of land and not actual occupation.

You have seen the various ways in which easements may be acquired. We now need to consider how they can be terminated.

8.5 Extinguishment of easements

If the owner of a piece of land has the benefit of an easement over another's land, they do not have to retain it. They may, if they wish, expressly release it by deed. That will bring the easement to an end.

Similarly, as we have seen, it is not possible for a landowner to have an easement over their own land. Consequently, if they own the dominant tenement and purchase the servient tenement, the easements they have over the latter will cease.

The owner of the dominant tenement may also abandon an easement.

In the case of *Moore v Rawson* (1824) 3 B & C 332, a house standing on the claimant's land enjoyed a right of light to certain windows in one of its walls. The claimant's predecessor pulled the wall down and built a replacement wall without windows. Fourteen years later, the defendant built a wall facing the claimant's blank wall. The claimant, some three years after that, created a window in the blank wall and claimed that the defendant's wall was blocking his light. The court decided that the claimant's rights had been abandoned. Holroyd J considered that by demolishing the original wall containing the windows and replacing it with a wall without windows, the claimant's predecessor had caused the right to light to be extinguished. If they had indicated an intention to put windows in the replacement wall within a reasonable time, that might have been sufficient to preserve the right. However, in this case, the fact that the replacement wall had no windows in it was a strong indication that the right was being abandoned.

8.6 Problem solving strategy

Set out below is a suggested approach to problem questions:

(1) Draw a diagram to represent the pieces of land involved, the owners, changes of ownership and dates in order to clarify the facts.

For each possible easement:

(2) Identify whether the right being claimed is capable of being an easement by applying the criteria in *Re Ellenborough Park*.

(3) Consider whether the easement has been validly created – by express creation, implication on a sale of part, or by prescription.

(4) If the dominant land has been sold since the easement was created, apply s 62 of the LPA 1925 to show that the benefit of the easement passed to the new owner.

(5) If the servient land has been sold since the easement was created, decide whether the owner of the land is bound by the easement or not. To do this, work out whether the easement is legal or equitable and whether title to the servient land is registered or unregistered.

The summary below will help you to select the correct option under (3) above.

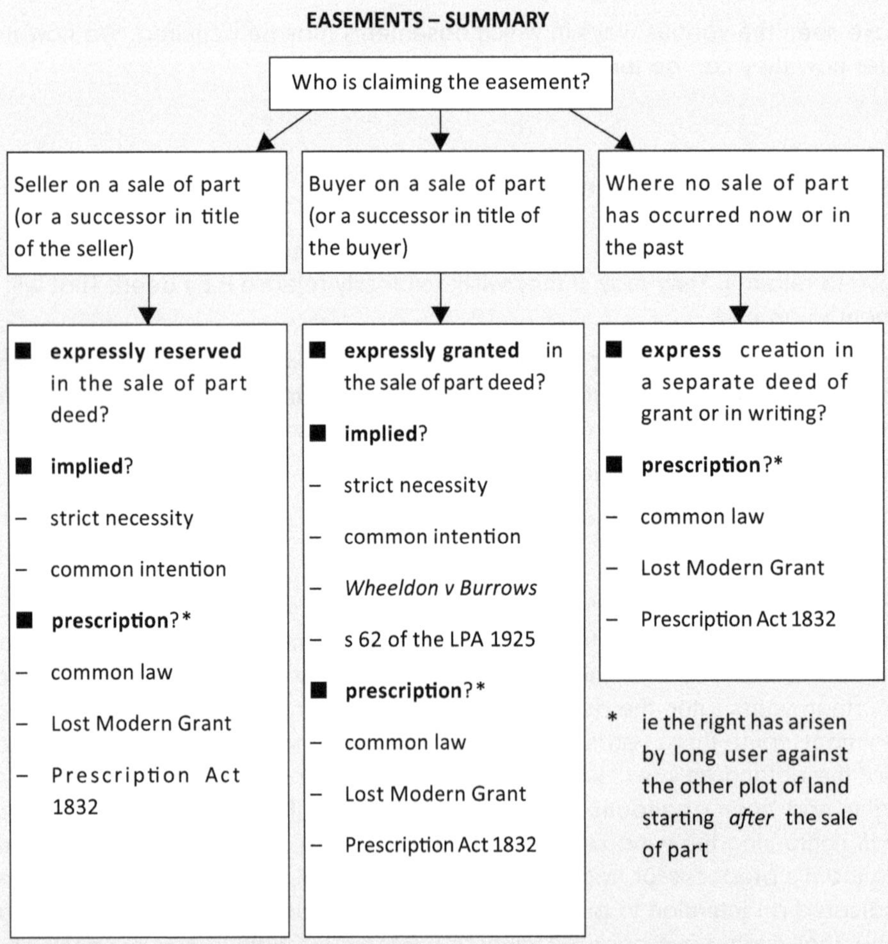

EASEMENTS – SUMMARY
Who is claiming the easement?
Seller on a sale of part (or a successor in title of the seller)
Buyer on a sale of part (or a successor in title of the buyer)
Where no sale of part has occurred now or in the past
■ expressly reserved in the sale of part deed?
■ implied?
– strict necessity
– common intention
■ prescription?*
– common law
– Lost Modern Grant
– Prescription Act 1832
■ expressly granted in the sale of part deed?
■ implied?
– strict necessity
– common intention
– Wheeldon v Burrows
– s 62 of the LPA 1925
■ prescription?*
– common law
– Lost Modern Grant
– Prescription Act 1832
■ express creation in a separate deed of grant or in writing?
■ prescription?*
– common law
– Lost Modern Grant
– Prescription Act 1832
* ie the right has arisen by long user against the other plot of land starting after the sale of part

8.7 Reform

On 8 June 2011, the Law Commission published a report on reform of the law of easements and covenants. The proposals relating to easements include replacement of the current method of implication of easements with a single statutory principle that easements will be implied where they are necessary for the reasonable use of the land at the time of the transaction. The report also proposes creating a single statutory scheme of prescription to replace the current methods.

ACTIVITY 2 Test your knowledge: easements

The aim of this activity is to allow you to practise applying some of the rules you have been studying in this chapter. Please look at the diagram, read the facts and then answer the questions that follow.

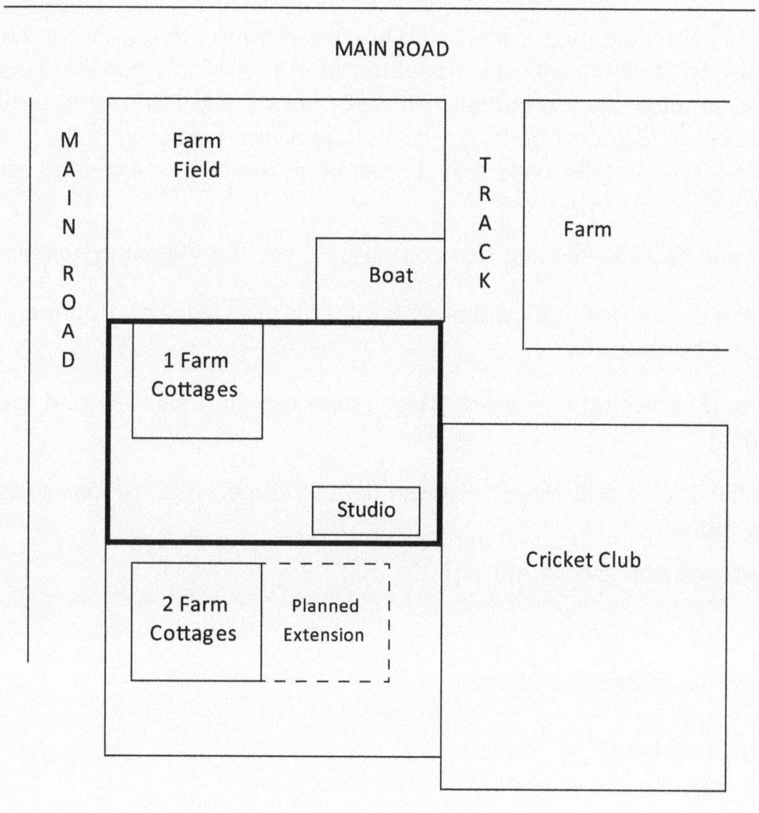

Facts

(Assume it is February 2025.)

In 1989 Adrian became the tenant of 1 Farm Cottages, shown surrounded by the thick black line in the diagram. His landlord was Duncan, the owner of the farm. Adrian is a keen sailor and had no room at 1 Farm Cottages to store his boat. Duncan agreed he could use a corner of the adjoining field for storage.

In 1993 Adrian bought the freehold of 1 Farm Cottages from Duncan. The conveyance contained no grant or reservation of any easement. Shortly afterwards, Adrian, who was finding it increasingly difficult to manoeuvre his boat across his own land and on to the main road at the front of his house, started to make use of the farm track for this purpose.

Duncan died in December 2017 and the farm passed to his nephew, Sidney. The only way in which Adrian can carry out repairs to the end wall of 1 Farm Cottages is by going on to the neighbouring field. He has done this on a number of occasions both before and after buying the freehold, having originally been given permission to do so by Duncan. Early in January 2024, as he was in the field repointing some of the brickwork, Sidney approached him and told him he had no right to be on the field. He also told Adrian that he was planning to develop the field and that Adrian would have to 'shift that boat of yours and stop using the track'. Immediately afterwards Sidney installed a gate across the track and has kept it locked ever since.

Adrian has also noticed that his other neighbour, Yasmin, who lives in number 2 Farm Cottages, is having an extension built. Adrian is a keen artist and, in April 2005, built a studio at the back of his property in a position where he could enjoy good access of light to the windows. Adrian is fearful that Yasmin's extension will interfere with the light and also spoil his view.

For the last 14 years, the local cricket club has been using the ground at the back of Adrian's property. Their cricket balls frequently land in Adrian's garden. Recently, he has been refusing to allow the members to enter his property to retrieve the balls. He now has a fine collection of 18 cricket balls. Adrian has received a letter from the club secretary demanding the return of the balls and claiming that the club has a legal right to enter Adrian's property to recover them.

Adrian comes to see you seeking advice and asks you the following questions:

(1) Can Sidney prevent him storing his boat, using the track and going on to the field to repair his property?

(2) Can he do anything to prevent Yasmin from blocking his view and taking away his light?

(3) Does the cricket club have any legal right to come on to his land to recover the cricket balls?

What answers will you give to Adrian?

COMMENT

Adrian should be advised as follows:

(1) Boat, track and field

The boat

Does the right to store the boat satisfy the criteria in *Re Ellenborough Park*? At the time of the sale of part in 1993, there was a dominant tenement (Adrian's land) and a servient tenement (Duncan's land). The right appears to accommodate Adrian's land, as a right to store a vehicle nearby would benefit anyone who owned that land. Although Duncan owns both pieces of land, Adrian is occupying the dominant land under a lease, so there is diversity of occupation. The main issue here is whether the right lies in grant.

One of the difficulties is the case of *Copeland v Greenhalf* [1952] Ch 488, in which the defendant was claiming as an easement the use of land for storing vehicles. Upjohn J considered that because the defendant could store any number of vehicles for any length of time, the right went 'wholly outside any normal idea of an easement' and amounted to a claim to joint user. This has given rise to doubts over whether it is possible to have an easement that has the effect of excluding the owner of the servient land. However, in

Wright v Macadam, Mrs Wright's use of the coal shed had the effect of excluding the use by the owner of the servient land, and in *Miller v Emcer Products Ltd* [1956] Ch 304, Romer LJ considered that exclusion of the servient owner was, to a greater or lesser extent, a feature of most easements.

The right to park cars was the subject of *London & Blenheim Estates Ltd v Ladbroke Retail Parks* [1992] 1 WLR 1278. In that case Judge Paul Baker QC held such a right could exist as an easement, at least as long as it did not 'leave the servient owner without any reasonable use of his land, whether for parking or anything else'. As Adrian's use is only of a corner of the field, it seems that there is nothing to prevent him claiming an easement.

When Adrian began to store his boat on Duncan's field, he did so with Duncan's permission. He had a mere licence. However, in 1993 Duncan conveyed the freehold to Adrian. The conveyance contained no express grant of any easement. Nevertheless, it is possible for an easement to be implied if it is an easement of necessity or an intended easement, or if the rule in *Wheeldon v Burrows* or s 62 of the LPA 1925 applies, as Adrian was a buyer on a sale of part.

Easement of strict necessity or intended easement

The storing of the boat is neither an easement of strict necessity nor an intended easement.

Wheeldon v Burrows

It will not fall within the rule in *Wheeldon v Burrows* as Duncan never exercised such a right when he owned both the farm and 1 Farm Cottages, ie there was no quasi-easement.

Section 62 of the Law of Property Act 1925

Section 62 implies words into a conveyance so that, when 1 Farm Cottages was conveyed to Adrian, the conveyance will have included all 'easements, rights and advantages ... appertaining or reputed to appertain to the land ... or, at the time of the conveyance ... enjoyed with ... the land'. In *Wright v Macadam* [1949] 2 KB 744, the Court of Appeal decided that the wording of s 62 enabled Mrs Wright, who had a mere licence to use a coal shed, to acquire an easement to do so on being granted a new tenancy of her flat. It is therefore possible for Adrian's licence to be converted into an easement as a result of s 62. However, in order for this to occur, the right must be one capable of existing in law as an easement. We saw above that this seems to be satisfied.

The only other requirement for the operation of s 62 is that there is diversity of occupation (*Long v Gowlett* [1923] 2 Ch 177; *Sovmots Investments Ltd v Secretary of State for the Environment* [1979] AC 144). Clearly there is here, as Adrian was at the time of the conveyance (sale of part) the tenant of the dominant land and Duncan was the owner of the servient land.

It appears that Adrian has the benefit of a valid easement, created by s 62 of the LPA 1925 upon the sale of part between Duncan and Adrian in 1993. However, Adrian will be able to continue to store his boat on the adjoining land only if Sidney (as successor to Duncan) is bound by that easement.

An easement created by implication is a legal easement which does not have to appear on the register of title. As it was created in 1993 it would have been an overriding interest under the pre-LRA 2002 rules. Schedule 12, para 9 to that Act provides that such protection will continue once the LRA 2002 is in force. Sidney will therefore be bound by the easement when he inherits the land from his uncle after Duncan's death in 2017 and cannot now prevent Adrian from storing his boat in the field.

Use of the track

Does the right to use the track satisfy the criteria in *Re Ellenborough Park*? When the use began, Adrian's land was the dominant tenement and Duncan's remaining land the servient tenement. A right of access appears to accommodate Adrian's land. Duncan and Adrian each own the freehold of their respective pieces of land, so there is diversity of ownership and occupation here. The right appears to lie in grant as Adrian does not have exclusive use, the parties are capable of creating the easement and it is the type of right that the courts have recognised. Therefore, the right to use the track is capable of being an easement.

Adrian's use of the track began after the conveyance to him of the freehold in 1993. The only basis on which he can claim to have an easement is by prescription.

Prescription Act 1832

In order to establish such a right under the PA 1832, Adrian's use of the track must have been 'as of right', that is he must have exercised the right without any objection having been raised, he must have done so openly and he must have done so without permission.

There is nothing to suggest that his use has not been as of right. He must have been a fee simple owner (yes) and so must the owner of the track (yes – Duncan and then Sidney owned the freehold). He will also have to show that he has been using the track for 20 years 'without interruption next before some suit or action' (s 4). He had been using the track for around 30 years when Sidney put the gate across the entrance and locked it. Had he taken action straightaway he would have been able to claim an easement under the PA 1832. However, Sidney has blocked Adrian's access and this interruption has continued for longer than a year. Adrian cannot, therefore, rely on the PA 1832.

Common law

This will not prevent Adrian falling back on the common law. He first must claim that the right has existed since time immemorial, that is, since 1189. It is obvious that it has not. However, if the right has been exercised for more than around 20 years, as here, the court will presume that it originated in a grant and that the grant has been lost. This is known as the doctrine of lost modern grant and may enable Adrian successfully to claim a right of way. That being so, he will succeed in claiming an easement by prescription under the doctrine of lost modern grant as he exercised this right against another fee simple owner and satisfied all the other common law conditions (see above).

The easement by lost modern grant would have arisen after 20 years' use of the track, ie around 2013 when Duncan was still the adjoining owner. As above, Adrian will be able to continue to use the track only if Sidney is now bound by the easement. An easement by prescription is a legal easement not requiring registration. It is overriding under the LRA 2002 rules and so protected when Sidney acquired the servient land in 2017, as for the boat easement above.

Repairs

Again, you need to consider whether the right to go onto the field to effect the repairs is capable of being an easement. The considerations here are very similar to those for the boat, above, as Adrian's use began while he was still a tenant of the cottage, with Duncan's permission. Applying the rules in *Re Ellenborough Park,* it seems that the right is a possible easement.

Wheeldon v Burrows

For the right to go on to the field to carry out repairs to have been implied under the rule in *Wheeldon v Burrows*, it must be shown to have been exercised by Duncan at the time he conveyed the freehold to Adrian. Clearly it was not, as Adrian was occupying 1 Farm Cottages at the time. Adrian will not, therefore, succeed under the rule in *Wheeldon v Burrows*.

Section 62 of the Law of Property Act 1925

However, as long as Adrian was obtaining access under the permission given by Duncan prior to the conveyance to him in 1993, he can rely on s 62 of the LPA 1925 as it was a privilege appertaining to the land. He is likely to succeed here.

Prescription

To succeed in claiming the right by prescription, Adrian would have to show not only that the right had been enjoyed for 20 years next before action, but also that it had been used 'as of right'. In view of the fact that Duncan originally gave him permission, this will prevent such a claim being successful.

(Note: Persons wishing to carry out work to their property that requires access on to a neighbour's land and who have no easement that allows them such access may now be able to gain access as a result of the Access to Neighbouring Land Act 1992. This requires an application to be made for a court order.)

Sidney will be bound by the implied easement, as for the boat above. He will not be able to stop Adrian from entering his field to do repairs.

(2) Studio

The view

In the case of the studio, Adrian will not be able to claim any right to a view, as such a right is not capable of existing as an easement.

Light

Does the right to light satisfy the criteria in *Re Ellenborough Park*? Adrian's land is the dominant tenement and Yasmin's land the servient tenement. A right of light will accommodate Adrian's land. Yasmin and Adrian occupy their respective pieces of land, so there is diversity of occupation here. The right appears to lie in grant as the parties are capable of creating the easement and it is the type of right that the courts have recognised, even though it is a negative right, so long as it is through a defined aperture (here to the studio windows). Therefore, the right to light appears to be capable of being an easement.

Adrian may be able to take action in relation to the interference with light to the studio. As the studio was built slightly less than 20 years ago, he cannot at present claim to have a right by prescription. However, any interruption not lasting for more than a year is ignored under the PA 1832. This means that if he waits until April and does not delay in bringing an action for more than a year from the start of the interruption, he will succeed under the PA 1832, s 3. If, on the other hand, Yasmin realises the possibility of Adrian claiming such a right, she may bring an action before April to prevent the acquisition of it. In the case of an easement of light, Adrian does not have to show that user was as of right, although if he was given written permission by Yasmin or one of her predecessors this will defeat his claim. As long as he can claim uninterrupted use for 20 years without any written consent, his claim to a right of light will be deemed absolute and indefeasible.

Adrian should be advised that although he may have an easement of light, it will only entitle him to 'sufficient light according to the ordinary notions of mankind' for the beneficial use of his studio. He may not, therefore, be able to claim a right to exactly the same amount of light as before.

(3) Cricket

Applying the rules in *Re Ellenborough Park* to this scenario, the cricket club has the dominant tenement and Adrian the servient tenement. It is questionable whether the right to retrieve cricket balls will accommodate the cricket club's land as it is very specific to their use and would not benefit a future owner of the land using it for a different purpose. There are different occupiers of the two tenements. Can the right lie in grant? It could, presumably, be granted by deed, but whether the courts would recognise it as a valid right is debatable - see comment on *Horton v Tidd* below.

As Adrian did not sell the ground to the cricket club, there is no question of an implied easement as there is no sale of part. The only possibility is that an easement may have been acquired by prescription. However, as the cricket club has been using the ground for only 14 years, the club cannot have acquired such a right.

(Note: In the case of *Horton v Tidd* (1965) 196 EG 697, the captain of Egham Cricket Club, Surrey, brought an action against the owner of a property claiming an easement to deposit cricket balls on to and recover them from a property adjoining the cricket ground. Lyell J decided that there was no implied easement and none had arisen by prescription; he did not consider whether or not the right was one that was capable of existing as an easement.)

SUMMARY

- In this chapter you have looked at easements, how they are created and how they may be enforced in a lot more depth than you did in **Chapter 1**.
- With this enhanced understanding you could now assess a simple pack of pre-contract title documentation containing, for example, official copies of the title and replies to the seller's inquiries, in order to determine whether any easements are likely adversely to affect or, conversely, to benefit the land being sold.
- The law of easements has been used to great effect by opponents of proposed developments, where planning permission has been granted already. Residents have been able to demonstrate that they have the benefit of a long-standing right to use land in a particular way, which has then prevented unwanted development of that land.
- You should use the test your knowledge activity contained in this chapter either as a means of checking whether you have met the learning outcomes, or in order to reinforce what you have learned.

9 Legal Mortgages

LEARNING OUTCOMES

When you have completed this chapter, you should be able to:

- understand how and why legal mortgages are created and protected;
- resolve issues relating to mortgagees' remedies by application of legal principles;
- understand and explain the rules relating to priority of legal mortgages as between themselves and other proprietary interests in order to solve multi-issue problems.

9.1 Introduction

Imagine that Sarah Morgan comes to see you. She has asked one of her friends (Pedro) if she can borrow some money from him to start a new business. Pedro is happy to lend Sarah the money as he has known Sarah for years and is sure that she will repay the loan. However, Sarah does want to borrow £30,000 and can only repay it by instalments over a number of years as her business grows.

If Pedro is sure that Sarah will repay the loan, he may take no security that the loan will be repaid. If Sarah fails to repay the loan, Pedro can sue her for the debt, but this may not mean that Pedro will get his money back (for example, if Sarah becomes insolvent). This is an unsecured loan.

If Pedro lends Sarah a considerable sum of money then, even if they are friends, Pedro will probably want Sarah to provide him with some form of security for the loan (ie some form of guarantee that the loan will be repaid). What kinds of security are available to Pedro? One way of categorising the different kinds of security is to divide them into personal security and real security.

First, as an example of personal security, Sarah has mentioned that, if necessary, her father would be happy to guarantee that Sarah will repay the loan. So, Sarah's father, Dennis, agrees with Pedro that if Sarah fails to repay the loan, Dennis will do so. As Dennis is a man of considerable financial standing, this seems attractive to Pedro. If Sarah fails to repay the loan, Pedro can then ask Dennis to do so. But what happens if both Sarah and Dennis become insolvent? Then Pedro is still left with the problem that the two people liable for the debt are not worth suing. He has no effective method of getting his money back.

To avoid the problems involved in personal security, Pedro may decide to take real security instead. This means attaching the liability to repay the loan to a specific item of Sarah's property. If Sarah fails to repay the loan, Pedro can demand that the security item is sold and the proceeds used to repay the loan. A very important example of real security is the mortgage or charge of land. If Sarah owns land, this can form the security for the business loan.

9.1.1 Terminology

In the above example, Sarah is the *mortgagor*. She is the owner of the estate in land who is borrowing a sum of money on security of the mortgage over the property. The mortgagor gives the mortgage to the lender.

Pedro is the *mortgagee*. He is the lender who is taking security over the borrower's land; he is being given the mortgage.

We shall now look at how mortgages can be created.

9.2 Creation of legal mortgages

A mortgage is one of the five interests capable of existing as a legal interest in land (Law of Property Act (LPA) 1925, s 1(2)). So, if created correctly, a mortgage takes effect as a legal mortgage. If those formalities have not been complied with, the mortgage may take effect as an equitable mortgage, details of which are beyond the scope of this textbook. In this section, you will start by considering the methods of creating a legal mortgage.

The first requirement of a legal mortgage is that it should be created by a deed (LPA 1925, s 52(1)). But are there any other requirements that must be satisfied for the mortgage to take effect as a legal mortgage?

Under s 85 of the LPA 1925, there are two ways of creating a legal mortgage. The first method is for the mortgage to take the form of a demise (lease) for a term of years absolute subject to a provision for the lease to end on redemption of the mortgage. This method is rarely used nowadays.

The second way of creating a legal mortgage is to use a charge by deed expressed to be by way of legal mortgage (or a legal charge). The legal charge must be made in the form of a deed and state that the charge is made by way of legal mortgage. This form of legal mortgage does not convey any estate in land to the lender and is the most popular method of creating a mortgage. Since the Land Registration Act (LRA) 2002 came into effect on 13 October 2003, mortgages over land with registered title can only be created in this way.

Look at **Reading 7** in the **Appendix** for an example of the form that a charge by way of legal mortgage may take.

9.2.1 Legal mortgage of a leasehold estate

A mortgage can be created over a leasehold estate either by way of the creation of a charge, or by the creation of a sub-lease for a term of one day less than the term of the lease being mortgaged (LPA 1925, s 86(1)). So, for example, if the mortgagor is mortgaging a lease of a flat for 99 years, the sub-lease granted to the mortgagee will be for 99 years less one day. However, as with freeholds, most mortgages are created by way of charges over the leasehold estate, and since 13 October 2003 this is again the only method by which a mortgage of a registered leasehold estate may be created.

9.2.2 Unregistered titles

Where a first legal mortgage is created over an unregistered title, s 85(1) of the LPA 1925 gives lenders the right to take custody of the title deeds. This first legal mortgage (if created after March 1998) will also trigger compulsory first registration of the title to the land (see **Chapter 2**).

9.2.3 Registered titles

Where borrowers create a mortgage over a registered title, the mortgage must be registered against the title at Land Registry. A mortgage over a registered title is a registrable disposition under s 27 of the LRA 2002. It will become a legal mortgage only when it is entered in the charges register of the title affected. Mortgages created prior to the LRA 2002 were treated in a similar way, so many will still appear on the register.

In the next section we will consider the remedies of a legal mortgagee. In **9.1** we saw that Pedro could have taken a legal charge over the land to secure Sarah's business loan. If he did so, what can he do if she fails to make the repayments as agreed?

9.3 Remedies available to a legal mortgagee

The first remedy is to recover the debt by an action for repayment.

9.3.1 Debt action

If the borrower has failed to make the payments they have agreed to make, the mortgagee can commence an action for the recovery of the debt. Before starting the action, they must check that the legal date for redemption has passed, as the right to ask for repayment does not arise until this date has passed.

Historically, the legal date for redemption was important because it set a fixed date in the mortgage agreement upon which the mortgagor could redeem (pay back) the mortgage. They were not allowed to redeem either before or after this contractual date. If they failed to pay on that date, the mortgagee could take the land *and* sue in contract for repayment of the debt! The intervention of equity has made this rule redundant, but the fixed date or 'legal date for redemption' still acts as an important trigger point for some of the mortgagee's remedies. It is usually set at one month from the date of the mortgage.

If the payments have been outstanding for some time, the mortgagee should also check that recovery is not barred under the Limitation Act 1980. Under the 1980 Act, the mortgagee cannot recover arrears of the capital repayments if more than 12 years have passed since the payments first became due. Likewise, the lender cannot recover arrears of interest payments if they have been outstanding for more than six years.

In practice, this remedy is of limited assistance. If the borrower has failed to make the repayments on the mortgage, it is highly unlikely that they will have the money to satisfy any court order for repayment that may be made against them; mortgagees are more likely to use one of their remedies against the property itself.

Mortgagees have a choice of remedies against the property, and we will start with the right to take possession of the property.

9.3.2 Possession

The right to take possession of land can mean one of two things:

(a) If the mortgaged land is not subject to a lease, the lender has a right to oust the borrower from the property and to take physical possession of the land.

(b) If the mortgaged land is subject to a lease, the lender takes possession of the land by directing that the tenant pay their rent to the lender instead of to the borrower.

The remedy of seeking possession of the mortgaged property is often exercised with other remedies. For example, if the lender wishes to exercise their power to sell the land, they may want to sell with vacant possession as this will obtain a higher price than a sale without vacant possession. This means they will obtain possession first, then apply to sell the land.

Remember, when you looked at leases in **Chapter 5**, you dealt with the effect of s 6 of the Criminal Law Act (CLA) 1977. Section 6 also applies to lenders who take physical possession of the mortgaged land. So most lenders go to court and obtain a court order when exercising their right to take possession against borrowers, as if the lenders use or threaten violence to get possession of the mortgaged premises they commit a criminal offence. Section 6(2) of the CLA 1977 provides that the fact that the lender has a right to possession of the mortgaged property does not give them lawful authority to use or threaten violence to obtain possession.

When can a lender under a legal mortgage take possession of the mortgaged property?

9.3.2.1 When does the right to take possession arise?

A lender under a legal mortgage can take possession of the mortgaged property 'before the ink is dry on the mortgage', ie as soon as the mortgage has been completed (*Four Maids Ltd v Dudley Marshall (Properties) Ltd* [1957] Ch 317). The borrower does not need to be in default. However, the terms of the mortgage deed executed by lenders and borrowers may expressly or impliedly postpone this right until the borrower is in default. See clause 6 of **Reading 7** in the **Appendix** for an example.

9.3.2.2 Reasons for exercising the right to possession

As we saw above, in some cases, mortgagees want possession of the property so that they can intercept the rents paid by tenants occupying that property. In this way they can recover the debt owed to them.

However, some lenders want to get vacant possession of the mortgaged property so that they can exercise another remedy, eg where the property is occupied by the borrower and the lender wants to sell with vacant possession.

9.3.2.3 Mortgagee's liability to account to the mortgagor

The mortgagee will take possession in order to sell the property or to intercept the income from it. Where the property is producing income, the mortgagee is entitled to use it to pay the debt owed to them. However, they are not allowed to take any sum beyond that which is due to them under the mortgage.

The mortgagee does owe the mortgagor a duty to manage the property with due diligence. Should they fail to do so, they must account to the mortgagor for the income they did receive and also for any income they would have received had they managed the property correctly. In *White v City of London Brewery* (1889) 42 Ch D 237, the mortgagor created a mortgage over their public house, a free house, in favour of the brewery. Due to the default of the mortgagor, the mortgagee took possession and leased the public house as a tied house, which had a detrimental effect on the level of the rent. The mortgagee was held liable to account to the mortgagor for the additional rent which would have been received had the property been let as a free house.

9.3.2.4 The procedure for taking physical possession

If the mortgagee wishes to take physical possession of the property, they must consider the provisions of the CLA 1977 and, where the property is a dwelling-house, s 36 of the Administration of Justice Act (AJA) 1970 and s 8 of the Administration of Justice Act (AJA) 1973.

If the mortgagor refuses to move out and the mortgagee ousts them, the mortgagee may well commit an offence under the CLA 1977. The mortgagee should apply to court for a possession order. If the mortgagor refuses to vacate in accordance with the order, the court bailiff will assist in the eviction.

Where the mortgaged property is a dwelling-house, there are two other provisions which must be considered:

(a) *Section 36 of the AJA 1970.* A prudent mortgagee would always obtain a court order before evicting a mortgagor from a dwelling. Under s 36, the court can adjourn the possession proceedings if the court is of the opinion that the mortgagor will be able to repay the 'sums due', or remedy the breach of mortgage, within a reasonable time.

(b) *Section 8 of the AJA 1973.* Section 8 provides that where the mortgage deed provides for the sum to be repaid by instalments, 'sums due' means only the instalments which are in arrears at the date of the possession proceedings, not the full amount outstanding on the mortgage. However, the court can exercise its powers under s 36 only if it thinks that the mortgagor will, within a reasonable time, be able to repay not only the arrears which were due when the proceedings were commenced but also any arrears which have become due since the commencement of the proceedings. If the court believes that the mortgagor can catch up on their payments within a reasonable time, it will give them the chance to do so.

Where the court exercises its discretion to postpone the order for possession, the court must be satisfied that the borrowers can remedy the default within 'a reasonable period'. This has been defined as the outstanding term of the mortgage. In most cases, borrowers ask the court to postpone the sale so that they can set up a repayment schedule, giving the borrower time to pay back the arrears. Or they may need a period of time to sell the land and use the proceeds to pay back the amount owed to the lender.

The Court of Appeal's decision in *Ropaigealach v Barclays Bank* [1999] 1 QB 263 makes it clear that a mortgagee remains entitled to exercise their right to possession by physical re-entry without bringing court proceedings. This is only likely to happen where the property is empty. By taking possession in this way, the mortgagee will bypass the protective provisions of s 36 of the AJA 1970. The mortgagor's only protection is s 6 of the CLA 1977, but this does not provide any civil remedy, only criminal sanctions. It appears that the Protection from Eviction Act 1977 does not apply to mortgagors in the same way that it applies to residential occupiers under leases and licences (see **Chapter 5**).

If the mortgaged property has been let out to tenants, and the mortgagee merely wishes to exercise the right to collect the rents, no court order will be required. The mortgagee will take possession by directing the tenants to pay their rent to them.

9.3.2.5 Possession and human rights

The Court of Appeal's decision in *Ropaigealach v Barclays Bank* (see **9.3.2.4** above) confirmed that a mortgagee can exercise its right to possession by peaceable re-entry, even where the property involved is a dwelling. It has been argued by some commentators that the Human Rights Act 1998 may provide a mortgagor with a legitimate challenge in such cases. The challenge would be based on the argument that their rights to 'respect for his private and family life' and 'the peaceful enjoyment of his possessions' have been infringed. This approach was rejected, however, in *Horsham Properties Group Ltd v Clark and Beech* [2008] EWHC 2327 (Ch). The court felt that any deprivation of possession by a mortgagee after a default by a mortgagor was justified in the public interest and reflected the nature of the necessary security which a mortgagee needed to take to offer substantial lending on property at affordable interest rates.

We have looked at lenders' duties whilst they are in possession of the mortgaged property where the mortgaged land is producing an income, and we saw that lenders can be made personally liable for any mismanagement. They may, therefore, prefer to appoint a receiver instead of taking possession of the mortgaged property. We consider this remedy next.

9.3.3 Appointment of a receiver

As an alternative to taking possession, the mortgagee can appoint a receiver to collect and redirect the income from the property. The advantage of appointing a receiver is that the mortgagee does not incur the personal responsibility which is involved in taking possession but nevertheless gets the ability to use some of the income to repay the debt owed to them. A receiver must be appointed in writing (see **9.3.3.1**).

If the mortgagee does appoint a receiver, the receiver takes control of the mortgaged land and then either sells it or manages it and uses the income from it to repay the loan. The receiver has been appointed by the lender, and therefore the duties and powers of the receiver are governed by the (mortgage) document under which they are appointed and by the law of agency.

A mortgagee has the power to appoint a receiver provided:

(a) the mortgage was created by deed. The power to appoint a receiver is implied into every mortgage made by deed (LPA 1925, s 101). The power will often be expressly included as one of the mortgage terms in any event (see clauses 6.5 and 7 of **Reading 7** in the **Appendix**); and

(b) the power has arisen (ie the legal date of redemption has passed – see **9.3.1** above) and has become exercisable.

Section 109(1) of the LPA 1925 states that the power becomes exercisable in the same way as the power of sale (see **9.3.4.1** below). Section 103 of the LPA 1925 sets out how the power becomes exercisable. This happens if any one of three situations applies:

(1) The lender has served notice on the borrower requiring repayment of the loan, and the borrower has failed to comply with that notice for three months after service.

(2) Interest due under the mortgage is two months or more in arrears.

(3) The borrower has breached a term under the mortgage deed (for example, a borrower's covenant not to grant a lease without first obtaining the lender's consent).

These requirements are often relaxed or modified in favour of the mortgagee in the mortgage deed. See clauses 6.4, 6.5 and 7.1(a) of **Reading 7** in the **Appendix** for examples of the detailed mortgage conditions.

9.3.3.1 Making the appointment

Once the mortgagee is satisfied, the method of appointment varies. Where the mortgage deed provides that the receiver should be appointed in a certain way (for example, by deed) then the mortgagee must appoint the receiver in that way. Otherwise the general rule is that the receiver should be appointed in writing (LPA Act 1925, s 109).

9.3.3.2 Application of the money held by the receiver

What should the receiver do with any income received from the mortgagor's property?

The receiver must apply the income in the order set out in s 109 of the LPA 1925. So they must apply any income as follows and pay:

(a) outgoings on the property;

(b) interest on any prior mortgages (ie if there are any mortgages on the property that have priority over the mortgagee which appointed the receiver – we will look at priority at **9.5** below);

(c) insurance premiums on the property and their own costs;

(d) interest on the current mortgage;

(e) capital on the current mortgage if directed to do so in writing by the mortgagee;

(f) the balance to the mortgagor.

So far we have looked at two remedies that the mortgagee has against the property of the mortgagor - possession and appointing a receiver. Both of these will enable the mortgagee to recover arrears but not to secure repayment of all sums owed by the mortgagor. The mortgage itself will continue.

In **9.3.4** and **9.3.5** we will examine two remedies which may allow the mortgagee to recover all sums owed under the mortgage - the power of sale and foreclosure. Both of these will bring the mortgage to an end.

9.3.4 The power of sale

When lenders exercise their power of sale, they sell the mortgaged property and use the proceeds of sale to pay themselves back the sum that they are owed under the mortgage. In this section of this chapter, you will look at lenders' duties when selling the mortgaged land and their duties in relation to the proceeds of sale.

9.3.4.1 Exercising the power of sale

As we have already seen in relation to appointing a receiver, the law distinguishes between the existence of the lender's power to sell the mortgaged property and the circumstances in which the lender can exercise that power of sale. The statutory power of sale is implied into every mortgage created by deed (LPA 1925, s 101) and is usually expressly included in the mortgage deed itself. However, before the mortgagee sells the property, the power of sale must have arisen and become exercisable. The power of sale arises on the legal date for redemption (s 101(1)(i)) and becomes exercisable when one of the conditions in s 103 of the LPA 1925 has been complied with (see **9.3.3**). Section 103 is usually varied by the mortgage deed to ensure that the power will become exercisable in additional circumstances (see clauses 6.2 to 6.4 of **Reading 7** in the **Appendix**).

Before selling, therefore, the mortgagee must check that the power has both arisen and become exercisable. The next step is to look at the position of the purchaser from the lender. How do far do purchasers need go to check that the lender does have a power to sell that has arisen and become exercisable?

Where lenders do exercise their power to sell the mortgaged property, the effect of sale is dealt with under s 104 of the LPA 1925. We have already seen that the mortgagee, before selling, must ensure that their power to sell has arisen, ie that the legal date for redemption has passed. Once they have done that, they must make sure that their power to sell has become exercisable under s 103 of the LPA 1925. The purchaser, on the other hand, under s 104(2) of the LPA 1925, has some protection if the mortgagee does not follow the correct procedure when they sell. The purchaser must still check that the mortgagee does have a power of sale which has arisen. They do not, however, need to check that the power has become exercisable.

9.3.4.2 The nature of the power

Remember that when lenders exercise their power to sell the mortgaged land, they intend to sell the mortgaged land and use the proceeds to pay themselves back what they are owed under the mortgage deed. Once the lender has paid themselves back what they are owed, any balance goes to the borrower. The lender has the choice of when and how to sell. This could be by private treaty (ie negotiating with buyers individually using an agent) or auction. However, lenders owe two duties to borrowers when exercising their power to sell the mortgaged land. A lender:

(1) must act in good faith and not cheat the borrower (eg the property must be properly advertised and the lender cannot sell hastily at a knock down price); and

(2) must take reasonable care to obtain the true market value of the property at the date of the sale. They are not under any obligation to delay the sale in order to maximise the price of the property.

Market values of property can vary and be difficult to estimate, so 'provided the lender has exposed the property to the market properly and fairly', it will have discharged its duty. If the lender fails to obtain the true value, it must account to the borrower for the difference. The onus of proof is on the borrower to show that there has been a breach in the lender's duty of care.

Example

Beren has mortgaged his land to Larry. Beren has planning permission to build some flats on a piece of land. He borrowed £50,000 from Larry and mortgaged his land to Larry. Beren then obtains another planning permission allowing him to build houses on the land. The land now has the benefit of two planning permissions. Beren could decide to implement either and build flats or houses on the land. Beren defaults on his repayments and Larry becomes entitled to exercise his power to sell the land and decides to do so. He instructs auctioneers to sell the land. The auctioneers advertise the land as having planning permission for houses and sell it for £44,000. Beren now claims that if the land had been advertised as having planning permission for flats, the sale would have achieved a figure of around £75,000.

These were broadly the facts of the case of *Cuckmere Brick Co Ltd v Mutual Finance Ltd* [1971] Ch 949 where the court found that the lender had failed to obtain the true market value. The lender had to account to Cuckmere for the difference in value between the price that could have been achieved (if the property had been properly advertised) less the price obtained. It is in this case that the Court of Appeal established a lender's duty when selling the mortgaged land.

9.3.4.3 The effect of the sale

The next thing to consider is the position of the purchaser from the mortgagee: what title to the property do they get and what third party interests, including other mortgages, will be binding on them?

Under s 104(1) of the LPA 1925, the sale by the mortgagee passes to the purchaser the whole estate of the mortgagor:

(a) free from any estates or interests (including other mortgages) which the selling mortgagee took priority over; but

(b) subject to any estates and interests which took priority over the selling mortgagee.

Section 104 talks about the selling mortgagees having 'priority'. We will look at the question of priority in **9.5**. It is based on the concept of enforceability of third party rights that you met in **Chapters 2** and **3**.

9.3.4.4 What happens to the proceeds of sale?

When the sale has been completed, the mortgagee must decide how to distribute the proceeds of sale. The order of the distribution is set out in s 105 of the LPA 1925. The selling mortgagee is a trustee of the proceeds of sale, and they must use them in the following order:

(a) to repay the cost of redeeming prior mortgages (ie mortgages with priority over the selling mortgagee's mortgage);

(b) to pay off the mortgagee's expenses of sale;

(c) to pay off the mortgagee's own mortgage;

(d) to pay any balance to the person entitled to the mortgaged property (ie a mortgagee with lower priority to the selling mortgagee, if there is one, or the mortgagor).

9.3.5 Foreclosure

The last remedy is foreclosure. This is rarely used in practice. The right to foreclose arises either when the legal date of redemption has passed *or* when the mortgagor has breached one of the terms of the mortgage.

Foreclosure is available by application to the High Court once the legal date of redemption has passed. There are two stages in the process. The first stage in the procedure involves the lender obtaining an interim court order. This order fixes a date by which the borrower should pay the outstanding money. If the borrower fails to do so, then the procedure moves to the next stage. The second stage is the final order (also known as the order of foreclosure absolute). Following this order, the borrower cannot redeem unless the court exercises its discretion to allow the borrower to redeem.

If the property is worth more than the sum owed, the lender is entitled to keep the surplus. Conversely, if the property is worth less than the sum owed, then the borrower is released from liability.

Example

Freddie mortgaged his freehold house by a legal mortgage to Base Rate Bank. Unfortunately, he has not kept up with the payments due under the mortgage and has fallen into arrears. He has just spoken to the bank manager, who has told him that if he does not pay the arrears the bank will foreclose. Freddie does not really understand what is meant by the term 'foreclosure' and has come to you for advice. He has just had his house valued and it is worth £200,000. The bank manager told him that the amount outstanding on the mortgage is £100,000 (including interest and costs). Freddie has been told that the effect of foreclosure is to vest ownership of his property in the lender and so Base Rate Bank would take the freehold estate in Freddie's house.

Although the property is worth £200,000 and the amount outstanding under the mortgage is £100,000, Freddie does not have a claim over the land for the remaining £100,000 after deduction of the mortgage. Because the effect of foreclosure is so drastic, equity gives the court discretion to allow the borrower to redeem even after the final order for foreclosure has been made. One factor that may influence the court to exercise its discretion is the value of the property as compared to the amount outstanding under the mortgage. If, as with Freddie's transaction, there is a lot of equity left in the property after deduction of the mortgage, the courts may be more willing to re-open the foreclosure.

The effect of foreclosure is so drastic that one would expect lenders to be more eager than they in fact are to use the remedy. Why, therefore, do lenders use foreclosure infrequently? Can a borrower prevent the foreclosure?

Section 91(2) of the LPA 1925 allows 'any person interested either in the mortgage money or in the right of redemption' to request that the court makes an order for sale instead of foreclosure. As the borrower is a person interested in the right of redemption, they can apply to court for an order for sale. Once this request has been made, the court can order that the property should be sold 'on such terms as it thinks fit'.

When you looked at the effect of lenders exercising their power of sale, you saw that the effect of sale is less drastic than foreclosure. When the property is sold, the lender will receive the amount it is owed under its mortgage, and the borrower will be entitled to receive any sums left over.

9.4 The protection of mortgages

Immediately after the creation of the mortgage, the mortgagee must always consider what steps they must take to protect their mortgage in the event that the mortgagor attempts to sell the property or create another mortgage over the property. Protecting the mortgage is essential to ensure that it is binding on any purchaser and (more importantly in practice) that it has priority over any later mortgages that the mortgagor may create over the property should the borrower default in the future.

We will briefly revise the rules for the protection of mortgages of registered and unregistered land. You should also look at the rules on enforceability of third party rights in **Chapters 2** and **3**.

9.4.1 If title to mortgagor's land is registered

A legal mortgage under s 1(2) of the LPA 1925 is a registrable disposition under s 27 of the Land Registration Act 2002, and so must be *completed* by registration against the title affected to be legal and to bind a purchaser or later mortgagee of the land.

On registration, the mortgagee is entered as proprietor of the charge. See entries 3 and 4 in **Reading 4** in the **Appendix** for an example of how a charge is recorded by Land Registry.

The method of protection required for a mortgage created before 13 October 2003 under the Land Registration Act 1925 was the same as under the LRA 2002.

If the mortgage is not registered, it will not be binding upon a purchaser for value, and this includes the owner of a subsequent mortgage.

9.4.2 If title to mortgagor's land is unregistered

Legal mortgages of a legal estate are not registrable on the Land Charges Register if the mortgagee has retained the title deeds. The first mortgagee has the right to take possession of title deeds (LPA 1925, s 85(1)). Remember that since 1998, creation of a first legal mortgage will trigger first registration of the title to the legal estate.

9.5 The priority rules

9.5.1 Priority between legal mortgages where title to the land is registered

You have considered what happens where land is subject to one mortgage and the lender under that mortgage exercises their power to sell. There is nothing to prevent borrowers from creating more than one mortgage over their land. Second or third lenders need to check, before lending on the security of the land, that the land is worth enough to repay all of the mortgages. Now you will examine what happens where land with registered title is subject to more than one mortgage and one of the lenders decides to sell. To decide what happens to the proceeds of sale, you have to work out the order of priority between the lenders.

Example

Beren owns the freehold estate in his house and decides to create a number of mortgages over it:

(a) Five years ago, Beren creates a first mortgage by deed over his house in favour of Larry for £50,000.

(b) Twelve months later, Beren creates a second mortgage by deed over his house in favour of Megan for £20,000.

(c) Last month, Beren creates a third mortgage by deed over his house in favour of Niall for £10,000.

Beren has defaulted under his mortgage with Megan (the second mortgagee), and she intends to exercise her power of sale. From studying this chapter, you know that when Megan exercises her power to sell the mortgaged land, she will use the proceeds to pay off her mortgage before anything goes to Beren. But here there are three mortgages. Which lender is entitled to be paid back first?

When the land is sold, the lender who ranks first in the order of priority is entitled to be paid back in full first before the other lenders get any money. The lender who ranks second in the order of priority is entitled to receive the proceeds next. To determine the order of priority, you need to apply the rules on enforceability of third party rights that you studied in **Chapters 2** and **3**. In this part of the chapter we are going to focus on the situation where the mortgaged land is registered.

Under s 48 of the LRA 2002, the order of priority for registered charges depends on the order in which they are entered on the register. This means that the mortgage that appears first ranks first.

ACTIVITY 1 Priority between legal mortgages where title to the land is registered

Answer the following questions. Read the comment on each question before answering the next:

(1) Consider the Beren scenario set out above. Assuming that each lender has taken the correct steps to protect their security, what will be the order of priority?

COMMENT

If each lender has taken the correct steps to protect their mortgage, they will have registered their mortgages as registered charges in the charges register of the title to the land. As each mortgage is registered, the register kept at Land Registry should therefore reveal all three mortgages against the property. The order of priority is generally governed by the order of registration. Assuming that Larry registered his mortgage first, his comes first in the order of priority; Megan, assuming that her mortgage was registered next, comes second in the order of priority; and Niall is last. (If the mortgages had all been created after the introduction of the LRA 2002, the position would have been the same.)

(2) If Megan has failed to register her mortgage, what effect would that have on the order of priority?

COMMENT

The order of priority would change to:

(a) Larry;

(b) Niall;

(c) Megan.

As Larry registered his legal mortgage as a registered charge in the charges register of the title to the land before the other two mortgages, his mortgage takes priority over the other two.

Megan has a mortgage that she should have registered as a registered charge for it to take full effect as a legal mortgage. As Megan did not do so, her mortgage only takes effect in equity. An equitable mortgage is an interest affecting a registered estate under the LRA 2002, and as it has not been registered it does not bind Niall who has taken his interest in the land for valuable consideration.

If we now return to the facts set out in question (1) above, the effect of s 104(1) of the LPA 1925 is that the lender (here Megan), when she exercises her power of sale, sells subject to prior incumbrances and free from those which do not have priority.

The basic position here is that Megan sells subject to the prior mortgage in favour of Larry but free from the later one in favour of Niall. This obviously causes a problem for the purchaser, who does not wish to buy the land subject to Larry's mortgage. In practical terms what will happen is that the purchaser will insist that Megan, the selling lender, agrees that she (Megan) will redeem the first mortgage in favour of Larry and sell free of that mortgage.

So the priority between lenders depends on a number of factors, for example whether or not lenders have correctly registered their mortgages. The issue of priority is also relevant between mortgagees and other third party rights. In this situation the lender is in a similar position to a purchaser of land.

9.5.2 Priority between legal mortgages and other proprietary interests where title to the land is registered

On occasion it is necessary to consider whether particular third party interests created by the mortgagor are binding on the mortgagee. For example, a mortgagee wishing to exercise its power of sale may discover that there is a tenant occupying the property. The mortgagee must find out whether it is bound by the lease in order to determine whether it can sell the property free of the lease or subject to it. In addition, those claiming other interests in the property can also cause problems for mortgagees.

For the purposes of the LRA 2002, a mortgage, like a purchase, is a registrable disposition.

To decide whether the interest is binding on the mortgagee, first, check whether the interest was created before or after the date of registration (but see (b) below) of the mortgage. If it was created before the mortgage, it is necessary to decide whether that interest takes priority over the mortgage, ie is the lender bound by the interest? (If the interest is created after the mortgage, the lender will not be bound unless it has given consent to the interest, eg the granting of a lease by the mortgagor.)

Remember the rules you looked at in **Chapter 3**. What follows is a brief summary of those rules. Again, we are going to focus on the registered system.

With regard to interests created on or after 13 October 2003, when the LRA 2002 came into force:

(a) all registrable dispositions must be registered and interests affecting a registered estate must be protected by a notice on the register by the date of registration of the mortgage to take priority over it (LRA 2002, s 29);

(b) all interests which override under Sch 3 to the LRA 2002 must exist by the date of completion of the mortgage to take priority over it.

Where the mortgage is taken to finance the acquisition of the property, any equitable trust interest, arising through a contribution to the purchase price, will be an overriding interest against a registered title only if the person holding the interest was in occupation of the property at the date the mortgage was created. In the vast majority of cases the purchaser does not take up occupation of the property until after the purchase has been completed. Therefore, where the mortgage finances the acquisition, it is highly unlikely that the equitable trust interest will bind the mortgagee (*Lloyds Bank Plc v Rosset*, *Abbey National Building Society v Cann* and see also *Bristol and West Building Society v Henning* [1985] 1 WLR 778).

Where a legal owner mortgages a property after its acquisition (or remortgages it), then the mortgagee may be bound by any trust interest that already exists (*Williams & Glyn's Bank Ltd v Boland* [1981] AC 487) (unless the mortgagee has overreached - see **Chapter 3**).

ACTIVITY 2 Test your knowledge: mortgages

The aim of this activity is to give you some practice in applying the rules that you have been studying in this chapter. Set out below is a suggested approach to problem questions that you may find useful.

(1) A problem question on this topic may include discussion of remedies available to a legal mortgagee and/or enforceability of other interests over the land against a mortgagee (known as priority).

(2) When discussing remedies, identify what, if any, aims the lender has in recovering its money. If it simply wants to recover arrears then the remedies of a debt action, possession or appointing a receiver are appropriate. If the lender wants to secure repayment of the entire sum loaned, ie the capital and interest, then the power of sale or foreclosure are possibilities. Remember that foreclosure is rarely ordered. It is important to select only relevant remedies on the facts provided.

(3) When analysing priorities, it may help to produce a 'timeline' or sequence of events to determine whether the interest or estate has been created before or after the mortgage in question. Generally, any rights created after the date of the mortgage will not bind the lender if the mortgage has been correctly protected.

To assess enforceability:

(a) identify the types of interest or estate present;
(b) determine whether they have been created properly, using the formality rules (see **Chapter 1**) and hence whether they are likely to be legal, equitable or statutory;
(c) consider enforceability against the mortgagee where title to the land is registered (again refer back to **Chapter 3**). The vital date for assessing enforceability is the date of registration of the mortgage (or completion of the mortgage in relation to interests protected by Sch 3 to the LRA 2002), not the date of any subsequent repossession or sale by the mortgagee.

In February last year Fiona purchased two freehold registered properties on an industrial estate. The properties were known as Units 1 and 2. She purchased with the aid of two loans from Mercantile Facilities Plc secured by legal charges by deed in favour of Mercantile over the two units.

Two months later Fiona needed finance in connection with another commercial venture. She took out two loans from Premier Finance Ltd secured by legal charges by deed in favour of Premier over the two units.

When Fiona purchased, there were existing leases in respect of both Units 1 and 2. Both leases were for five-year terms, and both had been granted by deed. The lease for Unit 1 expired in December last year, at which time Fiona immediately granted a fresh lease to a new tenant without seeking the consent of the mortgagees. Again the lease was by deed and for a five-year term. The lease for Unit 2 is due to expire in December next year.

Earlier this year Fiona began to experience cashflow problems. She has failed to pay the last three months' repayments on the loans from Premier.

Premier is becoming concerned about Fiona's failure to pay. Property prices have fallen in the area, and the values of Units 1 and 2 are less than the amounts outstanding on the two loans over each of them.

Explain:

(1) the effect that Mercantile's charges and the leases will have on any remedies available to Premier; and

(2) the remedies that would be most appropriate for Premier to pursue in the circumstances.

COMMENT

(1) Assuming that Mercantile has registered its mortgage first, Mercantile takes priority to Premier. Mortgages created over registered titles rank according to order of entry on the register (LRA 2002, s 48).

Premier takes subject to the lease of Unit 2 as it is an overriding interest under Sch 3, para 1 to the LRA 2002, being a legal lease for seven years or less. Premier cannot evict this tenant to sell the property with vacant possession; any sale will have to be subject to the tenant's occupation. However, Premier may want to consider the fact that the rent paid by the tenant could be used to repay the mortgage debt.

The new lease of Unit 1 was created after Premier's legal charge. However, the mortgage deed usually includes a provision whereby leases may be granted only with the mortgagee's consent. If Premier's mortgage contains this provision, then, as it has not given its consent to the lease, Premier will not be bound by the lease and may evict the tenant and sell the property with vacant possession. This is why a prospective tenant should always check whether his landlord has a mortgage!

(2) Remedies

Unit 1

Power of sale – The power arises after the legal redemption date, and the power becomes exercisable according to mortgage conditions or according to s 103 of the LPA 1925. Fiona has breached the terms of s 103 (and thus, probably, the mortgage conditions, which may be more stringent). Any sale will be subject to Mercantile's mortgage, but, in practice, Mercantile's mortgage must be discharged before the sale, and the proceeds will be used to pay off Premier's loan (LPA 1925, s 105). Any remaining balance goes to Fiona.

Foreclosure - The effect of foreclosure is to vest the mortgagor's legal estate in Premier but subject to Mercantile's mortgage and subject, at least in the case of Unit 2 (and possibly Unit 1), to the lease. The legal date of redemption must have passed. Premier cannot foreclose without going to court, and the procedure involves two stages.
The court has the power to order a sale in lieu of foreclosure (LPA 1925, s 91). The deficiency which a sale may produce makes foreclosure more likely and sale in lieu of foreclosure less likely to be ordered. Premier will certainly apply for this.

Unit 2

Because this Unit cannot be sold with vacant possession, a sale is unlikely in this case. Instead, Premier should consider taking possession to get hold of the rent or appointing a receiver.

Power to take possession - This is possible as soon as the legal charge is executed and is a remedy which can be used to intercept rents or to grant new leases. The rents may be used to pay the interest owned to Premier and any surplus may be used to pay off capital.

Power to appoint a receiver - This power arises and becomes exercisable in the same way as the power of sale. The appointment must be made in writing. The receiver is deemed to be the agent of the mortgagor. This power is usually used to enable the lender to intercept the rent for any leases. However, the rent must be used by the receiver in accordance with the statutory order under s 109 of the LPA 1925. In particular, interest due to Mercantile has a prior claim to Premier's repayments, as do the fees to be paid to the receiver.

SUMMARY

- In this chapter you have looked at legal mortgages, how they are created and how they may be enforced in a lot more depth than you did in **Part I**.
- With this enhanced understanding, you could now explain to a client the consequences of entering into a mortgage and the possible remedies available to a legal mortgagee should the client default on the loan payments.
- You could also analyse the priority of competing lenders where there are numerous loans secured on a piece of land and predict the order in which any income generated by the land or sale proceeds would be applied between the creditors.
- You could also start to advise someone claiming a third party interest over the land whether they are affected by the legal mortgage granted by the mortgagor and, if so, what the consequences are for them.
- You should use the test your knowledge activity contained in this chapter, either as a means of checking whether you have met the learning outcomes, or in order to reinforce what you have learned.

APPENDIX
Resource Materials

Reading 1

Contract for Sale of Land

For conveyancer's use only
Buyer's conveyancer: ....
Seller's conveyancer: ....
Law Society Formula: [A / B / C / Personal exchange]

CONTRACT
Incorporating the Standard Conditions of Sale (Fifth Edition)

Date	:	
Seller	:	Andrew Norman and Emily Smythe both of 8 West Park Road Oldcastle Mercia OD2 000
Buyer	:	David Evans of 4 High Street Cornland Wessex CO1 5ND
Property (freehold/XXXXXXXX	:	ALL THAT property known as 8 West Park Road Odlcastle Mercia OD2 000
XXXXXXXXXX/root of title	:	A Conveyance dated the 8th January 1975 made between Hubert Parry (1) and Basil Harwood (2)
Specified incumbrances	:	The covenants contained in a Conveyance dated 6th April 1959 and made between TT Noble (Builders) Ltd (1) and George Handel (2)
Title guarantee (full/XXXXXX	:	Full title guarantee
Completion date	:	
Contract rate	:	The Law Society's interest rate from time to time in force
Purchase price	:	£109,000
Deposit	:	£10,900
Contents price (if separate)	:	£2000
Balance	:	100,100

The seller will sell and the buyer will buy the property for the purchase price.

WARNING

This is a formal document, designed to create legal rights and legal obligations. Take advice before using it.

Signed

Seller/Buyer

SCS1 1 Laserform International 5/11

STANDARD CONDITIONS OF SALE (FIFTH EDITION)
(NATIONAL CONDITIONS OF SALE 25TH EDITION, LAW SOCIETY'S CONDITIONS OF SALE 2011)

1. GENERAL

1.1 Definitions

[illegible]

2. FORMATION

[illegible]

3. MATTERS AFFECTING THE PROPERTY

[illegible]

4. TITLE AND TRANSFER

[illegible]

SCS1 2

4.6.4 If after completion the seller will remain bound by any obligation affecting the property which was disclosed to the buyer before the contract was made, but the law does not imply any covenant by the buyer to indemnify the seller against liability for future breaches of it:
(a) the buyer is to covenant in the transfer to indemnify the seller against liability for any future breach of the obligation and to perform it from then on, and
(b) if required by the seller, the buyer is to execute and deliver to the seller on completion a duplicate transfer prepared by the buyer.

4.6.5 The seller is to arrange at his expense that, in relation to every document of title which the buyer does not receive on completion, the buyer is to have the benefit of:
(a) a written acknowledgement of his right to its production, and
(b) a written undertaking for its safe custody (except while it is held by a mortgagee or by someone in a fiduciary capacity).

4.7 **Membership of company**
Where the seller is, or is required to be, a member of a company that has an interest in the property or has management responsibilities for the property or the surrounding areas, the seller is, without cost to the buyer, to provide such documents on completion as will enable the buyer to become a member of that company.

5. **RISK, INSURANCE AND OCCUPATION PENDING COMPLETION**
5.1.1 The property is at the risk of the buyer from the date of the contract.
5.1.2 The seller is under no obligation to the buyer to insure the property unless:
(a) the contract provides that a policy effected by or for the seller and insuring the property or any part of it against liability for loss or damage is to continue in force, or
(b) the property or any part of it is let on terms under which the seller (whether as landlord or as tenant) is obliged to insure against loss or damage.
5.1.3 If the seller is obliged to insure the property under condition 5.1.2, the seller is to:
(a) do everything necessary to maintain the policy
(b) permit the buyer to inspect the policy or evidence of its terms
(c) if before completion the property suffers loss or damage:
(i) pay to the buyer on completion the amount of the policy monies which the seller has received, so far as not applied in repairing or reinstating the property, and
(ii) if no final payment has then been received, assign to the buyer, at the buyer's expense, all rights to claim under the policy in such form as the buyer reasonably requires and pending execution of the assignment hold any policy monies received in trust for the buyer
(d) cancel the policy on completion.
5.1.4 Where the property is leasehold and the property, or any building containing it, is insured by a reversioner or other third party, the seller is to use reasonable efforts to ensure that the insurance is maintained until completion and if, before completion, the property or building suffers loss or damage the seller is to assign to the buyer on completion, at the buyer's expense, such rights as the seller may have in the policy monies, in such form as the buyer reasonably requires.
5.1.5 If payment under a policy effected by or for the buyer is reduced, because the property is covered against loss or damage by an insurance policy effected by or on behalf of the seller, then, unless the seller is obliged to insure the property under condition 5.1.2, the purchase price is to be abated by the amount of that reduction.
5.1.6 Section 47 of the Law of Property Act 1925 does not apply.

5.2 **Occupation by buyer**
5.2.1 If the buyer is not already lawfully in the property, and the seller agrees to let him into occupation, the buyer occupies on the following terms.
5.2.2 The buyer is a licensee and not a tenant. The terms of the licence are that the buyer:
(a) cannot transfer it
(b) may permit members of his household to occupy the property
(c) is to pay or indemnify the seller against all outgoings and other expenses in respect of the property
(d) is to pay the seller a fee calculated at the contract rate on a sum equal to the purchase price (less any deposit paid) for the period of the licence
(e) is entitled to any rents and profits from any part of the property which he does not occupy
(f) is to keep the property in as good a state of repair as it was in when he went into occupation (except for fair wear and tear) and is not to alter it
(g) if the property is leasehold, is not to do anything which puts the seller in breach of his obligations in the lease,
and
(h) is to quit the property when the licence ends.
5.2.3 The buyer is not in occupation for the purposes of this condition if he merely exercises rights of access given solely to do work agreed by the seller.
5.2.4 The buyer's licence ends on the earliest of: completion date, rescission of the contract or when five working days' notice given by one party to the other takes effect.
5.2.5 If the buyer is in occupation of the property after his licence has come to an end and the contract is subsequently completed he is to pay the seller compensation for his continued occupation calculated at the same rate as the fee mentioned in condition 5.2.2(d).
5.2.6 The buyer's right to raise requisitions is unaffected.

6. **COMPLETION**
6.1 **Date**
6.1.1 Completion date is twenty working days after the date of the contract but time is not of the essence of the contract unless a notice to complete has been served.
6.1.2 If the money due on completion is received after 2.00pm, completion is to be treated, for the purposes only of conditions 6.3 and 7.3, as taking place on the next working day as a result of the buyer's default.
6.1.3 Condition 6.1.2 does not apply and the seller is treated as in default if:
(a) the sale is with vacant possession of the property or any part of it, and
(b) the buyer is ready, able and willing to complete but does not pay the money due on completion until after 2.00 pm because the seller has not vacated the property or that part by that time.

6.2 **Arrangements and place**
6.2.1 The buyer's conveyancer and the seller's conveyancer are to co-operate in agreeing arrangements for completing the contract.
6.2.2 Completion is to take place in England and Wales, either at the seller's conveyancer's office or at some other place which the seller reasonably specifies.

6.3 **Apportionments**
6.3.1 On evidence of proper payment being made, income and outgoings of the property are to be apportioned between the parties so far as the change of ownership on completion will affect entitlement to receive or liability to pay them.
6.3.2 If the whole property is sold with vacant possession or the seller exercises his option in condition 7.2.4, apportionment is to be made with effect from the date of actual completion; otherwise, it is to be made from completion date.
6.3.3 In apportioning any sum, it is to be assumed that the seller owns the property until the end of the day from which apportionment is made and that the sum accrues from day to day at the rate at which it is payable on that day.
6.3.4 For the purpose of apportioning income and outgoings, it is to be assumed that they accrue at an equal daily rate throughout the year.
6.3.5 When a sum to be apportioned is not known or easily ascertainable at completion, a provisional apportionment is to be made according to the best estimate available. As soon as the amount is known, a final apportionment is to be made and notified to the other party. Any resulting balance is to be paid no more than ten working days later, and if not then paid the balance is to bear interest at the contract rate from then until payment.
6.3.6 Compensation payable under condition 5.2.5 is not to be apportioned.

6.4 **Amount payable**
The amount payable by the buyer on completion is the purchase price and the contents price (less any deposit already paid to the seller or his agent) adjusted to take account of:
(a) apportionments made under condition 6.3
(b) any compensation to be paid or allowed under condition 7.2
(c) any sum payable under condition 5.1.3.

6.5 **Title deeds**
6.5.1 As soon as the buyer has complied with all his obligations under this contract on completion the seller must hand over the documents of title.
6.5.2 Condition 6.5.1 does not apply to any documents of title relating to land being retained by the seller after completion.

6.6 **Rent receipts**
The buyer is to assume that whoever gave any receipt for a payment of rent or service charge which the seller produces was the person or the agent of the person then entitled to that rent or service charge.

6.7 **Means of payment**
The buyer is to pay the money due on completion by a direct transfer of cleared funds from an account held in the name of a conveyancer at a clearing bank and, if appropriate, an unconditional release of a deposit held by a stakeholder.

6.8 **Notice to complete**
6.8.1 At any time after the time applicable under condition 6.1.2 on completion date, a party who is ready, able and willing to complete may give the other a notice to complete.
6.8.2 The parties are to complete the contract within ten working days of giving a notice to complete, excluding the day on which the notice is given. For this purpose, time is of the essence of the contract.
6.8.3 On receipt of a notice to complete:
(a) if the buyer paid no deposit, he is forthwith to pay a deposit of 10 per cent
(b) if the buyer paid a deposit of less than 10 per cent, he is forthwith to pay a further deposit equal to the balance of that 10 per cent.

7. **REMEDIES**
7.1 **Errors and omissions**
7.1.1 If any plan or statement in the contract, or in the negotiations leading to it, is or was misleading or inaccurate due to an error or omission by the seller, the remedies available to the buyer are as follows.
(a) When there is a material difference between the description or value of the property, or of any of the contents included in the contract, as represented and as it is, the buyer is entitled to damages.
(b) An error or omission only entitles the buyer to rescind the contract:
(i) where it results from fraud or recklessness, or
(ii) where he would be obliged, to his prejudice, to accept property differing substantially (in quantity, quality or tenure) from what the error or omission had led him to expect.
7.1.2 If either party rescinds the contract:
(a) unless the rescission is a result of the buyer's breach of contract the deposit is to be repaid to the buyer with accrued interest
(b) the buyer is to return any documents he received from the seller and is to cancel any registration of the contract.

7.2 **Late completion**
7.2.1 If there is default by either or both of the parties in performing their obligations under the contract and completion is delayed, the party whose total period of default is the greater is to pay compensation to the other party.
7.2.2 Compensation is calculated at the contract rate on an amount equal to the purchase price, less (where the buyer is the paying party) any deposit paid, for the period by which the paying party's default exceeds that of the receiving party, or, if shorter, the period between completion date and actual completion.
7.2.3 Any claim for loss resulting from delayed completion is to be reduced by any compensation paid under this contract.
7.2.4 Where the buyer holds the property as tenant of the seller and completion is delayed, the seller may give notice to the buyer, before the date of actual completion, that he intends to take the net income from the property until completion. If he does so, he cannot claim compensation under condition 7.2.1 as well.

7.3 **After completion**
Completion does not cancel liability to perform any outstanding obligation under this contract.

7.4 **Buyer's failure to comply with notice to complete**
7.4.1 If the buyer fails to complete in accordance with a notice to complete, the following terms apply.
7.4.2 The seller may rescind the contract, and if he does so:
(a) he may
(i) forfeit and keep any deposit and accrued interest
(ii) resell the property and any contents included in the contract
(iii) claim damages
(b) the buyer is to return any documents he received from the seller and is to cancel any registration of the contract.
7.4.3 The seller retains his other rights and remedies.

7.5 **Seller's failure to comply with notice to complete**
7.5.1 If the seller fails to complete in accordance with a notice to complete, the following terms apply.
7.5.2 The buyer may rescind the contract, and if he does so:
(a) the deposit is to be repaid to the buyer with accrued interest
(b) the buyer is to return any documents he received from the seller and is, at the seller's expense, to cancel any registration of the contract.
7.5.3 The buyer retains his other rights and remedies.

8. **LEASEHOLD PROPERTY**
8.1 **Existing leases**
8.1.1 The following provisions apply to a sale of leasehold land.
8.1.2 The seller having provided the buyer with copies of the documents embodying the lease terms, the buyer is treated as entering into the contract knowing and fully accepting those terms.

8.2 **New leases**
8.2.1 The following provisions apply to a contract to grant a new lease.
8.2.2 The conditions apply so that:
'seller' means the proposed landlord
'buyer' means the proposed tenant
'purchase price' means the premium to be paid on the grant of a lease.
8.2.3 The lease is to be in the form of the draft attached to the contract.
8.2.4 If the term of the new lease will exceed seven years, the seller is to deduce a title which will enable the buyer to register the lease at the Land Registry with an absolute title.
8.2.5 The seller is to engross the lease and a counterpart of it and is to send the counterpart to the buyer at least five working days before completion date.
8.2.6 The buyer is to execute the counterpart and deliver it to the seller on completion.

8.3 **Consent**
8.3.1 (a) The following provisions apply if a consent to let, assign or sub-let is required to complete the contract.
(b) In this condition 'consent' means consent in the form which satisfies the requirement to obtain it.
8.3.2 (a) The seller is to apply for the consent at his expense, and to use all reasonable efforts to obtain it.
(b) The buyer is to provide all information and references reasonably required.
8.3.3 Unless he is in breach of his obligation under condition 8.3.2, either party may rescind the contract by notice to the other party if three working days before completion date (or before a later date on which the parties have agreed to complete the contract):
(a) the consent has not been given, or
(b) the consent has been given subject to a condition to which a party reasonably objects.
In that case, neither party is to be treated as in breach of contract and condition 7.1.2 applies.

9. **CONTENTS**
9.1 The following provisions apply to any contents which are included in the contract, whether or not a separate price is to be paid for them.
9.2 The contract takes effect as a contract for sale of goods.
9.3 The buyer takes the contents in the physical state they are in at the date of the contract.
9.4 Ownership of the contents passes to the buyer on actual completion.

SCS1 3

SPECIAL CONDITIONS

1. (a) This contract incorporates the Standard Conditions of Sale (Fifth Edition).

   (b) The terms used in this contract have the same meaning when used in the Conditions.

2. Subject to the terms of this contract and to the Standard Conditions of Sale, the seller is to transfer the property with either full title guarantee or limited title guarantee, as specified on the front page.

3. (a) The sale includes those contents which are indicated on the attached list as included in the sale and the buyer is to pay the contents price for them.

   (b) The sale excludes those fixtures which are at the property and are indicated on the attached list as excluded from the sale.

4. The property is sold with vacant possession.

(or) XXXXXXXXXXXXXXXXXXXXXXXXXXXXXXXXXXXXXXXXXXXXXXX

•

XXXXXXXXXXXXXXXXXXXXXXXXXXXXXXXXXXXXXXXXXXXXXXXXXXXXXXXXXXXXXXXXXXXXXXXXXXXXXXXXX

6. **Representations**

   Neither party can rely on any representation made by the other, unless made in writing by the other or his conveyancer, but this does not exclude liability for fraud or recklessness.

7. **Occupier's consent**

   Each occupier identified below agrees with the seller and the buyer, in consideration of their entering into this contract, that the occupier concurs in the sale of the property on the terms of this contract, undertakes to vacate the property on or before the completion date and releases the property and any included fixtures and contents from any right or interest that the occupier may have.

   Note: this condition does not apply to occupiers under leases or tenancies subject to which the property is sold

Name(s) and signature(s) of the occupier(s) (if any):

Name ....

Signature ....

Notices may be sent to:

Seller's conveyancer's name: Gowing & Co
26 Newbridge Street
Oldcastle
Mercia
OD1 3XS

E-mail address:*

Buyer's conveyancer's name: Pooter & Co
4 the Square
Cornland
Wessex
CO1 8YY

E-mail address:*

*Adding an e-mail address authorises service by e-mail: see condition 1.3.3(b).

SCS1 4

Reading 2

Vikki Vincent's Conveyance

CONVEYANCE OF LAND

INLAND REVENUE PRODUCED FA 931	£800	£100	£50

This Conveyance is made the twenty first day of February 1980 BETWEEN

(1) MARK OLIVER SMITH (Vendor) of ROSEMEAD, LAWSHALL, SUFFOLK

(2) DAVID VINCENT AND VIKKI VINCENT (Purchasers) of 27 GREENWAY, LAWSHALL, SUFFOLK

NOW THIS DEED WITNESSES as follows:

1. RECITALS

1.1 The Vendor acknowledges receipt from the Purchasers of Ninety-five thousand pounds ('the Purchase Price')

1.2 In consideration of the purchase price the Vendor as beneficial owner conveys to the Purchasers the simple estate in the property known as Rosemead, Lawshall, Suffolk ('the Property') SUBJECT to the restrictive covenants contained in a conveyance dated 27th January 1927 made between Sibylla Audrey Slatter (1) and Arthur Herbert Jones (2) details of which are set out in the attached schedule

1.3 The Vendor reserves a right of way over the path in the garden of the Property shown with a broken green line on the attached plan (Note – this plan has not been reproduced)

1.4 It is certified that the transaction hereby effected does not form part of a larger transaction or of a series of transactions in respect of which the amount or value of the consideration exceeds Thirty thousand pounds

1.5 The Purchasers declare that they are beneficial Joint Tenants.

<u>SCHEDULE</u>

Covenants contained in a Conveyance dated 27th January 1927 between Sibylla Audrey Maud Slatter (1) and Arthur Herbert Jones (2)

1. The Purchaser hereby covenants with the Vendor her heirs and assignees that the Purchaser and his successors in title the owner or owners for the time being of the Property will at all times hereafter perform and observe the following stipulations and conditions.
2. The Purchaser shall erect within three months of the date of this conveyance and forever afterwards maintain good and sufficient fences on the eastern boundary of the Property.
3. Not to erect any building on the Property without first obtaining the Vendor's approval in writing to the plans of the said building
4. Not to carry out any trade manufacture or business of any kind at the Property

<u>SIGNED SEALED and DELIVERED</u>)
as a deed by the said <u>MARK OLIVER SMITH</u>) *Mark Smith*
in the presence of:-)

Leonard Pickering
62 Melrose Street
Leicester

<u>SIGNED SEALED AND DELIVERED</u>)
as a deed by the said <u>DAVID VINCENT</u>) *David Vincent*
in the presence of:-)

Ian Snell
1 Cooper Close
Ipswich

<u>SIGNED SEALED AND DELIVERED</u>)
as a deed by the said <u>VIKKI VINCENT</u>) *Vikki Vincent*
in the presence of:-)

Ian Snell
1 Cooper Close
Ipswich

Reading 3

Transfer of Land with Registered Title

Land Registry
Transfer of whole of registered title(s)

TR1

If you need more room than is provided for in a panel, and your software allows, you can expand any panel in the form. Alternatively use continuation sheet CS and attach it to this form.

Leave blank if not yet registered.	1 Title number(s) of the property: SH 98765
Insert address including postcode (if any) or other description of the property, for example 'land adjoining 2 Acacia Avenue'.	2 Property: 8 West Park Road Sunderland SR4 3LY
	3 Date:
Give full name(s). Complete as appropriate where the transferor is a company.	4 Transferor: Andrew Norman and Emily Norman <u>For UK incorporated companies/LLPs</u> Registered number of company or limited liability partnership including any prefix: <u>For overseas companies</u> (a) Territory of incorporation: (b) Registered number in England and Wales including any prefix:
Give full name(s). Complete as appropriate where the transferee is a company. Also, for an overseas company, unless an arrangement with Land Registry exists, lodge either a certificate in Form 7 in Schedule 3 to the Land Registration Rules 2003 or a certified copy of the constitution in English or Welsh, or other evidence permitted by rule 183 of the Land Registration Rules 2003.	5 Transferee for entry in the register: David Jones and Susan Jones <u>For UK incorporated companies/LLPs</u> Registered number of company or limited liability partnership including any prefix: <u>For overseas companies</u> (a) Territory of incorporation: (b) Registered number in England and Wales including any prefix:
Each transferee may give up to three addresses for service, one of which must be a postal address whether or not in the UK (including the postcode, if any). The others can be any combination of a postal address, a UK DX box number or an electronic address.	6 Transferee's intended address(es) for service for entry in the register: 8 West Park Road Sunderland SR4 3LY
	7 The transferor transfers the property to the transferee

Place 'X' in the appropriate box. State the currency unit if other than sterling. If none of the boxes apply, insert an appropriate memorandum in panel 11.	**8 Consideration** [X] The transferor has received from the transferee for the property the following sum (in words and figures): six hundred thousand pounds (£600,000) [ ] The transfer is not for money or anything that has a monetary value [ ] Insert other receipt as appropriate:
Place 'X' in any box that applies. Add any modifications.	**9 The transferor transfers with** [X] full title guarantee [ ] limited title guarantee
Where the transferee is more than one person, place 'X' in the appropriate box. Complete as necessary.	**10 Declaration of trust. The transferee is more than one person and** [ ] they are to hold the property on trust for themselves as joint tenants [X] they are to hold the property on trust for themselves as tenants in common in equal shares [ ] they are to hold the property on trust:
Insert here any required or permitted statement, certificate or application and any agreed covenants, declarations and so on.	**11 Additional provisions**

The transferor must execute this transfer as a deed using the space opposite. If there is more than one transferor, all must execute. Forms of execution are given in Schedule 9 to the Land Registration Rules 2003. If the transfer contains transferee's covenants or declarations or contains an application by the transferee (such as for a restriction), it must also be executed by the transferee.

12 Execution

Signed as a deed by ANDREW NORMAN
in the presence of
Signature of witness......................
Name ....
Address ....

Signed as a deed by EMILY NORMAN
in the presence of
Signature of witness......................
Name ....
Address ....

Signed as a deed by DAVID JONES
in the presence of
Signature of witness......................
Name ....
Address ....

Signed as a deed by SUSAN JONES
in the presence of
Signature of witness......................
Name ....
Address ....

Reading 4

Official Copies

Official copy of register of title

Title number WX65488 Edition date 30.04.20xx

- This official copy shows the entries subsisting on the register on 14 September 20xx at 10:55:50
- This date must be quoted as the 'search from date' in any official search application based on this copy.
- The date at the beginning of an entry is the date on which the entry was made in the register.
- Issued on 14 September 20xx.
- Under s.67 of the Land Registration Act 2002 this copy is admissible in evidence to the same extent as the original.
- For information about the register of title see Land Registry website www.landregistry.gov.uk or Land Registry Public Guide 1- *A guide to the information we keep and how you can obtain it.*
- This title is dealt with by Land Registry Hull Office

A: Property Register

This register describes the land and estate comprised in the title.

COUNTY	DISTRICT
CORNSHIRE	OVERTON

1. (18 December 2015) The freehold land shown edged with red on the plan of the above title filed at the Registry and being 4 Main Road, Cornland, Wessex CN2 000.
2. (18 December 2015) The property has the benefit of a right of way granted by deed of grant dated 19 April 1969 and made between (1) Ivan Walton and (2) Jonathan Hartley.

   NOTE: Copy filed

B: Proprietorship Register

This register specifies the class of title and identifies the owner. It contains any entries that affect the right of disposal.

Title absolute

1. (18 December 2015) PROPRIETOR(S): DAVID JONES and SUSAN JONES of 4 Main Road, Cornland, Wessex CN2 000.
2. (18 December 2015) The price stated to have been paid on 3 December 2005 was £180,000.
3. (18 December 2015) RESTRICTION: No disposition by a sole proprietor of the registered estate (except a trust corporation) under which capital money arises is to be registered unless authorised by an order of the court.
4. (18 December 2015) RESTRICTION: No disposition of the registered estate by the proprietor of the registered estate, or by the proprietor of any registered charge, not being a charge registered before the entry of this restriction, is to be registered without a written consent

signed by the proprietor for the time being of the charge dated 3 December 2015 in favour of NORTHERN WEST BUILDING SOCIETY of 54 Maine Road, Manchester, M2 3ER referred to in the charges register

C: Charges Register

This register contains any charges and other matters that affect the land.

1. (18 December 2015) A conveyance of the land in this title dated 1 April 1968 and made between (1) Ivan Walton and (2) Jonathan Hartley contains the following covenants:

   "The Purchaser with the intent and so as to bind (as far as practicable) the property hereby conveyed and to benefit and protect the retained land of the Vendor lying to the west of the land hereby conveyed hereby covenants with the Vendor that he and his successors in title will at all times observe and perform the stipulations and conditions set out in the schedule hereto."

   THE SCHEDULE ABOVE REFERRED TO

   "1. Not to use the property other than as a single private dwelling house; and
   2. Not to build or allow to be built any new building on the property nor alter or allow to be altered any building currently erected on the property without the written consent of the Vendor or his successors in title; and
   3. To keep the wall on the northern boundary of the property in good repair and condition."

2. (18 December 2015) A deed of grant dated 2 October 2001 made between Martin Leaf (1) and Patrick Harland (2) contains the following easement:

   "The Grantor grants to the Grantee and his successors in title a right to pass and repass on foot only over the footpath marked with a dotted red line on the Plan the Grantee and his successors in title contributing one half of the costs of maintenance of the footpath."

3. (18 December 2015) CHARGE dated 3 December 2015 to secure the monies including the further advances therein mentioned

4. (18 December 2015) PROPRIETOR - NORTHERN WEST BUILDING SOCIETY of 54 Maine Road, Manchester, M2 3ER.

END OF REGISTER

Note: A date at the beginning of an entry is the date on which the entry was made in the Register

Authors' note: These official copies should be accompanied by an official copy of the title plan. This has not been reproduced for the purposes of this worked example.

Reading 5

Result of Central Land Charges Search

FORM K18

LAND CHARGES ACT, 1972

CERTIFICATE OF THE RESULT OF SEARCH

CERTIFICATE NO	CERTIFICATE DATE	PROTECTION ENDS ON
A123456	11TH OCTOBER 2014	31st OCTOBER 2014

It is hereby certified that an official search in respect of the undermentioned particulars has been made in the index to the registers which are kept pursuant to the Land Charges Act, 1972. The result of the search is shown below

PARTICULARS SEARCHED

COUNTY OR COUNTIES: MERCIA

NAME(S) Particulars of Charge	PERIOD	FEES £
CYRIL CHARLES *EDGE* NO SUBSISTING ENTRY	1926 - 1937	1.00
T.T. NOBLE (BUILDERS) LIMITED NO SUBSISTING ENTRY	1937 - 1959	1.00
GEORGE*HANDEL* (1) D(ii) No. 196991 Dated 10 April 1959 (2) West Park Road (3) Oldcastle (4) Mercia	1959 - 1975	1.00
BASIL*HARWOOD* NO SUBSISTING ENTRY	1975 - 1992	1.00
ANDREW*NORMAN* NO SUBSISTING ENTRY	1992 - 2014	1.00
EMILY*SMYTHE* NO SUBSISTING ENTRY	1992 - 2014	1.00
--------------------END OF SEARCH---------------------		

APPLICANT'S REFERENCE	RM/BC12	APPLICANT'S KEY NUMBER	32493	AMOUNT DEBITED	£6.00

Reading 6

Official Copies Showing a Registered Leasehold Title

Official copy of register of title

Title number HU123456 | Edition date 01.02.1991

- This official copy shows the entries subsisting on the register on 5 October 2014 at 14:45:32
- This date must be quoted as the "search from date" in any official search application based on this copy.
- The date at the beginning of an entry is the date on which the entry was made in the register.
- Issued on 6 October 2014.
- Under s.67 of the Land Registration Act 2002 this copy is admissible in evidence to the same extent as the original.
- For information about the register of title see land Registry website www.landregistry.gov.uk or Land Registry Public Guide 1- *A guide to the information we keep and how you can obtain it.*
- This title is dealt with by Land Registry Durham District

A: Property Register

This register describes the land and the estate comprised in the Title

NORTHUMBERLAND : WARKWORTH

1. (1 February 1991). The **Leasehold** land shown edged red on the plan of the above title filed at the Registry and known as 4C Pele Villas, Pele lane, Biddlestone

2. (1 February 1991) Short particulars of the lease under which the land is held:

   Date: 1 January 1991
   Term: 99 years from 1 January 1991
   Parties: (1) Laurence Lilburn
   (2) William Akeld
   Note: Lessor's title registered under HU 654321

3. Unless otherwise mentioned the title includes any legal easements granted by the registered lease but is subject to any rights that it reserves, so far as those easements and rights exist and benefit or affect the registered land.

B: Proprietorship Register

This register specifies the class of title and identifies the owner. It contains any entries that affect the right of disposal.

Title Absolute

1. (1 February 1991) WILLIAM AKELD of 4C Pele Villas, Pele Lane, Biddlestone, Warkworth, Northumberland.

C: Charges Register

This register contains any charges and other matters that affect the land

1. (1 February 1991) - CHARGE dated 1 January 1991 registered on 1 February 1991 to secure the monies including the further advances therein mentioned.

2. PROPRIETOR - ROTHBURY BANK plc of Main Road, Rothbury, Northumberland, registered on 1 February 1991.

END OF REGISTER

Note: *The title plan has not been reproduced*

Reading 7

Legal Mortgage and Extract from Mortgage Conditions

C&G **Mortgage Deed**

Account Number:	Date:
We (the lender) are: **Cheltenham & Gloucester plc.** **Our address is Barnett Way, Gloucester, GL4 3RL**	
The **mortgage conditions** are: Cheltenham & Gloucester plc Mortgage Conditions 2000 (filed at HM Land Registry under reference MD668A/01).	
You (the borrower) are:	
The **property** is:	
	Title Number:

1. The **mortgage conditions** form part of this mortgage. You confirm that we have given you a copy of the **mortgage conditions**.
2. You charge the **property** by way of legal mortgage with payment of all the money and liabilities mentioned in condition 2 of the **mortgage conditions**. This mortgage is made with the full title guarantee.
3. This mortgage secures further advances, but we are not obliged to make any further advances.

Signed as a deed by you in the presence of the appropriate witness referred to below.

Signature of you (the borrower)	Signature, name and address of each witness

Form of charge filed at HM Land Registry under reference MD668A

YOUR HOME IS AT RISK IF YOU DO NOT KEEP UP REPAYMENTS ON A MORTGAGE OR OTHER LOAN SECURED ON IT

Section 2

Cheltenham & Gloucester plc Mortgage Conditions 2000

1. Interpretation

1.1 In these conditions, the words listed below have the meanings shown beside them:

"debt" All the money which the **mortgage** secures.

"expenses" All expenses you must pay under condition 11.

"head office" Our head office from time to time. The address of our current head office is: Barnett way, Gloucester GL4 3RL. We will give you written notice of any change of address.

"loan agreement" Any agreement under which we lend you money on the security of the **mortgage** and any other document (such as a guarantee) which makes you liable to pay the **debt** or any part of it.

"mortgage" The particular **mortgage** which these conditions apply to.

"neighbouring land" Any land which adjoins the **property** or is near to it.

"property" The property described in the **mortgage** or any part of that property.

"rebuilding costs" The amount needed to:
- rebuild the **property**;
- remove all debris;
- pay all professional fees;
- meet planning authority requirements;
- pay for alternative accommodation; and
- recover any rent lost during the rebuilding;

"relevant easements"
- rights of way;
- rights of support;
- rights to receive light and air;
- rights to receive or discharge water;
- rights to use wires and pipes which carry electricity, gas and other services.

"transferee" A person to whom we transfer, or agree to transfer, the **mortgage** or any of our rights under it.

"we" and "us" Cheltenham & Gloucester plc, its successors or any **transferee.**

"you" the person(s) named as the borrower in the **mortgage** and their successors

1.2 If there is more than one of you, these conditions apply to all of you together and to each of you on your own. This means that each of you can be held fully responsible for complying with these conditions.

1.3 The terms contained in the **mortgage** and these conditions are not intended to be enforceable by anyone other than you (including your successors) and us (including our successors and any **transferee**).

1.4 If these conditions are not consistent with the terms of a **loan agreement**, the terms of that **loan agreement** will apply to that part of the **debt** which you owe under it.

2. What the mortgage secures

2.1 Except where condition 2.2 applies, the **mortgage** secures the following:

(a) all money owing under:
- any existing or future **loan agreement** which you (or any of you) make with us, including any existing or future guarantee you give us;
- any bank account which you (or any of you) hold with us now or in the future;
- these conditions;

(b) all other actual or contingent liabilities which you (or any of you) owe us now or in the future.

2.2 The **mortgage** does not secure money which you owe us under an agreement which is regulated by the Consumer Credit Act 1974 unless:

(a) the agreement states that it is to be secured by the **mortgage**; or

(b) Part V of that Act does not apply to the agreement (for example, because it is an agreement to overdraw on a current account).

2.3 This paragraph applies if:

(a) we receive a payment from you or for your benefit;

(b) the payment is not made under an existing arrangement which makes it clear how the payment is to be used; and

(c) you do not tell us what to do with the payment.

Where this paragraph applies, we will use the payment to pay off any sums which are in arrears at the time when we receive the payment, and then credit it to whichever part of the **debt** we choose.

3. Your obligations

3.1 You agree to do the following:

(a) keep the **property** in good repair;
(b) make sure that any unfinished buildings on the **property** are completed without delay and are properly built;
(c) keep to any covenants which apply to the **property**;
(d) keep to any obligations which apply to the **property** under a statute or statutory instrument;
(e) prevent any contamination or other environmental damage to the **property**;
(f) comply with any legal obligation you have to put right any contamination or other environmental damage to the **property** or to **neighbouring land**;
(g) allow us to enter the **property** (after giving you reasonable notice) for either or both of the following purposes:
- to inspect the **property**;
- to put right any breach of your obligations under these conditions;

(h) immediately give us a copy of any notice or other document which you get from:
- any person exercising a statutory or other legal right over the **property**;
- any person claiming a new or increased interest in the **property**;

(i) immediately give us a copy of any notice which you give:
- to extend any lease under which you hold the **property**;
- to buy the freehold of the **property**;
- to get an interest in the freehold of any building which includes the **property**;
- to claim compensation concerning the **property**;

(j) give us a mortgage over any new or increased interest which you get in the **property**;
(k) keep the **property** in your possession (except where you have let the **property** with our written permission or it is let under a lease which has priority to our **mortgage**).

3.2 You agree not to do the following without first getting our written consent:

(a) grant a lease of the **property** or agree to grant one;
(b) grant any other rights in the **property** which might reduce the value of our security;
(c) allow anyone to acquire rights in the **property**;
(d) allow anyone to surrender a lease of the **property**;
(e) change the use of the **property**;
(f) allow the **property** to be used for a trade or business.

3.3 We may refuse our consent under condition 3.2 or place conditions on our consent:

(a) where we think our security might otherwise become inadequate; or
(b) on any other ground which is reasonable.

3.4 If:

(a) the **property** includes a dwelling; and
(b) you (or any of you) have given us a separate mortgage over any **neighbouring land**; and
(c) the **neighbouring land** is or could be used for agricultural purposes;

then the **property** must only be used as your private residence.

4. Insurance

4.1 You may insure the **property** with our written consent. If you insure the **property**, the following terms will apply:

(a) we must approve your choice of insurer;
(b) the insurance must be in the joint names of you and us;
(c) you must keep the **property** insured:
- against all risks which we reasonably specify; and
- for the amount of the current **rebuilding costs**;

(d) any excess under the policy must be kept down to a reasonable level;
(e) you will show us proof when we ask for it that the policy is in force and that you are paying the premiums under it.

4.2 We may insure the **property** if you do not insure it under condition 4.1, or if you do not keep to the terms of that condition. If we insure the **property**, the following terms will apply:

(a) we will insure the **property** at your expense;
(b) we will choose:
- the insurer;
- the amount of the insurance and any excess;
- whether the insurance is to be in our name alone, or in the joint names of you and us;
- the risks to be covered;

(c) you will repay us all premiums we pay to keep the **property** insured;
(d) unless we allow you to repay premiums by monthly instalments, you must repay each premium in full as soon as we ask you for it.

4.3 If you hold the **property** under a lease which provides for your landlord (or a higher landlord) to insure the **property**, the following terms will apply instead of conditions 4.1 or 4.2:

(a) you must see that our interest is noted on the insurance policy;
(b) you must do your best to make sure that the landlord keeps the **property** insured:
- with a reputable insurer;
- against all risks which we reasonably specify;
- for the amount of the current **rebuilding costs**;

(c) you must tell us immediately if you find out that the landlord is not keeping the **property** insured.

4.4 The following terms apply whoever insures the property:

(a) you must not do anything which could make it more difficult or expensive to keep the **property** insured, or which could make the insurance invalid;

(b) if you receive any money under the policy, you agree to hold it on trust for us;

(c) we may settle all claims under the policy which concern the **property**;

(d) we may choose whether any money paid under the policy must be used either to repair or rebuild the **property** or to reduce or pay off the **debt**;

(e) we may keep any remuneration or benefit which we receive if we arrange the insurance of the **property** and we are not under any duty to give you details of any remuneration or benefit we receive.

4.5 If we have the right to insure the **property** under condition 4.2 but cannot find an insurer who will insure it on acceptable terms, we may instead take out a policy to cover us against the risk of our suffering loss because the **property** is uninsured.

4.6 If we take out a policy under condition 4.5, you must repay us each premium we pay under the policy as soon as we ask you to.

5. Restrictions on your rights

5.1 These conditions exclude your power under statute:

(a) to grant leases of the **property** or agree to grant them;

(b) to allow anyone to surrender a lease of the **property**.

5.2 We may refuse to release the **property** from the **mortgage** until you have paid us all the money secured by any other mortgage you have given us.

6. Our rights and remedies

6.1 Our rights and remedies under these conditions are in addition to those we have by law.

6.2 A purchaser may treat the statutory power of sale as arising on the date of the **mortgage**.

6.3 The statutory power of sale applies to the **mortgage** free from the restrictions in section 103 of the Law of Property Act 1925.

6.4 We may exercise the power of sale immediately if:

(a) the money you owe us under a **loan agreement** becomes immediately payable;

(b) the money owed by the borrower under a **loan agreement** which you have guaranteed becomes immediately payable;

(c) a bankruptcy order is made against you (or any of you);

(d) you (or any of you) make a voluntary arrangement with your creditors;

(e) you are more than one month late in paying any money under these conditions;

(f) you break any other term in these conditions;

(g) the **property** is compulsorily purchased;

(h) the value of the **property** is going down because:

- you have abandoned it; or
- you are neglecting it or you are not looking after it properly.

6.5 If we are entitled to exercise the power of sale under condition 6.4, we may:

- take possession of the **property**;
- let the **property** on any reasonable terms (but without any other restrictions on the nature, terms and length of the lease, or on the rent due);
- allow anyone who holds a lease of the **property** to surrender the lease on any reasonable terms;
- agree to any reasonable variation in the terms of any lease of the **property**;
- appoint a receiver.

6.6 The following terms apply if we take possession of the **property**:

(a) we may remove, store or sell any goods or animals which you have not removed from the **property**. We will do this as your agent and at your expense and we will not be liable for any damage caused unless we fail to take reasonable care.

(b) we may carry out any repairs or improvement which we reasonably believe will make the **property** easier to sell or let.

6.7 You agree that we may transfer, or agree to transfer, the **mortgage**, or any of our rights under the **mortgage** to a **transferee** at any time.

6.8 On any transfer under condition 6.7:

(a) the **transferee** will be able to enforce the transferred rights against you in the same way and to the same extent that we could enforce them before the transfer;

(b) you will be bound by any statement of fact which we make to the **transferee**, provided that we make the statement in good faith and take reasonable care to check its accuracy;

(c) you agree that we may pass any information or documents relating to the **property**, the **mortgage**, or the **debt** to any **transferee** or prospective **transferee**.

6.9 Our rights under these conditions will not be lost or limited:

(a) by any earlier exercise of them;

(b) by any failure to exercise them;

(c) by any delay in exercising them; or

(d) by exercising them in part only.

7. Powers of a receiver

7.1 We may appoint a receiver:

(a) where condition 6.5 applies; or
(b) if you ask us to appoint one.

7.2 We may appoint a receiver for the whole of the **property** or for any part of it.

7.3 We may appoint one of our employees as a receiver.

7.4 We may fix the receiver's remuneration at any reasonable rate.

7.5 We may remove the receiver at any time and appoint another in his place.

7.6 The receiver will be your agent. Unless the receiver is one of our employees you will be responsible for his remuneration.

7.7 The receiver will have the following powers (in addition to those given to receivers by the Law of Property Act 1925):

(a) to take possession of the **property**;
(b) after taking possession of the **property**, to do any of the things which we could do under condition 6.6 if we had taken possession;
(c) to let the **property** on any reasonable terms (but without any other restrictions on the nature, terms and length of the lease, or on the rent due);
(d) to allow anyone who holds a lease of the **property** to surrender the lease on any reasonable terms;
(e) to agree to any reasonable variation, extension or renewal of any lease under which the **property** is let;
(f) to act as manager of the **property**;
(g) to insure the **property** on the same terms as we could insure it under condition 4 2;
(h) to complete any unfinished buildings on the **property**;
(i) if the **property** is held under a lease:
- to agree any reasonable variation, extension or renewal of the lease;
- to exercise any right which you have to renew or extend the lease, or to acquire the freehold or an interest in it.

7.8 We may exclude or limit any of the powers in condition 7.7 at the time when we appoint the receiver or later.

7.9 The receiver will use any money he receives from exercising his powers:
(a) firstly, to meet the costs connected with his appointment and with the exercise of his powers;
(b) secondly, to pay his remuneration;
(c) thirdly, to reduce or pay off the **debt**.

He will pay any balance to any person who has a mortgage over the **property**, or otherwise to you.

8. Power of attorney

8.1 You appoint us and (as a separate appointment) any receiver we appoint to be your attorney and to do the following things in your name and on your behalf:

(a) to execute any document which is needed to make good any defect in your title to the **property** or in our title to the **mortgage**;
(b) to execute any document which is needed to pass a good title to a purchaser or lessee of the **property**;
(c) to transfer to a purchaser any shares or other membership rights which you hold in a management company or residents' society by virtue of owning the **property**;
(d) to receive any money payable to you in connection with the **property** or any insurance of it;
(e) to do anything which we or the receiver need to do to exercise our rights under these conditions;
(f) where you have an interest in any **neighbouring land**, to grant to a purchaser or lessee of the **property** any **relevant easements** or other rights over the **neighbouring land**:
- which the purchaser or lessee of the **property** asks for;
- which you have power to grant; and
- which are needed to allow the **property** to be used or developed in a reasonable way, or which would arise under section 62 of the Law of Property Act 1925 or under the general law on a transfer or lease of the **property** by you.

8.2 The following provisions apply (in addition to those contained in condition 8.1) where there is more than one of you:

(a) if we take possession of the **property**, you appoint us to be your attorney for twelve months after we take possession and (during that period) to exercise in your name and on your behalf any rights and powers which you have as trustees of the **property**;
(b) if we appoint a receiver, you appoint the receiver to be your attorney for twelve months after we appoint him and (during that period) to exercise in your name and on your behalf any rights and powers which you have as trustees of the **property**.

8.3 You cannot revoke the appointments in conditions 8.1 and 8.2 while the **mortgage** remains in force.

8.4 If we ask you to, you will confirm anything done by us or a receiver while acting under the powers of attorney in conditions 8.1 and 8.2.

Index

D

E